American Society for Training & Development

Mark Krynovich

IN ACTION

Conducting Needs Assessment

SEVENTEEN

CASE STUDIES

FROM THE

REAL WORLD

OF TRAINING

JACK J. PHILLIPS

ELWOOD F. HOLTON III

EDITORS

ASTD

Ordering information: Books published by the American Society for Training and Development can be ordered by calling 703/683-8100.

Library of Congress Catalog Card Number: 95-076269

ISBN: 1-56286-017-8

Table of Contents

Introduction to the
In Action series

As are most professionals, the people involved in human resource development (HRD) are eager to see practical applications of the models, techniques, theories, strategies, and issues the field comprises. In recent years, practitioners have developed an intense desire to learn about the success of other organizations when they implement HRD programs. The Publishing Review Committee of the American Society for Training and Development has established this series of casebooks to fill this need. Covering a variety of topics in HRD, the series should add significantly to the current literature in the field.

This series has the following objectives:

- *To provide real-world examples of HRD program application and implementation.* Each case will describe significant issues, events, actions, and activities. When possible, the actual names of the organizations and individuals involved will be used. In other cases, the names will be disguised, but the events are factual.

- *To focus on challenging and difficult issues confronting the HRD field.* These cases will explore areas where it is difficult to find information or where the processes or techniques are not standardized or fully developed. Also, emerging issues critical to success in the field will be covered in the series.

- *To recognize the work of professionals in the HRD field by presenting best practices.* Each book in the series will attempt to represent the most effective examples in the field. The most respected organizations, practitioners, authors, researchers, and consultants will be asked to provide cases.

- *To serve as a self-teaching tool for people learning about the HRD field.* As a stand-alone reference, each volume should be a very useful learning tool. Each case will contain many issues and fully explore several topics.

- *To present a medium for teaching groups about the practical aspects of HRD.* Each book should serve as a discussion guide to enhance learning in formal and informal settings. Each case will have questions for discussion. And each book will be useful as a supplement to general and specialized textbooks in HRD.

The topics for the volumes will be carefully selected to ensure that they represent important and timely issues in the HRD field. The editors for the individual volumes will be experienced professionals in the field. The series will provide a high-quality product to fill a critical void in the literature. An ambitious schedule is planned.

If you have suggestions of ways to improve this series or an individual volume in the series, please respond directly to me. Your input is welcome.

Jack J. Phillips, Ph.D.
Series Editor
P.O. Box 1969
Murfreesboro, TN 37133-1969

Preface

One of the basic elements of the human resource development (HRD) process is needs assessment, or needs analysis. Before any HRD program can, or should, be developed and implemented, there must be some type of needs assessment. Unfortunately, this step is often overlooked or does not receive proper attention. More specifically, the literature does not contain enough applications of successful models to show precisely how organizations have conducted needs assessments.

HRD professionals around the world are seeking practical information about successful applications of the various assessment methodologies. Although a few case are available, they are scattered in the literature and are often hard to locate. A comprehensive collection of cases is needed.

This book responds to this challenge by providing a unique collection of 17 cases from a variety of real-world settings and involving a wide range of assessment methods. Each case presents the strategy, techniques, and methodologies utilized to determine the specific needs of the target group in the organization. The book should help to validate a variety of methodologies used in the needs assessment process.

Target Audience

This book should interest anyone involved in HRD. The primary audience is the practitioners who are attempting to conduct needs assessments as a basis for implementing new programs. Practitioners are the ones who request more examples from what they often label "the real world." This group also complains that many of the models, techniques, and strategies for needs assessment are incomplete or confusing. This publication should satisfy practitioners' needs by providing successful models of how the needs assessment process works. Also, the book should encourage more practitioners to tackle this important topic and help them avoid the problems of implementing programs without needs assessments.

The second audience is HRD instructors. Whether in university classes with students who are pursuing degrees in HRD, internal workshops for professional HRD staff members, or public seminars on HRD implementation, they should find this casebook a valuable reference for a very basic step in the HRD process. This book can be used as a supplement to a standard HRD textbook or complement a textbook on needs assessment or needs analysis. As a supplemental text, this casebook will bring practical significance to needs assessment, convincing students that the process is necessary and feasible, and represents an important part of the HRD function.

A third audience is the researchers and consultants who are seeking more applications of needs assessment technologies. This book provides insight into how to utilize a variety of assessment techniques, often in the same case. It shows the application of a wide range of models and techniques, most of which are based on sound theory and logical assumptions.

The last, but certainly not least, audience is those managers who must work with HRD on a peripheral basis—line and staff managers. Some of these managers are participants in HRD programs designed to develop their own management skills. Some managers send employees to participate in programs. Still other managers lead or conduct sessions in HRD programs. In these roles, managers must have some assurance that programs are based on legitimate needs and not designed or implemented for the wrong reasons. This casebook should improve their understanding of the needs assessment process.

Each audience should find the casebook entertaining and engaging reading. Questions are placed at the end of each case to stimulate additional thought and discussion. One of the most effective ways to maximize the usefulness of this book is through group discussions, using the questions to develop and dissect a case's issues, techniques, methodologies, and results.

The Cases

The most challenging part of developing this publication was identifying case authors. Thousands of letters were mailed. The response was very impressive, with more than 30 cases submitted. Cases had to meet specific guidelines and offer methodology that proved successful. (Only one case was not successfully implemented.) In the end, 17 cases were accepted for publication.

Although there was some attempt to structure cases similarly, they are not identical in style and content. It is important for the reader to experience each assessment as it developed and to identify the issues involved in each setting and situation. The result is a variety of presentations with a variety of styles. Some cases are brief and to the point, outlining precisely what happened and what was achieved. Others provide more detailed background information, including how the needs assessment was utilized and the subsequent results of the program.

There was no attempt to restrict cases to a particular range of methodologies. It is helpful to HRD professionals to show a wide range of approaches. Also, we have resisted the temptation to pass judgment on the various approaches, preferring to let the reader evaluate the different techniques and their appropriateness for the particular settings. Some of the assumptions, methodologies, and strategies might not be as comprehensive and sound as others.

In some cases, the name of the organization is identified, as are the individuals who were involved. In others, the organization's name is disguised at the request of either the organization or the case author. In today's competitive world, and especially in an attempt to explore a complex issue, it is understandable why an organization would choose not to be identified.

Case Authors

It would be difficult to find a more impressive group of contributors to an HRD publication than those contained in this casebook. These authors are experienced, professional, knowledgeable, and at the leading edge of HRD. Collectively, they represent practitioners, consultants, researchers, and professors. Individually, they represent a cross section of individuals involved in the HRD field. Most are experts, and some are well known in the field. A few are high-profile authors who have made a tremendous contribution in the field and have taken the opportunity to provide an example of their top-quality work. Others have made their mark quietly, have achieved success for their organizations, and have offered their approaches in this publication.

Suggestions

We welcome your input. If you have ideas or recommendations regarding presentation, case selection, or case quality, please send them to Performance Resources Organization, P.O. Box 1969, Murfreesboro, TN 37133-1969. All letters will be not only appreciated, but also acknowledged. Your opinions about this volume will help improve others in this series.

Acknowledgments

Although a casebook is the collective work of many individuals, the first acknowledgment must go to all the case authors. We are grateful for their professional contribution. We also want to acknowledge the organizations that have allowed us to use their names and programs for publication. We realize this action is not without risk. We trust the final product has portrayed them as progressive organizations interested in the HRD field and willing to try new techniques for needs assessment.

Our editorial assistant for this project, Tammy Bush, has served us admirably on this project. Without her untiring efforts, this publication would not have been developed or delivered within a reasonable time frame. To her, we say "thanks" for a job extremely well done.

Jack J. Phillips
Murfreesboro, Tennessee

Elwood F. Holton, III
Baton Rouge, Louisiana

May 1995

How To Use This Casebook

These cases present a variety of approaches to needs assessment. Collectively, they offer a wide range of settings, methodologies, and approaches, representing manufacturing, service, and government organizations. Target groups for the needs assessments vary from all employees to managers to technical specialists. Although many of the programs were aimed at determining needs for training and development, others were involved in determining needs for other types of potential initiatives, such as organization development, total quality management, and performance support systems. As a group, these cases represent a rich source of information on the thought processes and strategies of some of the best practitioners, consultants, and researchers in the field.

Each case does not necessarily represent the optimum or ideal approach for the specific situation. In every case, it is possible to identify areas that could benefit from refinement and improvement. That is part of the learning process—to build on the work of other people. Although needs assessment is sometimes contextual, these methods and techniques can be used in other organizations.

Table 1 summarizes the cases in the order in which they appear in the book. This table can serve as a quick reference for readers who want to examine a specific assessment method for a particular type of organization or target audience.

Using the Cases

There are several ways to use this book. In essence, it will be helpful to anyone who wants to see real-life examples of the needs assessment process. Specifically, four uses are recommended:

- This book will be useful to HRD professionals as a basic reference of practical applications of needs assessment methodologies. A reader can analyze and dissect each of the cases to develop an understanding of the issues, approaches, and, most of all, refinements or improvements that could be made.

Table 1. Overview of the case studies.

Case	Industry	Key strategies	Target audience
Ultrasound Coronary Systems Inc.	Medical instruments	Interviews	All employees
Maverick Inc.	Air conditioner manufacturing	Extant data analysis, interview, observation, survey	Production employees and floor managers
Northeast Community College	Academic institution	Evaluation research model, nominal group technique, behavior engineering model	Administrators, faculty, and staff
Reliance Electric Control Plant	Industrial systems manufacturing	Interactive assessment model	All employees
McDonnell Douglas Aerospace-East	Aerospace	Interviews, steering committee, focus groups, external benchmarking	Floor managers
Connecticut Department of Labor	State government	Job and task analysis	All employees in regional job centers
General Electric Aircraft Engines	Gas turbine manufacturing	Action research methodology	Technical staff of engineering division
AT&T Universal Card Services	Credit card services	Surveys, interviews, training histories, focus groups, human resource data, content analysis	Team leaders in Customer Services

Table 1 (continued). Overview of the case studies.

Case	Industry	Key strategies	Target audience
Oregon Department of Transportation	State government	Interviews, focus groups, structured surveys	All employees
Nestlé Beverage Company	Food company	Interviews	All employees
AER Inc.	Power and fuel production	Questionnaires	Middle managers and supervisors
Americana Insurance Company	Insurance	DACUM (developing a curriculum) method	Supervisors and project chiefs
Specialty Chemical Unit	Chemical processing	Performance analysis for training model	Technical employees
Kraft General Foods	Food company	Steering committee, conceptual demonstration, observation, focus groups	Customer service coordinators
Formation in Metal Inc.	Metal fabrication	Interviews, observation, document and record review	All employees
Izhorsky Zavod	Steel production	Interviews, strategic job analysis, person analysis, organization analysis	Managers
Promo Inc.	Direct-mail industry	Survey	All employees

- This book can be useful in group discussions; interested individuals can react to the material, offer different perspectives, and draw conclusions about the approaches and techniques.
- The questions at the end of each case can serve as a beginning point for lively and entertaining discussions.
- This book will serve as an excellent supplement to other training and development or needs assessment textbooks. It provides the extra dimension of real-life cases that show how the needs for training and development are determined.
- Finally, this book will be extremely valuable for managers who do not have primary training responsibility. These managers often provide support and assistance to the HRD staff, and it is important for them to understand how the needs for specific programs are identified.

It is important to remember that each organization is unique. What works well in one situation may not work in another, even if the situations are similar. Although the book offers a variety of approaches and provides an arsenal of tools from which to choose in the needs assessment process, it is not recommended that an approach or technique be duplicated without consideration of the complete situation.

Follow-up

Space limitations have resulted in some cases being shorter than both the author and the editors would prefer. Some information concerning background, assumptions, strategies, and results had to be omitted. If additional information on a case is needed, the lead author can be contacted directly. The address is listed at the end of each case.

A Snapshot of Needs Assessment

Elwood F. Holton, III

For readers new to the topic, the following discussion provides an introduction to conducting needs assessment for HRD programs. For others, it provides a framework for reviewing and analyzing the case studies that follow.

Overview

Our goal in preparing this case book was to present as broad a cross section of needs assessment methodologies as possible. Although these cases do not represent a scientific survey of needs assessment practices, they are an instructive collection of best practices that help to describe the field.

This chapter summarizes and synthesizes the methodologies used in the cases and analyzes the cases through several different frameworks. The chapter concludes with comments about what these cases say about the practice of needs assessment and what they suggest for future directions in developing needs assessment methodologies.

Levels of Analysis

Needs assessments have traditionally been classified as focusing on three levels of analysis: organization, job or task, and individual or person (Goldstein, 1993; McGehee and Thayer, 1961; Moore and Dutton, 1978; Sleezer, 1991). In essence this framework is Kirkpatrick's four-level evaluation model in reverse.

The three-level approach to needs assessment suggests that assessors should start by analyzing the organization to determine what results are not occurring and should be, and what organizational factors are contributing to that condition (Level 4 evaluation). The assessors should then analyze work, jobs, or tasks to determine what performance should be occurring (Level 3 evaluation). Finally, assessors should study individuals to determine who needs learning to accomplish those job tasks (Level 2 evaluation). Most assessors also collect information about trainees' preferences for how they receive the training (e.g., time, place, and format). This input corresponds to Kirkpatrick's Level 1 data in that it allows trainees to specify the types of training to which they will react positively. Figure 1 shows how these corresponding levels can be viewed as a U-shaped process of needs assessment leading to evaluation.

Figure 1. Integrating needs assessment and evaluation processes.

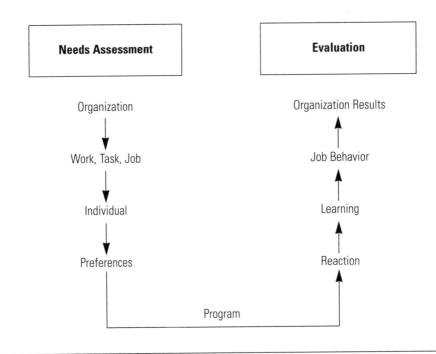

By starting at the organizational level, needs assessment is most likely to lead to well-designed interventions with a very good chance of solving real performance problems. Evaluation after the program is easy because the criteria for each level were determined before the interventions were designed.

Assessors are usually cautioned to be sure that a needs assessment encompasses these three traditional levels (organization, work or task, and individual). Failure to collect assessment data at all levels is likely to lead to misdirected resources and low-impact interventions that are difficult to evaluate. (In the rest of this chapter, I consider only these three levels, because preferences—and reactions to those preferences—are of questionable importance in program outcomes, at least as primary assessment and evaluation criteria (Holton, 1995).)

Kaufman and English (1979), however, pointed out that not all needs assessors are given the opportunity to perform an all-encompassing three-level analysis. They classified needs assessments as ranging from *alpha* to *zeta,* depending on the breadth of questions that the assessor is allowed to ask, with an *alpha* assessment having the broadest scope, encompassing all levels of analysis. The levels of analysis included in an assessment depend on such factors as the status of the assessor in the organization, available time and resources, management policy, and the assessor's biases (Sleezer, 1993). It should be no surprise, then, that not all the cases in this book are three-level assessments. Table 1 summarizes these cases by the levels of analysis used.

Table 1. Number of cases illustrating each combination of levels of analysis.

Levels of assessment	Number
Three levels (4 total):	
Organization, task, and individual	4
Two levels (9 total):	
Organization and task	2
Organization and individual	4
Task and individual	3
One level (4 total):	
Organization	2
Task	2
Individual	0

These cases support Kaufman and English's (1979) suggestion that practitioners have limited opportunities for full three-level assessments. Only four of the cases describe three-level needs assessments. The rest of the cases describe situations in which mandates, usually from management, limited the scope of the assessments. It should be noted, though, that space limitations may have kept some authors from reporting the full extent of their assessments, which may have included other levels.

The two cases that deal heavily with human resource development (HRD) interventions that have nonperformance-driven objectives (specifically, ethics and diversity) suggest that a three-level assessment is not always necessary. In both cases, organization-level analysis was conducted to assess the climate and cultural dimensions. Individual analysis followed to assess individual attitudes. Task analysis was not necessary because the objective was to remove organizational and individual barriers.

Another way of looking at the levels is to consider the total number of the cases that assessed data at each level. These numbers show that each level was considered in the majority of the cases :

Organization	12
Task	11
Individual	11

Swanson (1994) and other researchers have argued, though, that needs assessors need to be careful to take a systems approach to performance problems in organizations. Twelve of the cases used some type of organization-level analysis to identify system problems that could affect performance. It is encouraging to see so many cases including organization-level analyses.

In these 17 cases, individual-level analyses were always conducted along with at least one other level of analysis. The editors confess to creating this outcome because we were very specific in the case guidelines that we would not accept simple "felt-needs" surveys. All of the cases here address important business issues and support our contention that real solutions to critical performance issues are rarely found by simply asking people what they think they need or would like. Multilevel analyses are usually needed.

Methods Employed

Needs assessors have long been known for employing a wide variety of methods. The cases in this book support this claim. Table 2 summarizes the methods used in these cases.

Some notable and encouraging trends evident in these cases include the following:
- *Multimethod strategies.* Although surveys and interviews were the most popular methods, many others were used as well. In fact, all of the cases used multiple methods. Most combined qualitative and quantitative methods. Weaving together multiple data sources significantly

Table 2. Data collection methods used.

Category	Methods
Quantitative	Survey Task analysis Benchmarking
Qualitative	Interview Focus group Subject matter expert Committee
Blended	Nominal group technique Action research Observation Work sampling DACUM (developing a curriculum) Subject matter analysis
Extant data	Job descriptions Internal reports Performance appraisal Personnel records Industry data Annual report Literature

enhanced the assessments, particularly in multilevel analyses.

- *Integration of qualitative methods.* Every case employed some type of qualitative method, usually either interviews or focus groups. Needs assessors have sometimes been criticized as not being rigorous enough because they use so many qualitative methods. In these cases, their use is a strength, not a weakness. Interviews and focus groups provide open-ended information that enrich an assessment. True revelations tend to occur more frequently with qualitative methods, largely because quantitative data collection instruments constrain the range of responses. Interviews are often the primary way to explore problems at the organizational level.

All of the cases except three used qualitative methods in conjunction with more quantitative methods, and the exceptions were appropriate ones. One was an assessment focusing only on the organizational level, using a small group of executives. The other case focused on a small group of 30 employees. The third used a highly structured process to content analyze the data. Qualitative methods were also used to promote buy-in from participants.

- *Appropriate use of surveys.* Needs assessment has also been criticized for an overreliance on surveys. Surveys were certainly used in many of these cases, but not in six of them. Of these six, two dealt with small groups or organization-level-only analysis, and three dealt with some dimension of future uncertainty. The remaining case used a nominal group technique with 280 people to solicit more buy-in, even though a survey could have been used. Of the 11 cases that did use surveys, none used a survey by itself, but rather employed a survey in conjunction with some other type of analysis. The message to assessors is this: Surveys are powerful tools, but they are best used in conjunction with other methods, and they are not a necessary part of needs assessment, even with a large group.

Focus of Needs Assessment

The previous two sections have classified the cases according to two traditional approaches: level of analysis and methods used. These two approaches fail to capture another dimension of needs assessment that points out a critical issue facing needs assessors. Rothwell and Sredl (1992) described needs assessments as being either deficiency or opportunity oriented. Traditionally, needs assessment has been deficiency oriented, designed to identify and address existing deficiencies or gaps in performance. A deficiency approach is, by definition, focused in the present. Opportunity-oriented needs assessment is future oriented, identifying performance gaps likely to occur in the future and proactively implementing solutions to prevent them. And if organizations are to handle today's fast-changing business environments, needs assessments must be more focused on the future.

A useful classification scheme comes from the father of action learning, Revans (1994), although it has not been applied to needs assessment before now. He has suggested that organizations face four types of change, varying along two dimensions. One dimension is the type of problem—known or unknown. The other dimension is the conditions under which the problem occurs—also divided into known and unknown. The four-cell matrix that results (see Figure 2) can be used to describe the following four types of needs assessments:

Figure 2. Four types of needs assessments.

		Problem	
		Known	**Unknown**
Condition	**Known**	Corrective	Developmental
	Unknown	Adaptive	Strategic

- Corrective needs assessments are those that analyze existing problems in existing circumstances to identify performance problems. These are the traditional deficiency-oriented assessments, usually using discrepancy performance models, such as Mager and Pipe's model (1984).
- Adaptive needs assessments occur in organizations that find themselves performing under new conditions, but facing the same job demands as in the past. For example, an organization that restructures to work teams but faces essentially unchanged customer demands should conduct an adaptive needs assessment.
- Developmental needs assessments are those designed to improve an organization's ability to deal with additional problems in the existing environment and conditions. Navran's case in this book provides an excellent example of an organization seeking to improve its ability to deal with unknown problems in the current environment by strengthening its ethical practices.
- Strategic needs assessments require the anticipation of unknown problems or deficiencies that are likely to occur in the future under changing, but unknown, conditions. Such assessments usually occur in organizations facing fundamental and rapid change.

Traditional needs assessment and performance analysis methodologies are strong tools for corrective needs assessments, limited tools for adaptive and developmental needs assessments, and weak tools for strategic needs assessments.

The cases in this book are classified into these four categories in Figure 3. Eight of the cases were traditional corrective needs assessments. Of the other nine, four were adaptive because they were conducted in

Figure 3. List of cases by type of needs assessment.

Problem

		Known	**Unknown**
Condition	**Known**	**Corrective** Ultrasound Coronary Systems Inc. Maverick Inc. Northeast Community College McDonnell Douglas Aerospace-East GE Aircraft Engines AT&T Universal Card Services Nestlé Beverage Company Promo Inc.	**Developmental** Oregon Department of Transportation
	Unknown	**Adaptive** Reliance Electric Control Plant AER Inc. Kraft General Foods Formations in Metal Inc.	**Strategic** Connecticut Department of Labor American Insurance Company Specialty Chemical Unit Izhorsky Zavod

organizations trying to respond to changing conditions, and one was developmental because the organization faced new problems in existing circumstances.

Of great significance is the fact that four cases were strategic needs assessments. Needs assessors have traditionally avoided these because they require a great deal of "crystal ball" analysis. These four cases clearly demonstrate that future-oriented strategic needs assessments can be accomplished simply by adapting existing methods. Wiley's experience with developing managers in the former Soviet Union is an outstanding example of this. I can think of no better example of unknown problems in unknown conditions than organizations used to operating in a controlled economy preparing to operate in a market economy. Yet, Wiley was quite successful in employing a full three-level assessment, including a task analysis, with only modest adjustments to the methods.

Needs assessors must develop the capability to assist organizations with noncorrective assessments. Corrective assessments, by definition, place the HRD person conducting the assessment in a reactive mode. But no organization can afford to wait for performance problems to occur in order to figure out how to prevent them. To link HRD practice to the strategic goals of an organization requires needs assessors to have the ability to conduct strategic needs assessments.

The somewhat surprising message from these cases is that the basic assessment methods appear to work in strategic assessments with minimal adaptation. Perhaps the barriers lie more in a lack of strategic thinking in HRD, not in the lack of methodologies.

Results of the Assessments

All of the assessments in this book except one identified HRD needs and resulted in interventions. (The lone exception is Zuber and Swanson's case, which is included to illustrate some of the reasons needs assessments do not always succeed.)

Sleezer (1992) suggested three possible results of needs assessments: information, priorities, and management buy-in. I would extend her framework by adding recommended solutions and interventions. All but one of the cases yielded results in all four categories. That is, the cases resulted in new information, prioritized needs, recommendations for interventions to solve problems, and management buy-in. Zuber and Swanson's unsuccessful needs assessment resulted in information that was reported to management, but was blocked because management would not believe the data.

Thus, these cases represent not only assessments of needs, but also what has been labeled needs analysis (Kaufman, 1986; Mills, Pace, and Peterson, 1988). That is, they not only identify the needs, but also attribute causes and prescribe solutions. I suggest that this is the appropriate role for needs assessors in HRD. Practitioners need to be proactive leaders in performance and organizational enhancement, not mere analysts. Leadership requires assessors not only to collect and sort data, but also to interpret data to determine solutions and obtain buy-in from management to implement the solutions.

It should not be surprising that multilevel assessments seemed to result in a broader range of information, closer fit with organizational priorities, more buy-in, and different types of solutions than more limited assessments. Assessments that focused on the task and individual levels provided all four types of results, but in a much more narrowly focused arena. In such situations, HRD was participating mostly in decisions about the training itself as opposed to the broader issues of organizational effectiveness.

It is also useful to examine the types of interventions and solutions that were implemented. Of these 17 cases, 16 resulted in interventions. Of those 16, 11 resulted in both training and nontraining interventions, whereas five resulted in only training interventions. The distinguishing characteristic between the two groups is the levels of analysis conducted. Of the 11 cases reporting training and nontraining interventions, 10 included an organization-level analysis. Not surprisingly, the assessments concluded that training alone would be insufficient to address the needs and recommended that some intervention in the climate, culture, strategy, or structure of the organization accompany the training. The other case in this group assessed needs only at the task and individual levels and resulted in job redesign interventions along with the training.

Four of the five cases reporting only training interventions conducted just task- or task- and individual-level analyses. The common characteristic of these four cases is the fact that somebody in the organization had already decided that training was the appropriate solution and the assessor was charged only with determining what type of training should be conducted. The fifth training-only case (Wiley) describes a situation in which a group had been hired to conduct a training program. Although the group did conduct an organization-level analysis, it was limited to determining organization-level factors that would influence the training design.

These cases reinforce the importance of including organization-level analysis. In all cases in which the assessor was given the opportunity to ask the broader questions and not presuppose training as a solution, the result was a blend of nontraining and training solutions. The problem with the other cases is that the decision had already been made to offer training before the assessment was ever conducted. Although it is possible that training was the right solution, something could have easily been overlooked. It is also likely that blending training and nontraining interventions increases the effect on the organization. The obvious (though nonscientific) conclusion from these cases is that the decisions made about assessment methodology directly and significantly shape the results of the assessment. Assessors and managers need to be careful in the choices they make.

Messages for Needs Assessors

So what do these cases say to needs assessors? I think the following messages are important:

- *Learn all the methodologies.* Assessors must have command of all types of assessment tools. The art of needs assessment is knowing which tools to draw from a large tool kit.

- *Become skilled at qualitative methods.* Qualitative methods (e.g., interviews and focus groups) add richness to the data and solicit buy-in. They are essential for assessments dealing with future or unknown conditions. But assessors need to learn scientific methods of analyzing these data, such as content analysis.
- *Assess strategically.* Strategic assessment can be done and is essential for becoming a strategic partner to the organization.
- *Use multiple methods to collect data.* One of the key reasons these assessments were effective was the use of multiple data collection methods. Every method has limitations, but when you use more than one method, you avoid most blind spots.
- *Assess on multiple levels, preferably three levels.* Multilevel assessments really are the best. But the practical reality is that not everyone is given the chance to do three-level assessments. That does not mean you can do without the data or should be happy if you are not the person collecting the data at each level. First, resolve the questions applicable to each level (see Moore and Dutton, 1978; Sleezer, 1991, for more detail) even if you just get the answers from management. Second, fight like the devil to be the one sitting at the table to collect the data for each level.
- *Think performance analysis, not just training needs assessment.* Set out to solve performance problems, not to identify training needs. Assess all aspects of the organizational system that affect performance. An organization-level analysis is probably essential.

Future Trends in Needs Assessment

What do these cases say about the future of needs assessment methodologies? I think the following messages stand out:
- We need better guidelines on how best to integrate multiple methods. There is little question that multiple methods are best, but little guidance exists pointing to the best ways to integrate methods. Swanson (1994) is one of the few authors to have offered guidance in this area.
- We need better models for dealing with conditions of uncertainty (i.e., the noncorrective needs assessment). These cases indicate that conditions of uncertainty can be overcome, but this new frontier for needs assessment is only beginning to be explored. Strategic needs assessments will likely have to incorporate action research approaches.
- We need more sophisticated analyses. There is still too much "seat of the pants" analysis. Assessors need to adopt more valid, systematic, and systemic analysis strategies, especially with qualitative data.

Conclusion

In sum, these cases present some of the more sophisticated practices in the field. If one accepts them as a snapshot, then they are encouraging, as the level of sophistication is impressive. All readers should find something here to improve their own assessments.

References

Goldstein, I.L. (1993). *Training in organizations* (3d ed.). Pacific Grove, CA: Brooks/Cole.

Holton, E.F., III. (1995). In search of an integrative model for HRD evaluation. In *Proceedings of the 1995 Academy of Human Resource Development Annual Conference.* Austin, TX: Academy of Human Resource Development.

Kaufman, R. (1986). Obtaining functional results: Relating needs assessment, needs analysis, and objectives. *Educational Technology, 26,* 24-26.

Kaufman, R., and English, F.W. (1979). *Needs assessment: Concept and application.* Englewood Cliffs, NJ: Educational Technology Publications.

Mager, R.F., and Pipe, P. (1984). *Analyzing performance problems.* Belmont, CA: Lake Publishing.

McGehee, W., and Thayer, P.W. (1961). *Training in business and industry.* New York: John Wiley.

Mills, G.E., Pace, R.W., and Peterson, B.W. (1988). *Analysis in human resource training and organization development.* Reading, MA: Addison-Wesley.

Moore, M.L., and Dutton, P. (1978). Training needs analysis. *Academy of Management Review,* 532-545.

Revans, R. (1994). Keynote presentation at the 1994 Academy of Human Resource Development annual meeting.

Rothwell, W.J., and Sredl, H.J. (1992). *The ASTD reference guide to professional human resource development roles and competencies* (2d ed.). Amherst, MA: HRD Press.

Sleezer, C.M. (1991). Developing and validating the Performance Analysis for Training Model. *Human Resource Development Quarterly, 2,* 355-372.

Sleezer, C.M. (1992). Needs assessment: Perspectives from the literature. *Performance Improvement Quarterly, 5,* 34-46.

Sleezer, C.M. (1993). Training needs assessment at work: A dynamic process. *Human Resource Development Quarterly, 4,* 247-264.

Swanson, R.A. (1994). *Analysis for improving performance: Tools for diagnosing organizations and documenting workplace expertise.* San Francisco: Berrett-Koehler.

Organizational Assessment and Development

Ultrasound Coronary Systems Inc.

Michael Albert

This case shows the strength of the interview process as an assessment tool. Comprehensive interviews were conducted with a cross section of employees, with specific procedures for feedback. The factors that contributed to the success of the case are highlighted.

Background

This case describes a comprehensive needs assessment and follow-up actions and programs implemented at Ultrasound Coronary Systems Inc. (UCS) in 1993. The companywide needs assessment focused on organizational improvement and change, and analyzed specific strengths and developmental needs of the organization. An organization development (OD) model was used to design and implement actions and recommendations based exclusively on data collected from key personnel during a series of in-depth interviews. In this regard, the needs assessment process was used to analyze the priority of OD needs and to generate commitment to the subsequent implementation of key actions and programs. One key lesson from this case is: Line up your implementation dominoes, and manage commitment to future change throughout the needs assessment process.

This case illustrates the special demands and challenges of applying OD need assessments to rapid-growth, high-technology companies, an area about which very little has been written. The case highlights the issues experienced by the consultant during needs assessment and follow-

This case was prepared to serve as a basis for discussion rather than to illustrate either effective or ineffective administrative and management practices.

up. Readers may find it valuable to ask themselves, "What would I be doing at this stage of the process? What might I have done differently if this were the organization in which I work?"

Organization and Industry Profile

UCS develops, manufactures, and markets intravascular ultrasound imaging catheters and systems to aid in the diagnosis and treatment of cardiovascular disease. The company was founded in 1986 and introduced its products for commercial use in the United States in 1989. In 1992 the company completed its first public offering of 1.6 million shares, generating $10 million. A second offering of 1.1 million shares raised an additional $6.1 million in 1993.

The company's products include imaging consoles, which project ultrasound images of the heart on a video screen, and a family of disposable ultrasound imaging catheters, which are inserted into a vein in a patient's leg and then skillfully moved toward the heart's arteries.

The company's strategic goal is to become the worldwide leader in disposable imaging catheters. Clinical experience and experimentation by world-renowned cardiovascular surgeons have demonstrated that the company's products provide physicians with important diagnostic information about coronary arteries not available from conventional coronary x-ray technology.

As of 1994, the market for intravascular ultrasound was small—$25 million—but growing rapidly. The total market was expected to grow to $100 to $200 million within three to five years. UCS had between 40 percent and 45 percent of the market. Only two other companies were competing: Endosonics, with 10 percent to 15 percent of the market, and the combination of Hewlett-Packard and Boston Scientific, with about 45 percent of the market. (Hewlett-Packard manufactures the ultrasound system, and Boston Scientific manufactures the catheters.)

In 1993 UCS sales reached $8.1 million, a 33 percent increase from 1992. Sales projections for 1994 were approximately $14 million. The company was expected to reach profitability by late 1994. The development of products in the medical instruments and pharmaceutical industry has traditionally required the commitment of substantial resources to conduct the time-consuming research and development, testing, and clinical trials necessary to bring medical products to market, and to secure approval from the Food and Drug Administration (FDA).

The organization is functionally structured, with vice-presidents for finance, operations, research and development, and sales and marketing reporting to the chief executive officer (CEO). Various engineering project managers report to the operations and research-and-development executives. In June 1993 there were approximately 100 employees, and the positions of vice-president for sales and marketing and director for quality assurance and regulatory affairs were open. UCS markets its products in the United States through its direct sales force of four sales personnel, and in Europe and Japan through independent distributors.

Issues and Events

After hearing the consultant's presentation on "How High-Performance Companies Manage Corporate Culture" at a monthly dinner gathering of 140 human resource (HR) professionals in March 1993, the HR manager contacted the consultant. In her contact letter, she stated that many of the issues discussed that evening were relevant to UCS and that a similar presentation to a few senior executives would be very beneficial.

The consultant called the HR manager to get more information about the situation and the company. After this discussion, the consultant had a basic understanding of

- UCS's products and general business focus
- the particular circumstances that, from the vantage point of the HR manager, created a need for discussing culture and corporate performance at that time
- who would be attending the in-house session
- what issues and discussion format might best meet the needs and style of the executives
- what experiences they had had with external consultants.

A three-hour discussion session was scheduled for late April and was attended by the HR manager, the CEO, and the vice-president for finance. This initial meeting provided an opportunity for the consultant and UCS executives to have a preliminary dialogue about various management practices and organizational issues that supported or constrained UCS's ability to attain key goals. Prior to the meeting, the HR manager had informed the consultant that the CEO was sincerely interested in looking candidly at his organization and at ways to improve its effectiveness.

During the meeting, the consultant reviewed his prior discussion with the HR manager, and both executives agreed that it was important for the organization to look systematically at itself and at ways to improve its overall management and organization. Most important, they both stated that they believed in the value of OD and improvement. From their perspective, the demands of developing, manufacturing, and marketing their products in an environment characterized by a high degree of technological and marketing uncertainty constrained UCS from focusing its efforts toward emerging management and organization issues. In a nutshell, the fact that its products reflected new applications of an emerging technology to an emerging market required the company to focus most of its resources toward new product development, clinical testing, and getting the product to new customers. This focus on technical-functional priorities was generally at the expense of creating and developing the management and organizational infrastructure to support the technical-functional focus. Further pressure and problems evolved from the past use of such practices as overly optimistic product release dates and premature shipping of product to customers to generate cash flow.

As the consultant discussed the corporate culture practices of high-performance companies, he provided a forum for the two executives and the HR manager to describe and analyze current and past situations at UCS. The purpose of the session was to provide the executives with an opportunity to understand and assess some key managerial and organizational factors related to the development of an appropriate culture and how culture affected corporate performance at UCS. To aid in this discussion, a few models illustrating how corporate culture develops and affects performance were briefly described. One model was based on the work of Schein (1985), who portrayed culture as the learned behavior of a group of people as they learn to cope with external environmental and internal problems. The other model was based on a strategic model developed to assess needs for cultural change (Albert, 1985). The consultant also described the essence of an OD needs assessment model, as illustrated in Figure 1.

This needs assessment model was described as a way for organizations to assess what their key OD needs are, and then to plan and implement actions, programs, and changes in light of the needs assessment. Subsequent to the implementation of change, follow-up assessment occurs as the cycle from assessment to planning to implementation continues. To a moderate degree, the consultant used the three-hour meeting to engage the executives in an informal, preliminary needs assessment, hoping that they would experience the potential benefits of an organizational needs assessment.

The meeting concluded with a request from the CEO for a proposal to work with the organization for a 12-month period. The proposal was discussed with the same three individuals during a two-hour meeting in mid-May. The consultant felt it would be best to begin the needs assessment process by meeting individually with the CEO and each of the vice-presidents. The purpose of these interviews was to help the consultant understand key strategic and operating goals and issues, develop rapport

Figure 1. Needs assessment model for organization development.

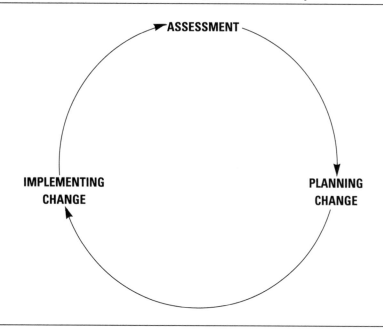

and communicate expectations about his values and work focus, and understand the background and work experiences of the executives. In a series of follow-up meetings with each of the executives, the consultant would have them discuss such issues as UCS's structure, HR issues, and the executive team from the perspective of strengths and developmental needs. Afterwards, the consultant would interview approximately 25 other key personnel, including all managers and some engineering, sales, and support staff.

The day following this meeting, the HR manager informed the consultant that the CEO would like to go ahead with the OD project. The consultant would work on average four days per month and receive a monthly retainer of $3,000.

Methodology and Objectives

The initial needs assessment, conducted from June to August 1993, collected information from managers and staff about ways they thought UCS could improve its effectiveness. The assessment was developed solely from the information gathered during a series of individual interviews with 29 employees, including all senior and midlevel managers. Various engineers, application specialists, sales personnel, and other staff also were interviewed.

All personnel interviewed were asked to discuss their views in three broad areas: the strengths of the executive staff as a team, and what they needed to do more of or less of; the corporate structure, focusing on reporting relationships, coordination, communication, and additional needs; and HR issues. A sample of interview questions appears in Table 1.

Twenty-five interviews were conducted at the UCS headquarters, located in the western United States; these lasted between one and

Table 1. Sample of interview questions.

Broad questions that allowed interviewees to discuss areas they felt were important:

1. To help me better understand your organization, please tell me a little about your job.

2. How is your job related to Ultrasound Coronary Systems's (UCS's) products and services?

3. From your point of view, what does UCS do that is very effective?

4. Regardless of how effective they are, all organizations have some things that get in the way of their success. What things, to some degree, get in the way of UCS's effectiveness?

Questions used to have the interviewees elaborate on specific areas they may have not discussed in answering the first four questions.

5. Describe how coordination occurs between your function and other key functions and levels.

6. What about communication? What is it like? How does it happen? What works well? What gets in the way of effective communication?

7. Focusing on human resource (people) issues and programs, tell me what it is like to work here.

8. Are there any human resource issues or programs that need more attention?

9. Focusing on the executive staff as a team, rather than individually, what do you think the executive team needs to do more of? less of?

10. What are two or three specific recommendations that might result in improving any of the areas you have discussed?

one and one-half hours each. In addition, four 30- to 40-minute interviews were conducted with off-site staff by telephone. All personnel interviewed were assured strict confidentiality; no one individual would be referred to by name in any reports or in any follow-up discussions. As people discussed their perspectives, they were periodically asked what recommendations they had to improve UCS.

Because the focus of the needs assessment was on broad-based, companywide issues, a cross section of key personnel from all major functions and management levels was interviewed. Every manager from all three levels was interviewed because of the relatively small number of supervisors, managers, and executives (18). In addition, the consultant wanted to involve all managerial personnel so that they would be committed to the change process that would result from the needs assessment.

The needs assessment had four objectives: to collect candid, honest views and recommendations about areas that UCS should focus on to become a more effective organization; to provide extensive qualitative data from which areas needing improvement would be developed; to explain the purpose and focus of the change process that the CEO and senior management had made a commitment to; and to develop commitment among company personnel to the follow-up change.

Every effort was made to help the people interviewed feel comfortable discussing both positive and negative aspects of UCS. Creating a climate of trust during interviews is a key skill for conducting needs assessments for organizational or training and development interventions. Poor data gathering will contribute to poor needs assessment and poor program development.

I have found that the following guidelines create a climate of trust during the interview process:
- I try to ensure that employees understand my role and the focus of the project before meeting me. I generally ask the CEO or the sponsoring manager to briefly discuss the project and the role of the consultant to employees at company meetings prior to the interviews.
- I try to create a two-way discussion early in the interview process to create rapport. In essence, before I ask any interview questions, I express my appreciation for the employees' availability; I state that I want them to understand how I work as a consultant; I ask them about their experiences with external consultants; I clarify such issues as my role and the confidentiality regarding what they say; I explain that any organizational changes and program development will be based on the information collected from employees during

the interviews; and I emphasize that I do not ever make recommendations or provide any input whatsoever regarding anyone's job effectiveness, qualifications, or promotion potential.

- I emphasize that each person sees an organization from a unique vantage point and use this theme to focus the interviews. In this regard, I try not to be judgmental when listening during the interviews, and I tell employees that it is fine if they have no views about some issues.
- In every interview, I try to maintain good eye contact; exhibit good listening skills; communicate authentic interest in what the person is saying; and use a soothing voice, acknowledgment responses, and supportive body language.

Data Analysis

After all the interviews were conducted, a content analysis was used to identify key company issues and areas for improvement. Content analysis is a method of analyzing qualitative verbal data in a systematic, objective, and quantitative manner. In essence, it involves analyzing and classifying all the verbal data into major content categories, based on the frequency of responses. The process generally begins by reading all the responses and, based on one's experience and conceptual knowledge, developing preliminary content categories that account for most of the responses. Then, each verbal response is coded into specific categories or subcategories. During this process, the original categories may be modified as the analyst gains more in-depth understanding of the range and variations of the verbal data.

Results

The content analysis of the needs assessment identified five key companywide issues and areas for improvement:

- develop a strategic focus
- meet staffing needs and modify organizational structure
- modify the performance evaluation system
- improve communication
- create a positive, supportive, motivating climate.

Key perspectives and recommendations for each of these five areas are summarized in this section. Recommendations were developed solely by UCS personnel during the interviews. The results were included in a report given to all 29 personnel who were interviewed. The following summary represents about 75 percent of the information contained in the main section of the report, which also included an overview and a concluding section on implications of change.

Develop a Strategic Focus

The need to develop a strategic focus was discussed by a cross section of personnel from a variety of vantage points. Some senior managers stated that UCS's strategy was to be the leading supplier of disposable catheters and to continue to advance and develop a portfolio of products that produce better images, have better designs, are smaller, and can be used for different applications. At the same time, some senior managers acknowledged that UCS lacked a strategic plan and that a shared strategic vision was needed. As one senior manager stated, "There are a lot of opportunities outside our main business; we need a strategic planning mechanism to discuss and analyze these opportunities." Another executive stated that "UCS needs a process that helps us decide what products get developed in the market. It should focus on the needs of customers and perceptions in the marketplace—a process that helps us boil down decisions about what our key products should be." Many midlevel managers and staff expressed similar views.

Meet Staffing Needs and Modify Organizational Structure

Another area for improvement focused on two distinct but related issues: key staffing needs and aspects of UCS's structure. (Because many specific communication needs were mentioned by UCS personnel, these needs were discussed as a separate category in the report.)

STAFFING NEEDS. One pervasive view was that senior management was "stretched too thin and doing too many things." Many people also felt that UCS lacked certain key skills, notably in the areas of quality and regulatory affairs. Whereas UCS was seen as saving money by not hiring executives in some key areas, this strategy was questioned and viewed as costing more than it saved.

The interviews pointed to staffing needs in five specific areas: quality, regulatory affairs, national sales, human resources, and hiring decisions. (Note that personnel were not asked about any of these areas; no function was even mentioned by the consultant until after it was first discussed by the interviewee.)

- *Quality.* There was widespread concern about the lack of a skilled executive with expertise in quality to provide leadership in this area and about the corresponding lack of a quality focus at UCS. Some managers and staff stated that quality was an issue of key strategic importance and was a companywide issue. Moreover, they did not understand why an executive had not been hired for the quality assurance position.

- *Regulatory affairs.* The need for an executive with skills in regulatory affairs was discussed from a similar perspective. (Such an executive would have responsibility for both quality and regulatory affairs.) In addition, various personnel discussed the negative impact that the absence of a regulatory affairs executive was having on productivity. Some notable comments on this need were
  — "We had two deficiencies with a recent product; had we had a regulatory executive in house, perhaps we could have saved 10 months of time."
  — "Some key engineers' skills are mismanaged. Instead of working on critical projects needing our technical skills, we have to focus on regulatory reports for the FDA. This slows down progress on projects."
  — "The FDA work that my manager has to do gets in the way of his spending important time with his subordinates. As a result, he gets involved only when our projects have significant problems—but that's too late."
- *National sales.* The need for hiring a national sales manager was emphasized by a variety of in-house personnel as well as by individuals in the field. One executive stated that the sales function was the weakest part of the organization (not the salesforce, but the fact that there was no full-time sales manager for them to report to). Both sales personnel who were interviewed felt that there had been recurring instances when it was important for them to discuss issues with their manager, but that he was not always available because of his very busy schedule. An individual who was not involved in sales stated, "UCS is saving money by not hiring a sales vice-president, but there are costs associated with this. The salespeople don't have the focused direction they may need on any day."
- *Human resources.* A few individuals stated that it might have been better to replace the past HR manager with a more experienced manager. But others were comfortable with the decision because they thought the company was right to give an inexperienced person an opportunity for professional growth. Some concern was also raised about leaks during discussions with HR personnel and the critical need to rekindle a climate of confidentiality. Some personnel stated that the HR function should be oriented more toward employee relations; others focused on the need to ensure that termination decisions had performance-based documentation. Widespread concern regarding problems with the system for performance evaluation is discussed in a separate section.

- *Hiring decisions.* With pride and enthusiasm, many managers and staff stated that very talented people worked at UCS and that was an attractive dimension of the company. Some individuals, though, expressed concern about a few past hiring decisions that turned out to be unproductive for the organization. Most of the examples focused on sales and quality. Some individuals felt that perhaps poor performance in some cases was partly the result of hiring a person for one job and then putting that person in a job for which he or she did not have the skills. Other people interviewed stated it was important to use a more systematic approach when hiring key personnel in the future.

    ORGANIZATIONAL STRUCTURE. Three specific areas of organizational structure were discussed: the merging of two major engineering departments, reporting relationships, and the formation of engineering project teams.

- *Merging of two engineering departments.* A variety of individuals stated that the consolidation of the departments was very beneficial. Reporting to one executive was thought to improve project coordination and resource utilization.

- *Reporting relationships.* Many individuals stated that they did not understand why quality, customer service, and HR personnel reported to a chief financial officer (CFO). (This concern was not directed to the current CFO, but rather to the position of CFO.) For example, one person stated, "It was inappropriate to have HR report to a CFO, whose primary function is to control costs, because of the conflict of interest." Other personnel stated that any CFO would not have technical understanding concerning quality issues and such a reporting relationship does not promote quality.

    Other concerns regarding reporting relationships focused on the conflict of interest that occurs when the same personnel who are doing the design and development work are also doing quality assessment. Other individuals noted that there was no one person responsible for customer service and that a person who had a problem in the field had no system available to get the problem resolved.

    One person commented that an international liaison was needed to promote sales abroad.

- *Formation of engineering project teams.* Many managers and staff stated variations of the theme that UCS had major inefficiencies in applying people's talents to projects:
    — "There needs to be more coordination at the executive level to ensure that project teams include engineers with the skills

required for project success. At times, someone vital to the project's success may not get his or her manager's approval."

— "Projects have suffered because of a lack of ability to commit technical resources. We needed an electrical engineer to work on the catheter development team because we found the transmission line inside the catheter was susceptible to noise. We were not able to get one, and the project suffered."

— "Because more experienced engineers were involved in other projects, a new, less experienced engineer had to be assigned to a recent project. This contributed to some of the validation problems we experienced."

A set of comments regarding the use of engineers focused on the very positive effects of sending some engineers into the field:

— "When some of the engineers went to talk with the customers, the engineers got excited. We need to do more of this in the future."

— "We need to send some instrument engineers to the field once a month for them to get a market perspective."

Modify the Performance Evaluation System

On the one hand, there was widespread acknowledgment that, in concept, the performance evaluation system was very important and potentially a very good communication tool to focus people on quarterly goals and projects. However, all managers and staff below the executive level, plus some senior managers, expressed major concerns and overall dissatisfaction with various aspects of the system. In essence, there was a consistently strong opinion that the system was not working.

The performance evaluation system was called Strategic Breakthrough Analysis (SBA). In concept, the SBA system was a planning and evaluation tool developed to focus the work of a variety of company personnel on critical activities related to key projects. In essence, key strategic projects were identified by managers at the beginning of each quarter and analyzed to determine critical activities for achieving success. Key personnel were then expected to be part of a variety of SBA project teams for the following quarter or longer. Performance evaluation of the team project was then assigned a specific weight in a team member's performance evaluation, which, in turn, was a component of the employee's bonus compensation for the following year.

In practice, the system was characterized by many problems, including lack of flexibility, poor coordination of personnel across SBA projects, and subjective evaluation of subsequent project performance, as indicated in the following comments:

- "The process for coordination is poor. We submit our SBAs for the next quarter, and later we learn that other people need our assistance on some projects. However, this later need was not factored into the original SBAs. We need a better way to communicate other people's expectations for us on their projects before each of us submits our individual SBAs."
- "Unexpected events that interfere with the SBAs occur all the time. There also is no flexibility in the SBAs, and there needs to be!"
- "There is little correlation between how hard engineers work and their SBA ratings."

Improve Communication

The need to improve communication in a variety of areas was emphasized by most managers and staff, including senior management. As stated by one executive, "It is important to have a mechanism to change the way communication occurs in the company." Three broad areas discussed by UCS personnel were: the need for greater input from managers and staff, more openness, and project and interdepartmental coordination.

INPUT FROM MANAGERS AND STAFF. Most personnel below the executive level said there was a need for opportunities and processes to encourage greater input from UCS employees. Senior management, in contrast, did not discuss this need much. The following quotes illustrate views in this area:
- "Senior management has meetings every Monday, but they don't even inform the midlevel managers what was discussed. We would like to know what is happening."
- "We need a mechanism for bringing our problems to senior management. Some information gets filtered or sugarcoated by some executives when it gets discussed with other executives. Perhaps we could have monthly or bimonthly meetings at which three or four people from one function meet with the executives to give them our candid views about issues, projects, and so forth."
- "We need to have weekly meetings with our senior managers to discuss how things are going. They're mostly too busy and have little time to meet with us."

OPENNESS. The need to communicate with more openness was emphasized by most personnel below the executive level, but not by senior management. The following comments are examples of how this need was expressed:
- "Being a straight shooter and candidly communicating your views is a norm that is not accepted around here. We need to be able to talk

about problems; if there is a problem, be open!"

- "Senior management subtly says, 'We don't want to hear about your problems.' The tone should be, 'How are things going? Tell us about your concerns.' People often don't speak up because of the subtle tone, 'Don't come in here complaining.'"
- "Senior management needs to be more open to listen to our views of issues and problems."

PROJECT AND INTERDEPARTMENTAL COORDINATION. A final area of communication problems focused on project and interdepartmental coordination. Many managers and staff below the executive level discussed problems they saw resulting from communication practices and systems:

- "The communication of change is sometimes lacking, which affects our ability to plan for our areas."
- "During new product development, all relevant product perspectives should be considered, such as quality, service, testing, and built-in diagnostics."
- "We are all busy doing little pieces, but we need to get together as one cohesive group (the entire organization). We have to get more specific information about company issues, such as who needs to know about what and who has this information."

Create a Positive, Supportive, Motivating Climate

Most managers and staff, including senior management, expressed the need to create a positive, supportive, motivating climate. It appeared that UCS may have been sidetracked in this area because of the extensive work senior management had been devoting to issues of significant external importance. In essence, their unrelenting attempt to develop, manufacture, and distribute products in an environment characterized by a high degree of market and technological uncertainty may have had the unintended effect of reducing the focus on the people within the business.

Senior management understood the situation and was committed to focusing more on this important area. One executive stated, "We seem to know some of our needs, but we need to show it through our actions. Senior management should develop more rapport and a conducive management style with employees so as to create more trust." Conveying a similar theme, another executive discussed the need for UCS to develop a greater sense of community.

To a large degree, some of the concerns discussed in the first four improvement areas directly affected the work climate at UCS. The needs for greater input in some decisions, more openness, more substantive interactions between senior managers and employees reporting to them, improvements in communication, and modifications in the SBA process were directly related to creating a positive, supportive, motivating climate.

Managers and staff below the executive level discussed a variety of views in this area. Many stated how hard working, enthusiastic, committed, and motivated the senior managers were. Other comments focused on the need for senior managers to

- provide more opportunities for input
- spend more time with subordinates on a day-to-day basis
- be more involved, attend meetings, go to social activities
- develop a supportive communication style when interacting with one another and with employees
- be aware of the subtleties in their day-to-day behavior
- be role models
- foster an appropriate corporate culture
- provide more positive reinforcement and a climate of positive interaction.

The Feedback Process

Perhaps the most critical stage of an OD needs assessment is managing the feedback process. One needs to create conditions for the organization to use the information collected to plan and implement appropriate change. Collecting data, however, is a much simpler process than using the data for the purpose of planned organizational change. Because of the potential for managers and staff to resist change in any organizational setting, the success of an OD needs assessment is significantly affected by how the feedback process is managed.

To maximize the potential for the development and implementation of plans and follow-up action, the consultant and key personnel took the following actions:

- During the initial and follow-up meetings with the CEO, vice-president for finance, and HR manager, the consultant candidly explained that he wanted to work only with organizations that would implement change based on a needs analysis. If UCS was not interested in implementing change based on the views of a cross section of key personnel, it was best not to begin at all.
- The CEO discussed his support for the entire needs assessment process and the subsequent change with the rest of the executive team, as well as with all personnel at the end-of-month companywide meeting.

- A task force was formed to support the OD process. The task force, known as the OI (Organizational Improvement) Task Force, comprised seven people: the CEO, the HR manager, three project managers from research and development and one from operations, and the manager of clinical affairs. Other than the CEO, the members were from middle management and provided a cross-functional perspective. The task force was formed in early June 1993, two weeks after the needs assessment process began, and met once a month for three hours at a nearby hotel.

  The four roles of the task force were discussed and clarified during the first meeting: to provide input to assist in the design of planned change programs, to support and assist in the implementation of planned change, to communicate key change themes and programs to employees, and to be a role model for the organization improvement model that UCS was developing. These roles, in turn, were communicated to all employees by a member of the task force at the companywide meeting at the end of June.

- During the initial meeting with each person who was to be interviewed, the consultant clarified his role and the needs assessment process, and emphasized that planning and implementation of changes would begin after three to four months. Feelings of ownership and commitment to the change process were also encouraged by emphasizing that any future changes would be based on the issues and recommendations developed from the interviews. In addition, all personnel were told they would be getting a copy of the report summarizing the views and recommendations of the 29 interviewees.

- The consultant discussed the feedback report with the CEO before he gave it to his executive team. In addition to clarifying follow-up actions and programs, which are discussed in the following section, the consultant and the CEO discussed the critical role of the CEO in the change process.

- The CEO and his executive team discussed the feedback report and follow-up actions and programs at their weekly senior staff meeting.

- When the report was distributed to other company personnel by the HR manager, the CEO attached a memo stating his support for the OD process and the need for the company to begin planning actions and changes based on the needs assessment. These themes were repeated by the CEO at the next companywide meeting. Although all 29 personnel interviewed received a copy of the report, a representative of the OI Task Force told the employees that anyone who wanted to read it could borrow a copy.

Follow-up Actions and Programs

The comprehensive feedback report was distributed after Labor Day, three months after the needs assessment interviews began. Although the report was actually completed in mid-August, the CEO and consultant thought it would be best to wait until after the vacation season ended to focus companywide attention and time to the report. After the report was distributed, the OI Task Force met to determine which issues and recommendations discussed in the report were priorities, and what the implications were for follow-up actions and programs. As already noted, the executive team also discussed implications of the report for follow-up actions and programs.

Changes in a variety of areas were developed and implemented from mid-September to mid-February, including

- The development and implementation of a modified goal-setting and performance evaluation system to replace the SBA system. The new program was viewed very favorably by all employees. Most important, it incorporated flexibility into the goal-setting and performance evaluation process so that employees would not be penalized financially for modifying their tasks and project focus. This kind of flexibility is of critical importance for companies working on products characterized by high technological and market uncertainties.

- The reassessment of all meetings for senior staff, departmental personnel, and cross-functional personnel and the modification of the focus of these meetings, the issues discussed, and the people attending. In addition, meetings and other communication mechanisms were modified to facilitate upward and downward communication.

- The vice-president of research and development began having his engineering staff discuss key skills and staffing issues related to project success. Subsequently, engineering project teams incorporated these previously neglected factors when analyzing requirements for technical projects.

- The executives began a series of monthly dialogues about strategic issues. This new forum began with a one-day program conducted by a strategy expert.

- A vice-president of sales and marketing was hired in mid-November, and a director of quality and regulatory affairs was hired in mid-February 1994. These additions, in turn, led to a variety of significant changes in the organizational structure: The director of quality reported directly to the CEO rather than the CFO; the sales force was doubled from four to eight and reported to the sales and marketing executive; and field service support reported to the sales and marketing executive rather than to the operations function.

- A series of team-building programs for senior management was planned to begin by March or April 1994 with a two-day session off site; three-hour programs were planned for the following four months.

Conclusions and Recommendations

Four key factors contributed to the successful needs assessment process at UCS. These factors suggest recommendations for human resource development professionals involved in organization change and development programs.

- Create active support of the change process among top management. The CEO and other executives at UCS played an active role in the OD process. When employees understand senior management supports a program and expects everyone to support a program, they realize "this is not just another HR program." Programs focusing on companywide needs assessment and organization improvement should not be led by an HR manager; they should be championed by the CEO or another senior executive.
- Develop and manage expectations for the needs assessment. During the first contact with the company, the consultant began communicating and managing expectations: Information would be gathered from interviewing diverse personnel, and this information would be used to assess high-priority issues for organizational improvement. The consultant communicated this point to each of the 29 personnel interviewed. In addition, the CEO discussed this process with all the employees at a companywide meeting.
- Build commitment processes into the needs assessment. An OD needs assessment has the potential to generate companywide commitment. When personnel realize that their views and recommendations will be used to assess organizational strengths and development needs, and that actions and programs will be implemented based on their views, the foundation for employee commitment has been developed. OD needs assessment processes that actively involve employees in assessing needs and planning and implementing change result in high employee commitment. Perception that top management supports the needs assessment process is another factor related to building companywide commitment. Finally, external or internal personnel conducting interviews need to have skills in creating a trusting communication climate, or commitment to the process will be hindered.
- Maintain an action-oriented focus to the needs assessment. Human resource development and OD programs are doomed to fail if they are

not focused on action. If one cannot secure top management's support for taking action, it is best not to proceed with the data-gathering stage of needs assessment. It is far better not to proceed than to proceed and create the perception that the company is conducting "another one of those surveys that have no real impact on anything." In contrast, timely implementation of appropriate actions and programs based on employees' input creates greater employee commitment to the long-term process of organization change and improvement.

Although there were no barriers to program implementation, there has been one periodic roadblock at UCS—emerging operational problems and strategic threats. There were times when task force meetings, discussions with senior management, and actions and programs had to be delayed. This is to be expected in any program of planned change. Real-time problems in such areas as quality, production volume capabilities, new product development, product roll-out, and patent infringement will take precedence over discussions and actions related to the needs assessment process. This is especially true in companies characterized by rapid growth, operating in an evolving, uncertain technological and marketing business environment.

Questions for Discussion

1. What were the various factors that contributed to the success of the needs assessment?
2. If the needs assessment conducted at Ultrasound Coronary Systems were conducted in the company in which you currently work, what things would you do similarly? What would you do differently? Provide rationales for your answers.
3. Develop an approach to evaluate the costs and benefits of the needs assessment process.

The Author

Michael Albert is a professor of management at San Francisco State University, teaching courses in advanced management, organizational behavior, and organization development. He is the author of *Effective Management: Readings, Cases and Experiences* and a coauthor of *Management: Individual and Organizational Effectiveness*. Both books were published into third editions (1988) by Harper & Row. He also has written numerous articles in the area of human resource development and corporate culture and has provided consulting services to numerous organizations in these areas. Albert can be contacted at the following address: San Francisco State University, 15 Sotelo Avenue, San Francisco, CA 94116.

References

Albert, M. (1985, May). Assessing cultural change needs. *Training & Development Journal, 39*, 94-98.

Schein, E. (1985). *Organizational culture and leadership: A dynamic view.* San Francisco: Jossey-Bass.

Safety Problems

Maverick Inc.

Rhonda Clemmer

This case shows how a combination of methods can be utilized to improve the validity and accuracy of the assessment process. Interviews, observation, and surveys were combined with extant data analysis to complete the needs assessment.

Background

This story begins several years ago, but for the purpose of this case, we begin in May of 1992. Maverick Incorporated, the client organization, hired an external consultant to investigate the excessively high number of accidents occurring in its shop area. Based on the findings, the consultant was to make recommendations concerning what safety training was needed. In essence, the consultant was contracted to perform a training needs assessment that would serve as the basis for the development of all safety training. However, the assessment revealed that the solution to Maverick's accident problems entailed much more than training.

Organizational Profile

Maverick Inc. is a midsized, custom air conditioner manufacturer located in Tulsa, Oklahoma. Maverick began operations as a small, family-owned business 15 years ago. Approximately four years ago, Maverick's owners made the decision to sell the business. The company would continue operations, but as a subsidiary of its new parent company, Lornex. With the change in ownership came new management, new policies, and a new marketing strategy.

This case was prepared to serve as a basis for discussion rather than to illustrate either effective or ineffective administrative and management practices.

Maverick employs more than 200 workers, the majority being production employees. The production group works two shifts. In addition to the production group, the organization consists of the senior management team and the human resources, engineering and design, quality control, and sales and service departments. Maverick designs, manufactures, distributes, and services custom units, concentrating on the commercial market. An example of one Maverick product is a 3,000-square-foot unit for a shopping mall. These large units have become increasingly complex over the past decade, and demand for them has increased. The future looks very bright for this growing organization.

Maverick's physical facilities include three buildings located over a three-block area. The human resources and sales and service departments are located in one building, the administrative and management offices in another building, and the shop area in yet another building.

Although quality is becoming more important at Maverick, output (i.e., the number of units produced) is still the primary performance criterion. Sales have increased dramatically over the past two years; consequently, the production team has been asked to produce more and more.

Key Players

The need for this assessment was identified by Lance Ashton, quality control and safety manager. Ashton also served as the assessor's point of contact and champion of the assessment process. His background was in engineering, and he had been employed by Maverick for just over one year. He was very enthusiastic about his quality control responsibilities, as well as personnel safety issues. (One other note: Ashton is the grandson of one of Maverick's senior vice-presidents.)

Robert Hanes was the president of Maverick. He supported the idea of training and development and made the final decision to conduct the assessment. However, human resource development was low on his list of priorities. Like many other executives, he felt sales and product development were much more important and failed to see how sales and safety training were related. Hanes had to be shown how safety training could improve the bottom line.

Don Collins was the vice-president of production. Collins had been with the company for 12 years. His management style was autocratic, and he was indifferent about his involvement in the assessment.

James Harmon was the shop manager. He had been with Maverick since it began business and was very knowledgeable about building air conditioners. Each of the five shop floor managers reported directly to Harmon. In addition, he was responsible for safety in the shop area until recently, when Ashton was assigned responsibility for the safety program, including ensuring compliance with Occupational Safety and Health Act (OSHA) regulations.

The final player in the needs assessment conducted at Maverick was Lynn Jones, the personnel director. She had been with the company for seven years and was responsible for all personnel actions, including occupational injury, workers' compensation, and accident reports. Her role in the assessment was to supply safety-related records and historical data.

Organizational Issues

Several organizational issues and attitudes had some bearing on the conduct and outcome of the assessment. First, the recent change in ownership brought with it new management and a more democratic and future-oriented management style. Second, Maverick was in the process of expanding its shop area to accommodate the increased sales. Additional production employees would have to be hired. The floor space for production would double within the year. Third, training and employee development had been relatively nonexistent in the past at Maverick. Safety training was no exception. Fourth, many of the production employees had been employed by Maverick for several years. These employees were somewhat set in their ways and reluctant to change or support training of any kind. These were all issues the assessor considered while conducting the assessment.

Initiating Events

The primary catalyst for the decision to conduct a needs assessment was the assignment of the safety program to Ashton. Safety, as well as training, was a new frontier for him, but he knew it would require much work to develop and implement an effective safety program. Maverick did not have a training department, and the personnel department did not have the skills or the staff to conduct a needs assessment. Therefore, Ashton approached his supervisor and Hanes about the possibility of contracting with an external consultant to conduct an assessment to identify the essential elements of the safety program. Ashton was most concerned about the high number of accidents being reported at Maverick. The proposed project was approved and the consultant was hired. Ashton proposed that the assessment should investigate the accident rate and suggest possible training programs needed.

Target Audience

The production employees were identified as the group of employees most affected by the safety program or lack thereof. Ninety-nine percent of occupational injuries occurred in the shop area. Thus, production employees and floor managers were targeted for this assessment and the resulting training. The turnover rate at Maverick was low compared with the industry average, so the majority of the employees were skilled in their particular jobs. No formal training was offered. The production employees learned their jobs through on-the-job training and trial and error.

Approximately 95 percent of the 150 production employees were male. Their average education level was high school graduate. All training recommended as a result of this assessment would be mandatory. In addition, employees would have to attend some safety training in accordance with OSHA guidelines.

The Process

A very systematic and well-planned process was used in conducting the assessment. The six steps in the assessment process were problem identification, data collection, data analysis, problem restatement, recommendations, and a report to management. However, many smaller actions had to be accomplished as a part of the six major steps. The assessor first established a liaison within the organization. She then identified some "cheerleaders" in upper management who would champion the assessment and proposed training. Ashton had already convinced the president of Maverick of the importance of the assessment, but promoting buy-in from the target population was still ahead. The assessor also set goals, wrote assessment objectives, prepared written outlines and procedures for each step, and evaluated and selected appropriate data collection techniques before any investigation took place.

Additionally, the assessor submitted short progress reports after each stage of the assessment process. Each progress report was either a short memo or a verbal report to Ashton, who, in turn, briefed senior management. The reports were an important vehicle for ensuring cooperation, buy-in, and ultimately implementation. The assessor was careful not to reveal so much information as to contaminate any subsequent data collected from individuals who received one of the reports.

Data Collection

The assessor felt that several methods were needed to validate and confirm the initial problem statement. Using the target population and the information needed as the guide, she chose four independent data collection methods: record (extant data) analysis, personal interview, observation, and survey. These tools were selected based on appropriateness to the assessment and the constraints placed on the assessor by Maverick—for example, time, money, and access to employees.

The assessor began the data collection process by conducting a personal interview with the newly appointed safety manager. It was during this interview that Ashton identified the excessively high accident rate as the problem the assessor should investigate and indicated that training was needed. (Telling the assessor the problem and solution before the assessment began immediately sent up a red flag.) The assessor also collected information concerning personal biases, the organizational culture, and current and past safety training, policies, and programs. Ashton also briefly explained the air conditioner manufacturing process and the equipment used in the shop area. From this interview, an observation guide was developed. The guide would remind the assessor to look for certain safety concerns while observing the shop area.

The observation of the shop was the second data collection method used. The assessor observed Maverick employees building air conditioner units, trying to remain as inconspicuous as possible so as not to disrupt or bias employees' actions. Next, the assessor interviewed Jones, the personnel director. The assessor collected accident reports for the previous 12 months, OSHA reports, appraisals, employee suggestions, and workers' compensation forms. Information was collected on the numbers, types, causes, and costs of accidents, as well as on demographics, such as length of service of injured employees. The assessor also reviewed safety policies and the OSHA guidelines relating to workplace safety at Maverick. This phase took approximately 24 hours to complete.

At this point, enough "optimal" and "actual" data were collected to begin collecting data on attitudes, causes, and solutions. An interview guide was developed (see Table 1) to serve as a road map for interviewing the vice-president of production, the shop manager, and the floor manager for each of the production areas. Follow-up and spontaneous questions were also an important part of the interviews. The guide reflected the importance of setting the stage (e.g., building trust) at the beginning of an interview. The information collected during the interviews would serve as a baseline for the development of the fourth data collection method, the production survey.

Table 1. Interview guide.

Introductions	• Background on needs analysis project • Facilitator's background • Why selected as interviewee • Safety program improvement • What steps have been taken to date
Professional background	• Past experiences • Length of employment with Maverick • Connection with company safety issues
History of safety program	• Past 10 years • Changes since company purchase • Task of safety office and Lance Ashton

Current safety issues	• Personal perception of current situation
	• Company perception of current situation
	  — Management
	  — Floor manager
	  — Line workers
	• Emphasis and procedures followed by workers
	• Current safety program in use
	• Factors contributing to accidents
	• How injured personnel are disciplined
	• Work environment's effect on accident rate
	  — Organization, facility, equipment
	  — Cleanliness of shop
	• Lifting involved in the job
	• Types of injuries most common

Other	• Relation of production expectations to safety • Current safety equipment in use • Management's commitment to safety
Occupational Safety and Health Act requirements	• Accident reporting • Safety gear

Once all the interviews were completed and the data compiled, a report to Ashton and Maverick's president was prepared. At this point in the investigation, the assessor had some idea of what the symptoms, problems, and causes were. She used this information to design a survey to collect information from the employees most involved with the safety issues: the production employees. It took a full week to design the survey and test it using a panel of employees, both frontline and supervisory. In essence, the survey was designed to validate data previously collected. The survey was distributed to 120 production employees, who returned their responses anonymously to a collection box beside the time clock. A return rate of 92 percent was achieved.

Cost and Benefits

The cost of the assessment was minimal compared with the potential savings on medical insurance premiums, workers' compensation claims, lawsuits, absenteeism, and turnover, although the assessor did not have the opportunity to follow-up after the recommendations were implemented and determine the financial benefits or outcomes precisely. The total cost of the needs assessment was $6,500. This may seem like a large amount of money, but defending one personal injury suit could cost more than $20,000, and the cost to replace one injured employee (i.e., recruitment, training, etc.) would almost offset the assessment cost.

Data Analysis

Time constraints, lack of resources, and organizational constraints demanded a simple, quick, but reliable process for data analysis. Therefore, the assessor relied on simple descriptive statistics (such as means or percentages) and summary graphs and tables to analyze the data collected. The assessor followed the same steps for each data collection method. She began by reviewing the raw data thoroughly and then deciding on the best way to condense and summarize the information. Then, she tabulated the data. The next step was comparing the raw data with the condensed data to ensure the information had not been distorted. Finally, the assessor recorded any personal comments or observations. An important part of the data analysis was to discover some of the issues that were being avoided and to recognize the nonverbal information provided during the interviews.

Extant Data

From the records, reports, evaluations, and policies reviewed, the assessor extracted only information she felt was relevant. For example, a

Figure 1. Relative frequencies of common injuries reported from June 1991 through March 1992.

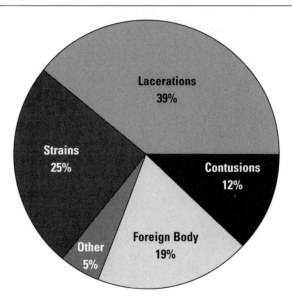

pie chart showing the most common injuries and accidents was prepared. The extant data were then kept accessible so the assessor could refer to them for support or clarification of data collected using other methods.

Observation

The assessor recorded the safety precautions taken, how the safety equipment was used, and all safety-related actions that she noticed while observing employees in the shop area. In one instance, she broke down one of the tasks to determine which particular step or steps appeared to be responsible for the excessive injuries. The observation notes were read and reread to find significant behaviors, events, patterns, or environmental flaws (such as old equipment) that could have contributed to the high accident rate. These findings were summarized and presented in the observation report.

Interviews

The extant and observational data were objective and, therefore, easily tabulated and analyzed. The challenge began with the analysis of the interview and survey data. An assistant who was not a Maverick employee assisted in capturing pertinent data during the interviews.

This note taker recorded the responses of each interviewee. The interviewer also took some notes. The interviewer assured the employees that all comments would be kept confidential and that the note taker was present only to ensure accurate recording of the information.

The interview data were summarized and analyzed using two different methods: summary sheets and frequency counts. First, the assessor reviewed each interview record in the context of that interview. Any comments, trends, or themes that appeared to be important were recorded. The assessor also compared the interviews against one another to identify any recurrent themes. The summary that resulted from this method was somewhat subjective, because the assessor had to read between the lines and remember nonverbal information as well as the context in which comments were made.

Second, the assessor used a color-coded frequency count as a more objective and quantitative vehicle for analyzing the data. A legend was developed for each theme or problem area previously identified. The legend was as follows:
- green = communication problems
- red = lack of training or skills
- blue = management or supervisory problems
- yellow = organizational or policy issues.

Each interviewee's original interview notes (interview record) were highlighted according to the color code. The assessor then cut apart each interview record based on the color-coded answers and prepared a frequency count of each color-coded theme. The frequency count proved to be an effective tool for managing a large number of somewhat dissimilar responses.

A report that included the totals from the frequency count and the written summary of the interviews was prepared for management's review as a part of the final report.

Survey

The production survey was designed to include primarily closed-ended questions, which simplified the data analysis. The most common responses on the open-ended questions and the percentages for each of the closed-ended questions were tabulated and recorded on a blank survey. The surveys were tabulated manually, because a relatively small population was surveyed. However, a computer and a scanner could have easily been used for a longer survey or larger population. Tables 2 and 3 present some of the results for the two kinds of questions on the survey.

Table 2. Sample of the results from the production survey: Closed-ended questions.

Question	Response
06. Do employees read the safety manual?	Yes 43%, No 57%
07. Does your floor manager set a good example for using safety precautions?	Yes 43%, No 57%
08. Are the tools and machinery you use in safe working condition?	Yes 43%, No 57%
09. When an accident occurs, is the cause of the accident corrected immediately?	Yes 43%, No 57%
10. Does your floor manager enforce safety regulations?	Yes 43%, No 57%
11. Do you feel safety is a problem?	Yes 43%, No 57%
18. Please check all items that contribute to accidents in your area.	Carelessness of workers 59%
	Cluttered work area 75%
	Insufficient training on safety 40%
	Production rush 65%
	Cannot be avoided 29%
19. What safety training have you received in the last year? (Check all that apply)	Forklift 53%
	Equipment safety 18%
	Sheet metal 12%
	Lifting procedures 41%
	Respirator 5%
	First aid 6%
	CPR 3%

The assessor felt that the work area and tenure of an employee played a significant role in his or her answers on the survey. Therefore, she cross-tabulated the responses and analyzed some of them according to work area and tenure. Chart and graphs were then developed to help summarize the data and relationships visually.

The charts were prepared primarily as a tool for presenting the findings to senior management. Significance tests and other statistical calculations were not a part of this data analysis. Simplicity remained the order of the day. Figures 1 and 2 show examples of the graphs prepared.

Table 3. Sample of results from the production survey: Open-ended questions.

Question	Responses	
12. Safety areas not given enough training[a]	CPR, location of oxygen Forklifts (3) Housekeeping (2) All areas (6) Insulation Saws and cutting devices Lifting (2)	Welding practices Storage of hoses and electrical cords Safety without rushing Sheet metal safety Training new workers Equipment safety (3)
13. Response received when reporting unsafe conditions	Ignored No action taken Oh, well Don't worry about it; go back to work Repaired after time No action Didn't listen	Just live with it Not bad enough; it still works Promptly handled the matter Don't worry about it Okay, but was too busy to handle it No response
15. Where the first aid is kept	First aid cabinet by the bathroom Vice-president of production's office Upstairs Floor manager's desk	
17. Communication channel for safety regulations[a]	Word of mouth (2) Not informed (27) Letters sent by company Letters from vice-president of production (3) Floor manager (6)	Bulletin board Monthly worksheet Safety meeting Safety guidelines (2) Handouts (2)

[a] *For this question, each answer listed was given once unless inidicated otherwise by a number in parentheses.*

Summary

Data analysis involved both subjective and objective data. All data were analyzed and considered, keeping in mind personal biases, organizational norms, previous comments made, and what each person had

Figure 2. Perceived causes of accidents, by tenure.

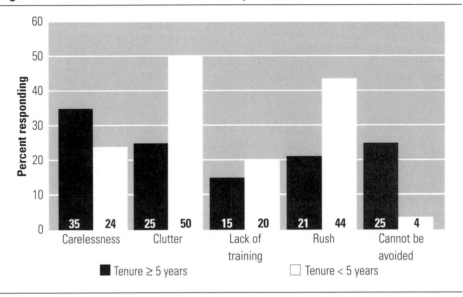

Tenure ≥ 5 years
Tenure < 5 years

to gain. Summary sheets were developed to assist in final analysis and were included in senior management's final report. (Samples of the summary sheets are shown in Tables 4 and 5.)

Needs assessment is an investigation process, and like any good private investigator, the assessor must rely on past experience and basic knowledge. The key is to balance the emphasis placed on subjective information with the facts and figures gathered.

Table 4. Summary of comments from interviews with floor managers.

- Floor managers do not have the authority to enforce safety regulations
- No orientation is given to new employees
- Work environment is not conducive to safety
- Safety is not considered a problem by many floor managers
- Management is very supportive of safety
- Forklift training and respirator training are most common
- Safety equipment is always worn
- Accidents happen, and they cannot be prevented sometimes
- Safety is basically reactive at Maverick
- Floor managers do not feel the accident rate is high
- Most accidents occur because people are not paying attention

Table 5. Summary of interview with the vice-president of production.

Current safety program
- According to policy, all employees should be receiving some safety training
- Accident reports are kept but scattered throughout the organization
- There is no communication of safety
- Only some of the training is documented
- All employees are required to wear safety shoes and goggles
- Some employees must wear hearing and breathing protection
- Ashton's knowledge of safety practices is limited
- Personnel handles the bulk of the safety documentation
- There is no accountability for lost hours and money

Subjective comments
- Accidents are inevitable (a fact of life)
- Importance of safety is increasing
- Some employees abuse the use of free medical treatment
- Maverick is very lenient concerning safety and visiting the doctor
- Strains and sprains are the number-one injury
- Safety training is basically on-the-job training
- Employees perceive training as a break from their jobs
- Maverick does not really react to accidents unless they are serious
- Congestion results in some accidents

Interviewer's comments
- Interviewer did not stress confidentiality (could have had an effect)
- No surprising information was received
- Maverick has a relatively lax attitude about safety
- Vice-president seemed to be cooperative and supportive of project
- Vice-president did not know the Occupational Safety and Health Act guidelines (odd)

Results

The data from each collection method were reviewed separately, and the summarized data from the various sources were analyzed collectively to ensure some repetition and consistency existed among the sources. Based on the sum of all the data, the assessor restated the problem facing Maverick, made recommendations, and drew conclusions. During the preparation of the recommendations, as during the analysis, she checked the frequency counts and summary sheets often to ensure the data supported the conclusions she had drawn.

The data indicated that the excessively high accident rate, originally thought to be the major problem, was actually a symptom of a very serious situation. A lax attitude toward safety was the real problem. By placing more emphasis on a safe work environment and implementing a safety program, Maverick would reduce the overall accident rate. The assessor presented three major recommendations to Ashton. The recommendations were not presented in order of preference, and each could stand alone or be used in conjunction with the others. Thus, choosing which recommendations to implement was management's decision, not the assessor's. The recommendations are listed in Table 6. (Note that only one recommendation involved training.)

Both written and oral reports of the needs assessment results were presented to senior management. In addition, the assessor provided a letter summarizing the findings to each employee who participated during the investigation stage. No confidential information was revealed in the letter.

Conclusions and Recommendations

This project was a relatively straightforward and simple assessment. The assessor received full cooperation, at least outwardly, from the organization. (This may not always be the case when an internal assessor conducts an assessment.) Many safety-related needs were identified, and implementation of all the recommendations will require great effort and commitment by Maverick, including a substantial investment of time and money. However, working on even one of the major recommendations will be an important first step in implementing a comprehensive safety program. A safe work environment will be even more important once the organization's expansion is completed. The success of the effort will hinge on the support Ashton receives from senior management and the production employees.

Senior management's reaction to the final report was very positive. However, even the best plans fail if not followed up with decisive action. A more focused assessment including task analysis may be appropriate before developing or implementing the proposed training interventions. Such an assessment would assist in developing the course objectives and content.

The assessor experienced a few stumbling blocks during the assessment process and learned several lessons:

- Encourage the organization to allow sufficient time for the assessment. Some steps were rushed.

Table 6. Recommendations.

1. Maverick should develop formal and informal communication channels in order to promote safety and implement an effective safety program.
   - Use a safety bulletin board to post safety regulations, meetings, accident reports, and other pertinent safety information.
   - Keep floor managers and production employees abreast of all safety information.
   - Appoint a safety representative for each area.
   - Clarify who has the authority to correct unsafe acts by employees and emphasize accountability.
   - Centralize all safety records for easy access.
   - Keep more accurate documentation of training.
   - Review safety policies and procedures.

2. Maverick should place more emphasis on the importance of workplace safety by making management, floor managers, and production employees accountable for safety.
   - Present a monthly safety award to areas with no accidents or injuries.
   - Reduce clutter in work areas by placing more emphasis on good housekeeping.
   - Include safety as part of the employee appraisal system.
   - Implement an employee involvement program to promote safety accountability by all employees.
   - Establish stiffer penalties for unsafe acts and unsafe working conditions.
   - Place safety signs throughout the shop area to remind employees about safety.
   - Encourage employee participation via the use of a suggestion system and safety slogan contest.

3. Maverick should provide each new employee with a four-hour safety orientation and provide follow-up training as needed each year.
   - Train each employee in lockout (tagout) procedures.
   - Train each employee on the types of machinery safeties.
   - Verbally cover the rules and regulations written in the employee handbook.
   - Train each employee in hazardous communications.
   - Train each employee in the use of personal protective equipment.
   - Train each employee in lifting procedures.
   - Train each employee on the importance of safety in a manufacturing environment.
   - Provide supervised on-the-job training for job-specific safety precautions.

- Use a sufficiently large pilot group to ensure a range of comments. The individuals who participated in the pilot provided very little useful information. The group did not want to comment.
- Eliminate all biases during the interviews. More time should have been spent gaining the interviewees' trust. Some interviewees seemed to give pat answers that they thought the assessor wanted to hear.

- Encourage management to make a decision regarding the recommendations presented, and then offer your services for implementing the recommendations. Someone must assist the organization to ensure that some action is taken.

Questions for Discussion

1. What other data collection methods might have been appropriate?
2. How did attitudes and organizational culture affect the outcome?
3. How could management support have been fostered?
4. Were additional recommendations warranted? If so, what recommendations would you have made?
5. Did the assessor make assumptions not based on the data (i.e., "read between the lines")?
6. Were data needed from any other group?
7. What steps should be taken now to implement the training recommendations?

The Author

Rhonda Clemmer is the president of Eagle Systems and Services Inc., based in Lawton, Oklahoma. Eagle provides training services, including assessment, program design, facilitation, and evaluation. Clemmer holds a bachelor's degree in business administration and marketing from Cameron University and a master's degree in human resource development from Oklahoma State University. She has performed numerous front-end analyses for government agencies, service organizations, and manufacturers. Clemmer is an active member of the American Society for Training and Development and has been named to Outstanding Young Women in America and Who's Who in the South. She can be contacted at the following address: Eagle Systems and Services Inc., P.O. Box 207, Lawton, OK 73502.

Assessing the Performance Improvement Needs at a Community College

Northeast Community College

Peter J. Dean, Martha Ray Dean, and Elizabeth C. Guman

In this needs assessment, the evaluation research model was used to guide the process overall. The nominal group technique was used to gather accurate data, and the behavior engineering model was used to demonstrate the difference between training and nontraining performance improvement solutions.

Background

The professional development committee of a midsized community college in suburban Philadelphia had responsibility for developing a one-year professional development plan for the administrators, faculty, and support personnel at the college. Past professional development programs were held on two consecutive days just before the second semester. All employees at the college were mandated to attend. In light of concern about these programs, we were hired as outside consultants to help develop the plan.

This case describes the needs assessment we conducted with the 280 support staff, faculty, and administrators of the community college. We used the evaluation research model (Geroy and Wright, 1988) as a guideline for planning and implementing the assessment. We taught the nominal group technique (Debeque and Van de Ven, 1971), a comprehensive data-gathering process for large groups, to representatives

This case was prepared to serve as a basis for discussion rather than to illustrate either effective or ineffective administrative and management practices. All names, dates, places, and organizations have been disguised at the request of the organization involved or the case author.

from each of these three groups. These representatives then facilitated the participation of virtually all employees at the college in identifying a prioritized list of items that would enable these persons to "do their job better." Analysis of the suggested performance improvement needs used the behavior engineering model (Gilbert, 1978). Five categories of intervention emerged from the data: high-yield training, direction and flow of information, resources, performance incentives, and medium-yield training.

Issues

After three lengthy meetings with the committee and focus groups, including representatives from each of the functional areas, we identified seven problems that would have to be dealt with in planning the professional development program. The problems included

- the commonly held perception that professional development automatically meant training
- the lack of a link between professional development and performance improvement
- the lack of agreement among committee members as to how to select professional development opportunities, with some members feeling they already knew the needs of each functional group
- limited communication of operating information across functional groups
- negative employee perceptions regarding previous professional development efforts
- the perceived unresponsiveness of decision makers to employees' past suggestions related to professional development needs
- the recent loss of incentive due to reduced power and autonomy within the faculty structure.

It appeared that a failure to address these problems would reduce the benefits of the professional development program. Specifically, the final professional development plan for the 1991-1992 academic year had to

- involve and empower all employees (i.e., stakeholders) equally in identifying professional development needs, regardless of whether their perceptions were viewed as valid by their peers
- develop a means by which the planning committee itself would recognize that performance improvement can be achieved by nontraining actions and that such actions might be required in order to maximize the effectiveness of the training that is done
- elicit data that would represent both the perceived wants and the actual needs of the employees of the college

- elicit accurate data while facilitating a process with 280 participants at one time
- provide decision makers with a systematic process for selecting professional development activities that would yield maximum results for the cost and effort invested.

In light of these challenges, the professional development committee agreed to conduct an assessment to identify the training needs of each functional group. They asked us to submit a plan for conducting the needs assessment.

Method

In designing the needs assessment plan, we wanted not only to address the problems and challenges listed, but also to shift the attention of the committee members from "professional development training" to "performance improvement solutions" so that they would concentrate on improving performance, which might mean recommending nontraining actions. Therefore, we needed to involve the committee members in each phase of the needs assessment design and implementation so they would have confidence in the accuracy of the data and the systematic way in which it was gathered. We also needed to provide them with the technical information they needed to make the right decisions about the data.

We selected the strategies of the evaluation research model to guide this process, the nominal group technique to gather accurate data, and the behavior engineering model to demonstrate to the committee the difference between training and nontraining solutions for performance improvement.

Evaluation Research

Evaluation research (Geroy and Wright, 1988) is a pragmatic, program-focused research strategy of analysis for decision makers. Its purpose is to provide data that can enable decision making through analysis of pros and cons, through prioritizing, or through the application of decision-making criteria.

A unique feature of evaluation research, and the source of its strength, is the involvement of stakeholders throughout the research process. Input and feedback from the stakeholders influence a project's feasibility in terms of cost, timeliness, and manner of implementation, as well as utility, accuracy, and ownership of the outcome.

Beginning with Phase One, selecting the purpose of the evaluation research (see Figure 1), the research evaluators and the stakeholders

Figure 1. Phases in the evaluation research model.

1. **Select the purpose of the evaluation research.**

   ❏ needs assessment   ❏ small-scale testing   ❏ policy analysis
   ❏ basic research   ❏ evaluation   ❏ fiscal accountability
   ❏ coverage accountability   ❏ input assessment   ❏ economic analysis

2. **Identify the technique to be used.**

   ❏ front-end analysis   ❏ program monitoring   ❏ impact evaluation
   ❏ formative evaluation   ❏ evaluability assessment   ❏ evaluation of evaluation

3. **Develop the research question.**

   "What do I need to meet my professional goals and objectives?"

4. **Establish a collaborative, utilization-focused process.**

   A. Compose a task force   B. Design task force activities
   ❏ All stakeholders are represented   ❏ Clarify focus
   ❏ Power exists to act on findings   ❏ Select methods and measurement
   ❏ Time is committed   ❏ Review instruments and strategies
   ❏ Process and results are valued

5. **Determine the research focus.**

   ❏ evaluation research with goals   ❏ evaluation research without goals

6. **Determine the evaluation research strategy.**

   ❏ scientific, hypothetical, deductive   ❏ anthropological, holistic, inductive

7. **Select the data collection method.**

   ❏ formal instruments (e.g., survey)   ❏ nonformal instruments (e.g.,
                                            structured or nonstructured interview)

8. **Implement the research.**

9. **Analyze the research.**

Adapted from Performance Improvement Quarterly, 1 *(3), 17-26, by Gary Geroy and Phillip Wright. Used by permission of PIQ.*

"become collaborating partners in the search for useful information" (Geroy and Wright, 1988). From then on, collaboration is included in each phase of the process. This collaboration provides a means of monitoring the appropriateness, relevance, and feasibility of each activity and strategy. As a result, the information gathered is more likely to be on target in addressing the needs of the stakeholders than if the process had been noncollaborative. The collaboration also facilitates decision making because of both the accuracy of the information and the useful way in which the information is reported. Furthermore, the stakeholders who have helped structure the process, as well as those from whom the data

Table 1. Steps in the nominal group technique.

Step One: Generating responses to a question individually
- Initially, no talking takes place.
- Each individual has a sheet of paper with the "nominal question" on it. This question provides the primary focus of the meeting and is carefully constructed prior to the meeting in order to generate the required information.
- Participants, independently and silently, write down as many answers to the questions as possible.

Step Two: Collecting responses from all participants
- After approximately 10 minutes, the facilitator, going round-robin, calls on each member of the group to give one of his or her ideas.
- A letter designation is given to each item. (Letters are used to avoid the implication that Item #1 might be the most important.)
- The round-robin continues until all participants have shared all their ideas.
- Tally marks can be used if the exact same idea is generated by several participants. If ideas are slightly different, each is listed separately.
- The purpose of this stage is to make sure that each participant is given equal opportunity to share his or her ideas, so that highly verbal individuals do not dominate the group process. Thus, all discussion and judgment are postponed.

Step Three: Clarifying ideas
- The facilitator reviews each idea sequentially, encouraging clarification questions, elaborations, and expressions of support, as well as rebuttals or hitchhiking to new ideas. This phase is complete when all ideas have been reviewed.

are derived, have greater ownership of the results than if they had not contributed to the process, and their potential buy-in to the recommendations that stem from the research is increased.

Another unique feature of evaluation research is the option of focusing on the stated goals and objectives of a program. These may include decisions to be made, problems to be solved, the degree of similarity between what someone says and what he or she is doing, or perceptions about program effectiveness. In each case, the data gathered are used to create, maintain, or improve program policy, implementation practices, or both.

Nominal Group Technique

The nominal group technique (Debeque and Van de Ven, 1971) uses a structured group meeting conducted by a group leader or

Table 1 (continued). Steps in the nominal group technique.

Step Four: Categorizing ideas

● This stage is optional, depending on the number and kind of responses generated in Step Two.

● When there is great overlap of ideas, the group can categorize ideas by topic. Each category is given a descriptive name and a category designation, such as C-A, C-B, or C-C. Each category name is followed by a number indicating how many individual responses were subsumed into it.

● This step can facilitate the ranking that follows in Step Five by reducing the number of items that have to be considered. It is necessary, however, for members of the group to agree on the categories established and the items that go into them.

Step Five: Ranking ideas

● Each participant silently and privately ranks the revised list of ideas and categories by assigning a numerical value to each.

● Depending on the purpose, the ranking criteria could be cost of implementation, feasibility, importance, etc. Similarly, the number of ideas and categories that are ranked can vary.

● Each member's rankings are recorded, and the average rank of each item is derived. These average rankings indicate the group's priorities.

---

facilitator in five steps: generating ideas, reporting ideas sequentially, clarifying ideas, categorizing ideas, and ranking ideas by importance (see Table 1).

Consistent with evaluation research, one of the advantages of the technique is the involvement of stakeholders. The nominal group technique ensures that each person has an equal opportunity to express his or her ideas. It stimulates the generation of ideas through silent writing in Step One and the round-robin listing in Step Two. This procedure prevents closure on ideas before all are equally considered.

All participants can reflect on all ideas and have their questions and concerns addressed in the third step, when ideas are clarified.

In Step Four, ideas that are highly similar are grouped into one category to avoid redundancy and to make the data easier to report by reducing the number of items. It has been our experience that when you get to the data analysis and reporting stages, categories frequently carry more weight than single items because of the number of responses they represent.

Ranking, the fifth step, gives equal weight to each person's opinion and reduces peer pressure to support one idea. After individuals silently rank the items they consider most important, a group tally of rankings is completed.

The fact that the nominal group technique can be used to gather large amounts of data in a short period of time without incurring great expense adds to its flexibility (Scott and Deadrick, 1982).

Behavior Engineering Model

The behavior engineering model (Gilbert, 1978) is one of the components of performance engineering (Dean, 1994). The premise of performance engineering is that a variety of factors in the workplace have bearing on performance effectiveness and that adjusting these factors appropriately can yield exemplary performance, often without training. Thus, it behooves people responsible for the performance of others to identify environmental and individual factors that will not only improve performance, but also maintain exemplary quality without costly training. By looking at employees and their work environments through the lens of the behavior engineering model, one can identify what can be done to improve and maintain performance—one of the goals of any professional development project.

The model, shown in Figure 2, includes six cells organized into rows and columns. The three cells along the top row of the model—information, resources, and incentives—represent factors of the work environment that influence performance. When these performance support factors are provided for, employees are empowered to perform at an exemplary level. When employees are given the responsibility and authority to perform at an exemplary level, but the support factors are not provided, the employees are not, in fact, empowered.

The absence of performance support factors in the work environment is probably the single greatest cause of performance deficiencies. This is why, in identifying the solutions that will yield performance improvement, we begin by examining the support factors in the work environment. Gilbert believes that the majority of the time, performance improvement can be achieved by addressing the environmental support factors. Yet traditionally, managers and human resource specialists assume that the individual, not the environment, needs "fixing," and thus training is provided as the solution for improving performance. It does not take much effort to identify the consequences of this misdiagnosis:

- Performance does not improve to the degree that managers expect, leading them to discredit the training, the employee, or both.
- The disparity between the average and exemplary employees remains.

Figure 2. The behavior engineering model.

Stimuli	Response	Consequences
Cell 1 **Information**	**Cell 2** **Resources**	**Cell 3** **Incentives**
• Descriptions of what is expected of performance • Clear and relevant guides on how to do the job • Relevant and frequent feedback about the adequacy of performance	• Tools, resources, time, and materials designed to achieve performance needs • Access to leaders • Sufficient personnel • Organized work processes	• Adequate financial incentives contingent upon performance • Nonmonetary incentives • Career development opportunities • Clear consequences for poor performance
Cell 4 **Knowledge**	**Cell 5** **Capacity**	**Cell 6** **Motives**
• Systematically designed training that matches requirements of exemplary performers • Opportunity for training	• Match between person and position • Good selection processes • Flexible scheduling of performance to match peak capacity of workers • Prostheses or visual aids to augment capacity	• Recognition of worker's willingness to work for available incentives • Assessment of worker's motivation • Recruitment of workers to match realities of work conditions

Adapted from Human Competence, *1978, p. 87. Used with permission from T.F. Gilbert.*

Of course, there are many instances in which the appropriate solution does involve the employee directly. The bottom row of the behavior engineering model represents factors related to the employee. The first, knowledge, comes into play when training is needed for

- meeting new job responsibilities
- participating in cross-functional teams
- using new equipment
- addressing gaps in knowledge and skills.

In these instances, it is often not necessary to use the model to identify the cause of performance deficiencies.

The second cell on the bottom row of the behavior engineering model, capacity, represents the match between the employee and the job requirements.

Gilbert contends that motivation, the third factor related to the individual, will be high if all the other cells, especially those related to the work environment, are provided for. Thus, he believes that evidence of low motivation is a red flag to look for deficiencies in information, resources, or incentives.

It is Gilbert's (1978) claim that any job that is supported in all six of the areas of the model should "carry a guarantee of high competence, provided that management was structured so as to really deliver these things and had a clear focus on the mission of the job in the first place."

Research and experience verify that without good needs assessment, training is likely to be the performance improvement intervention of choice. As a result, wants instead of needs are frequently addressed, the value of training yields less than optimal return on the dollar and time investment, and training has little long-term effect on the organization as a whole.

Strategies related to evaluation research and performance engineering have proven effective in both carrying out front-end identification of needs (Debeque and Van de Ven, 1971; Geroy and Wright, 1988) and deciding how to address the needs so the training that is eventually done will have high yields to both the trainee and the organization (T.F. Gilbert, personal communication, June 1991). Performance engineering helps to show where training is not the best choice of intervention and, if training is the best intervention, what kind of training will best meet the need (Dean, 1994).

Action Items

The needs assessment process we employed illustrates the integration of the nominal group technique and behavior engineering model into the strategies of the evaluation research model. In the following description of the stages of the needs assessment planning and implementation, this integration is apparent.

Step One: Establish Goals

As described in the introduction, we, along with the professional development committee, determined an assessment was necessary to identify professional development needs and their appropriate solutions. This step corresponded with Phase One of the evaluation research model, selecting the research purpose.

Step Two: Design the Needs Assessment Technique

We selected the nominal group technique (Debeque and Van de Ven, 1971) as the primary method for collecting data because it addressed the need to involve and empower all employees equally. This step fulfilled Phase Two of the evaluation research model, identifying the technique to be used. The first of the five applications of the nominal group technique occurred at this point. We used it with the professional development committee for two reasons. The committee members needed to experience the technique firsthand in order to buy into it, and they needed to achieve consensus on the definition of professional development (versus training) and the purpose of the committee. Therefore, the nominal question we asked them in this step was how to define professional development, and they followed the technique to reach consensus. We addressed Phases Two and Four of the evaluation research model during this activity.

Step Three: Conduct Focus Groups

We then held focus groups with representatives from each of the functional areas (administration, faculty, and support staff) in order to identify any perceptions or problems in the workplace that might affect planning the professional development program. The information we gathered verified some of the problems listed in the introduction and reinforced the need for a collaborative needs assessment process. The perceived professional development needs we identified during the focus groups corresponded with data gathered later using the nominal group technique. The focus groups provided another opportunity for collaboration of the stakeholders. This activity was also part of Phase Four of the evaluation research model, establishing a collaborative, utilization-focused process. We carried out Phase Four before Phase Three, developing the research question, because we wanted to use the results of the focus groups in finalizing the research question.

Step Four: Design the Methodology

We used the information provided by the professional development committee and the focus group interviews to develop the question that we eventually asked each of the 280 employees of the college: "What do I need to meet my professional goals and objectives?" This step completed Phase Three of the evaluation research model.

Our biggest design challenge was how to use the nominal group technique with 280 people at one time. Generally, this technique is conducted with no more than 10 members in a group, so we decided to conduct 28 concurrent nominal groups by training group facilitators. Data would be collected through three separate nominal group processes. The first would identify needs, the second would prioritize the needs, and the third would generate solutions to the previously identified needs.

At this point, we selected performance engineering for analyzing and reporting the data. This step of designing the methodology represented Phases Five, Six, and Seven of the evaluation research model. We had selected an evaluation research without goals as the research focus, an anthropological (i.e., holistic and inductive) research strategy, and a data collection method that involved a nonformal instrument—namely, the nominal group technique.

Step Five: Train Facilitators

We spent one afternoon training more than 40 people from the three functional areas on how to facilitate the nominal group technique. Each of these facilitators would be in charge of leading a group of 10 individuals from his or her functional area through the needs assessment process during the two-day program. This training was the second application of the nominal group technique.

The training consisted of information on the technique and a walk-through in which we modeled the nominal group technique process and the facilitators, as the group members, responded to the same question that the remaining 240 college employees would consider during the actual needs assessment. Each facilitator received job aids, including scripted directions to read during the three phases of the needs assessment program, tips for facilitators on group dynamics and how to encourage the free flow of ideas, and forms for reporting the data (see Figure 3).

Step Six: Conduct the Needs Assessment

On the first morning of the two-day program, we introduced the needs assessment process and used icebreaker activities to encourage the free flow of ideas when it came time for the nominal group technique.

After lunch, members of the three functional areas met in separate locations, where they divided into smaller groups of about 10 people each. Then, the trained volunteers simultaneously facilitated the 28 groups through the processes of need identification and prioritization.

At the end of the afternoon, each facilitator transferred the ideas and rankings that had been generated by his or her group onto a Facilitator's Report Form (see Figure 3). The forms were then collected and taken to the computer center, where volunteers from the support staff and professional development committee had assembled to help input the data and

Figure 3. Facilitator's report form.

Group Number _____ Facilitator _____

Fill in the ideas from the highest ranking to the lowest ranking. The top 10 are the ones addressed in Round Two and so should have a priority assigned to them. All ideas from your group should be recorded. If you need more pages, please see your master facilitator.

Codes Used in Report Form:

# 1, #2, etc.	Indicate order in which the items and categories were named during the ranking, not their importance
Name	Record the name of the item or category
Points	Record the total number of ranking points of the item or category
Category Description	When several ideas were combined into a category, describe the category
Explanation of Idea	Briefly explain any idea that is not clearly described by its name
Priority	Urgent, very important, important. Use only for the top 10.

#1

Name _____   Points _____
Category Description _____
Explanation of Idea _____
Priority _____

(Use one form for each idea.)

---

create a summary booklet for each functional area.

There were several reasons for developing the summary booklets after the first day. We wanted each group to be able to review the ideas from the other groups within its functional area before the second day, when the groups would be identifying solutions to the needs identified on the first day. We felt, and the feedback from the groups indicated, that the additional information would stimulate a wider range of solution ideas than the groups might have generated had they not had booklets.

Also, we believed that the effort we put into developing the summary booklets would demonstrate the commitment of the professional development committee and the college to "hearing" what the employees were saying. This was important, given the employees' negative perceptions of previous professional development efforts.

Not all of the information from the Facilitator's Report Form was included in the summary booklets. Table 2 illustrates how the professional development needs identified by one group of administrators were reported. Similar lists were generated for each of the other 27 groups. Each group was identified by number (e.g., Staff Group One, Faculty Group Three, Administrator Group Eight). The needs were then listed by order of importance. When categories were listed (e.g., "positive caring climate"), all the individual items within the categories were listed as well.

The volunteers worked late in the evening until all responses generated by all of the groups were typed and copies of the summary booklet from each functional area had been made.

On the second morning of the two-day program, we gave each participant a copy of the summary booklet. Each group was encouraged to review the responses of all the other groups within its functional area prior to generating solutions to each of the needs the group had identified on the previous day. Participants were encouraged to consider both training and nontraining solutions.

By lunch of the second day, the project had evolved through the first eight phases of the evaluation research model and used the nominal group technique in three separate contexts: establishing the goals of the project (15 participants), training the facilitators (40 participants), and conducting the needs assessment (240 participants).

Step Seven: Analyze the Data

Over the next six weeks, the volunteers summarized the solution ideas of all the groups within each functional area, just as had been done with the need ideas after the first day of the needs assessment program. The next goal was to summarize the needs and solutions identified by each functional area. Working with one area at a time, the volunteers reviewed each group's summaries, looking for similarities or themes across groups. Then they organized the needs and solutions by theme in order to facilitate analysis. For instance, they grouped together all needs that had to do with clarifying or revising policies and procedures, increasing communication of information, or purchasing equipment. The result of this grouping process was a unique list of

Table 2. Sample of raw data: Professional development needs identified by Administrator Group One.

Need 1: Positive caring climate
- Attitudinal adjustment
- More positive organizational climate
- Greater recognition of achievement
- Better coordination and cooperation among units

Need 2: Additional resources
- Consistent source of capital funds
- Time and space necessary to do the job
- Full-time, 12-month contract to do a full-time job
- Evaluative information about programs in the division
- Increased budget for equipment, supplies, staff development, and support staff
- More release time for faculty for program development and designing instructional materials
- Higher dollar definition of capital

Need 3: Instructional development and evaluation
- Consultants to help develop and improve divisional programs and teaching methodologies
- Innovative, new ideas and efforts from faculty
- Instruction development support for faculty
- Comprehensive faculty development and evaluation system

Need 4: Improved administrative skills
- Personal facility with computer applications programming
- Organization, time management, and supervision skills
- Long-range planning skills
- How to facilitate faculty growth and development
- Conflict resolution skills
- Computer skills
- Budgeting skills

Need 5: External professional networking and development
- Contact with colleagues at other institutions
- Attendance at more national conferences
- Interaction with colleagues with similar problems
- Professional workshops

Need 6: Clarity in college goals and processes

Need 7: Flexible participatory budget process

Need 8: Opportunity for new challenges

Need 9: Network with campus colleagues

Need 10: Mentoring

---

need themes and solution themes for each functional group.

This list was turned over to us, the consultants, to interpret and report the data. We organized the solution themes by type to illustrate that the majority of the performance improvement needs and their solutions were nontraining in nature. The solution categories were high-yield development programs (training), information, resources, incentives, and moderate-yield development programs (training).

Next, we had to develop a means of representing the need themes and solution categories to help the professional development committee decide what training and nontraining activities to recommend. This task involved synthesizing pages of data into a summary that was easy to interpret. We created a matrix that illustrated the need themes on one axis and categories of solutions on the other.

Within each cell of the matrix was the number of times a particular kind of solution was recommended for the indicated need theme, thus revealing the priorities placed on both themes and categories of solutions. When necessary, the committee was able to refer back to the organized lists of solutions to identify the specific solutions that fell into each solution category. This step completed the evaluation research methodology.

Discussion of Solution Categories

Although we had chosen the behavior engineering model as a means of organizing and reporting the data prior to the needs assessment, we did not force responses into the model. The needs identified through the nominal group technique naturally fell into categories according to the types of solutions called for: information, resources, incentives, and knowledge and skills training. Moreover, these solution categories corresponded to many of the cells in the behavior engineering model (see Figures 2 and 4). A review of the data indicated that not all solutions were of equal yield (i.e., cost-to-benefit ratio). For instance, although personal computer training was frequently identified as a need, its yield was minimal because, in many cases, there were a limited number of personal computers in the workplace. The distinction between high and low yield was most

Figure 4. Solution categories and corresponding cells of the behavior engineering model.

High-yield development programs (Cell 4)	Information (Cell 1)	Resources (Cell 2)	Incentives (Cell 3)	Moderate-yield development programs (Cell 4)

evident in the knowledge and skills (training) category. As a result, we subdivided training solutions into two categories.

Category One: High-Yield Development Programs

Solutions in this category could meet needs through effectively designed training that matched the skill and knowledge requirements of a specific job function. For training in this category, the benefit to be gained was greater than the cost of implementing the program. For instance, communication skills training for administrators was considered a high-yield solution to the need for sensitivity and interpersonal skills. Not only had this need been rated as very important by the administrators, but there were many needs identified by all functional groups that required information solutions. The administrators would need good communication skills to address those needs.

Category Two: Information

Three general solutions fit this category. The first solution was to provide descriptions of what performance was expected. This solution included providing job descriptions. The second kind of information solution was providing clear and relevant policies and procedures to guide job performance. The third information solution was providing relevant and frequent feedback about an employee's level of performance relative to the expectations.

Category Three: Resources

This category involved needs that could be solved by more equipment, better tools, a more effective working environment, or other solutions that would require additional funding.

Category Four: Incentives

This category included adequate financial and nonfinancial incentives, such as recognition and rewards. Optimally, these incentives should be based on performance. Also, opportunities for career development were in this category.

Category Five: Moderate-Yield Development Programs

This category was similar to Category One except that, for solutions in this category, the cost of the program would not have been balanced by the benefit, probably because of another related need with a solution in the second, third, or fourth categories. For instance, personal computer training would be of little benefit to employees until they had regular access to computers during the workday. A resource need for computers would have to be met before the computer training would be high-yield. It was recommended that programs in this category not be implemented until the other related needs were met. Once the related needs were met, however, the yield of a program might change, or the need for the program might be eliminated entirely.

Similarities in Responses Across Functional Groups

In Tables 3, 4, and 5, we report the number of suggestions each of the functional groups made for each need theme and solution category. The patterns of suggestions shown in the tables led to several interesting insights. The support staff, faculty, and administrators all suggested information needs and solutions more than any other category. The specific themes dealt with the need for information about policies, department structure, decision making, and "what the other fella is doing." This result is consistent with the experience of many performance technologists, who often find that needs assessments pinpoint information, in the form of clearly defined performance expectations, policies, procedures, and feedback, as the greatest need related to performance improvement (T.F. Gilbert, personal communication, June 1991).

Providing information is less time-consuming and less costly than providing training. In some cases, it is also more likely to result in performance improvement. When training occurs but employees are still not clear about performance expectations and do not receive feedback that will help them assess their progress toward performance expectations, they cannot achieve maximum performance improvement. The result is frustrated employees and a frustrated organization.

The second most common needs and solutions identified across the three functional groups involved resources. The administrators' responses focused on the need for more staff, the support staff needed more equipment, and the faculty expressed a need for funding to support professional development travel and for more equipment.

The relatively small number of suggested solutions in the incentives category might lead to the conclusion that employees were highly motivated and felt no need for incentives. However, it appeared that employee motivation was affected by environmental factors that were not directly associated with incentives. For instance, all groups expressed frustration about communication and resource needs. When these kinds of needs are addressed, frustration levels are usually reduced, and employees become more motivated.

Table 3. Summary of responses from administrators.

Need theme	Solution category					Total by needs
	High-yield development programs	Information	Resources	Incentives	Moderate-yield development programs	
Training: sensitivity, interpersonal relations, trust	12				10	22
Clarification of goals, objectives, policy, procedures, practices		16				16
Communication		15				15
More help: additional personnel			11			11

Table 3 (continued). Summary of responses from administrators.

Need theme	Solution category					
	High-yield development programs	Information	Resources	Incentives	Moderate-yield development programs	Total by needs
Equipment needs			6			6
Recognition, appreciation				6		6
Budget	3	3				6
Space requirements			3			3
Delegation, attainment	1	1				2
Total by solutions	16	35	20	6	10	87

Table 4. Summary of responses from support staff.

Need theme	Solution category					Total by needs
	High-yield development programs	Information	Resources	Incentives	Moderate-yield development programs	
Equipment needs, environment, space needs		3	30			33
Communication: cooperation between departments	4	21			3	28
Uniformity of policies and practices		17				17
Recognition, respect		8		4	1	13
Total by solutions	4	49	30	4	4	91

Table 5. Summary of responses from faculty.

Need theme	Solution category					Total by needs
	High-yield development programs	Information	Resources	Incentives	Moderate-yield development programs	
Money, resources, budget			64	12		76
Return to former department structure, staff development	8	25		24		57
Communication ● interdepartmental ● expectations ● open forum ● streamline procedures ● budget procedures		18 1 5 6 8				38
Equipment needs	3	3	22		3	31

Table 5 (continued). Summary of responses from faculty.

Need theme	Solution category				Moderate-yield development programs	Total by needs
	High-yield development programs	Information	Resources	Incentives		
Self-determination issues		24				24
Faculty-administrator relationships		19				19
Training: subject matter, teaching techniques, test writing, personal computers	12	2			5	19
Helping special students	3	4	3		2	12
Recognition				4		4
Team building		2			2	4
Total by solution	26	117	89	40	12	284

Differences in Responses Across Functional Groups

The administrators identified the highest proportion of training needs and solutions. Their particular interest was communication and interpersonal problem-solving skills that would contribute to a more positive organizational climate. This need for a more positive climate reflected the "feeling of being overworked" that was voiced by many administrators and was consistent with their expressed need for more staff. Faculty members, in contrast, were interested in training related to their subject matter areas, perhaps because of their negative feelings about the previous professional development programs at the college.

Recommendations

After identifying the similarities and differences across the three functional groups, we made recommendations to the professional development committee. Our nontraining recommendations included the following:

- Establish a new committee to oversee non-instructional performance improvement solutions.
- Present an overview of performance engineering and the behavior engineering model to the professional development committee.
- Review results of training and non-instructional interventions after one year.

    Training was recommended as well:

- Conduct a reorientation program for all employees, to provide information regarding the operation of each functional group.
- Use the reorientation program as the new employee orientation program.
- Implement the following high-yield training program:
    — interpersonal problem solving for administrators
    — communication skills for faculty and staff
    — personal computer teaching methods for faculty
    — delegation skills for administrators
    — budget planning for administrators.

Additional nontraining professional development solutions were recommended for each functional group. For instance, we suggested that the faculty division structure be reviewed to address faculty member's feelings of loss of power and alienation as a result of a recent restructuring. Unless faculty alienation was dealt with, it was going to be impossible to build trust and communication across functional groups.

Results

The value the professional development committee placed on the needs assessment and our recommendations was demonstrated by the actions they took after receiving the recommendations. For example, they immediately began planning the recommended high-yield training and scheduled a meeting to learn more about the performance engineering model. However, they chose not to directly address the solutions related to resources and incentives for two reasons. First, the original committee was not empowered to authorize the budget expenditures that might be necessary to implement resource and incentive solutions. Second, the committee's mission was to plan professional development activities within the traditional paradigm of professional development. Once their vision had shifted from professional development training to performance improvement solutions that include nontraining options, they felt that the most responsible strategy would be to have a committee established to focus exclusively on nontraining performance improvement solutions. Consequently, they recommended to the president of the college that such a committee be established.

Benefits of the Process

The models and methods used in planning and implementing the needs assessment provided the data that supported the committee's actions and facilitated making decisions about the relative worth of the actions for promoting both professional growth and institutional development. The models and methods also addressed the challenges that we identified at the beginning of the project.

- All employees (i.e., stakeholders) were equally involved in identifying professional development needs. The support staff indicated in their evaluations that it was the first time they'd felt anyone had listened to their concerns or ideas.
- The planning committee recognized that certain nontraining actions were required to increase the worth of training.
- The step of the nominal group technique in which ideas were clarified provided an opportunity for group members to question and even challenge one another's suggestions. Although this process did not guarantee that the ideas generated in the first nominal group process represented needs instead of wants, it increased the likelihood that they did. One part of the clarification step requires group members to substantiate their needs. If they had filled out a questionnaire or participated in a traditional focus group instead of the nominal group

technique, their responses might have been more spontaneous, less thoughtful, and subsequently of less value.

- Decision makers were provided with a systematic process for selecting professional development activities likely to yield maximum results for the cost and effort. The matrices used to report the data enabled the committee to compare the number of responses in the various need themes and solution categories. The trends that emerged have become the focal points for future professional development planning. When necessary, the committee can look back at the original data, which were keyed by themes.

This project illustrates the number and kind of responses generated through the nominal group technique, as well as the range of professional development options that emerge from the responses. It also models how to introduce performance engineering to decision makers without giving them the theory up front. The project also reveals the benefits of performance engineering:

- Professional development for all employees is new to many academic institutions, and performance engineering is seldom used to improve professional performance. This project illustrates how performance engineering can address the desire of academic institutions for training, while simultaneously presenting alternative performance improvement solutions.

- The findings of this project were quite different from those anticipated by the professional development committee. As a result, the committee members became convinced of the value of a needs assessment. The project provided techniques, references, and examples that could be used to convince other decision makers of the value of conducting a needs assessment and using performance engineering as the decision-making model for all human resource development functions of the organization.

- Presenting the needs assessment data within the framework of the performance engineering model added validity to the high-yield training. A training course in interpersonal communications and problem solving was offered to administrators. Some had signed up for it because the president of the college encouraged them to, not because they wanted to. During the introduction to the course, the data in Tables 3 through 5 were presented. The participants saw that communication was one of the greatest needs for all functional groups and that there were more solution suggestions in the information column than any other. Their perception about the training suddenly changed. Their comments indicated that they no longer saw the training as remedial, an effort to "fix" their poor communication skills. Instead, they saw it as providing them with tools for addressing the communication and information needs of other people. Their body language relaxed immediately, and they began participating in the group discussion. The communication skills training was used as an opportunity to teach the performance engineering model to the administrators.

Limitations

There were some limitations to the process as well:

- Typing and categorizing the data were time-consuming. It is unlikely that many organizations would commit as much staff support to a needs assessment project.
- Although focus groups were used to gather pre-assessment information, the nominal group technique was the primary source of needs assessment data. This methodology placed great reliance on the perceptions of the community college personnel. Studies have shown that people see or perceive what they are prepared to see or hear (Dean, 1986). The fact that there was consistency of responses within functional groups, coupled with the large number of responses, increased the likelihood that the responses represented genuine needs, and not just wants. Validity of the data could have been better assured, however, by triangulation of methodologies (Baker, Grubbs, and Ahern, 1990; Dixon, 1990). Triangulation is the use of two or more different types of measures of the same thing to arrive at one conclusion for the purpose of strengthening the validity of the conclusion. A questionnaire could have been used, or random interviews could have been conducted. Neither was done, because of time and money constraints.
- The professional development committee understood the role of nontraining professional development opportunities and was receptive to the recommendation that nontraining solutions should be implemented along with high-yield training. However, the committee members had no experience in determining the worth of development opportunities. As a result, they needed follow-up information about how to select the solutions with greatest potential for performance improvement.

Conclusion

The needs assessment we report in this chapter used a combination of models and methods to strengthen the accuracy and usefulness of its conclusions. The evaluation research model provided a guideline for involving stakeholders throughout the needs assessment process. It also demonstrated for the planning committee a new strategy for selecting professional development options. The nominal group technique strengthened ownership and accuracy by involving all employees equally in a process whereby they reflected on all ideas and had their questions and concerns addressed. Perhaps the most powerful aspect of this project was the way the data were reported. Organizing the needs and solutions according to the behavior engineering model enabled the decision makers to recognize the need to address both training and nontraining options for professional development.

Not until organizations and institutions are willing to conduct needs assessments such as this will they be able to identify appropriate solutions to their performance problems. Whether the assessment is in the context of planning for professional development or examining ways to improve and maintain performance, whether it is carried out by a special committee or becomes an integral part of human resource development, it must be done if the organization plans to remain a competitive participant in today's increasingly complex market.

Questions for Discussion

1. If you were on a professional development committee that had initially been empowered to plan professional development training for employees, but found that the employees believed that the greatest professional development needs and solutions were in the areas of information and resources—not training—what would you encourage the committee to do?

2. If you don't have the resources in your organization to conduct a needs assessment as comprehensive as the one described in this case study, how could you adapt some of the techniques to your situation?

3. How would you use the behavior engineering model described in the case study to convince your organization to address the influence of the work environment on employee and organization performance?

4. What pitfalls could you envision in adapting the techniques of this case study to your organization and how would you avoid them?

The Authors

Peter J. Dean established and coordinated the master's degree program in instructional systems, with an emphasis in training design and development, at Pennsylvania State University at Great Valley from 1988 to 1991. Currently, he is an assistant professor of management and organization, Smeal College of Business Administration, Graduate

Management Program, Pennsylvania State University at Great Valley. His research interests are performance improvement and ethics. He is the editor of *Performance Improvement at Work* (International Board of Standards for Training, Performance, and Instruction, 1994) and has written numerous articles on the roles of ethics, performance competencies, and performance support systems in organizational improvement. He received his Ph.D. from the University of Iowa. Dean can be contacted at the following address: Pennsylvania State University at Great Valley, Management and Organization, 30 East Swedesford Road, Malvern, PA 19355.

Martha Ray Dean has extensive experience in design, development, implementation, and evaluation of instruction, performance improvement, and management systems in the public and private sectors. A partner in the consulting firm Excellence by Design, she also teaches graduate education courses at Philadelphia College of Bible. Her areas of expertise include curriculum development, performance evaluation, and increasing creative behavior and thinking skills.

Elizabeth C. Guman's business, Performance Insights, has helped a variety of organizations pinpoint performance challenges and implement creative solutions. She consults in the areas of performance improvement, needs analysis, training design, and facilitation skills. Guman teaches graduate courses at Pennsylvania State at Great Valley in training design, needs analysis, instructional media, and presentation skills.

References

Baker, G.E., Grubbs, A.B., and Ahern, T.M. (1990). Triangulation: Strengthening your best guess. *Performance Improvement Quarterly, 3*(3), 27-35.

Dean, P.J. (1986). *A critical incident study investigating the perceived effective and ineffective leadership behaviors of Iowa community college presidents.* Iowa City: University of Iowa, College of Education. (ERIC Document Reproduction Service No. ED318,504).

Dean, P.J. (Ed.). (1994). *Performance engineering at work.* Batavia, IL: International Board of Standards for Training, Performance, and Instruction.

Debeque, A.L., and Van de Ven, A.H. (1971). A group process model for problem identification and problem planning. *Journal of Applied Behavioral Science, 7*, 466-492.

Dixon, N.M. (1990). *Evaluation: A tool for improving HRD quality.* San Diego: University Associates.

Geroy, G.D., and Wright, P.C. (1988). Evaluation research: A pragmatic, program-focused research strategy for decision makers. *Performance Improvement Quarterly, 1*(3), 17-26.

Gilbert. T.F. (1978). *Human competence: Engineering worthy performance.* New York: McGraw-Hill.

Scott, D., and Deadrick, D. (1982, June). The nominal group techniques. *Training and Development Journal,* 26-33.

A Work-Culture Renaissance Through Effective Assessment

Reliance Electric Control Plant

Sherrie Ford and Susan Dougherty

This case shows the use of the interactive assessment model, which combines structured brainstorming, affinity mapping, and relations diagramming. The case also illustrates the necessity of exploring legitimate needs instead of offering a list of training programs as the client had requested.

Background

This case describes an assessment process used at the Reliance Electric Control Plant in Athens, Georgia. Based in Cleveland, Ohio, Reliance is the leading maker of industrial and telecommunications equipment. For more than 90 years, it has been making products that enhance the way other products are made and packaged. The industrial equipment group produces standard controls, motors, and mechanical devices to develop customized systems that speed up and improve material handling, mining, food processing, waste water treatment, and other industrial operations. This case study concerns an assessment of one factory within the industrial equipment group.

The Reliance Electric Control Plant is responsible for producing both standard products to sell on the open market and products for use in customized systems designed by Reliance engineers. The plant was built and opened in 1969. It employs approximately 350 people. Forty-five percent of the employees have been at the plant for more than 15 years, creating a very stable workforce.

The plant is required to sell and ship products worth $110 million

This case was prepared to serve as a basis for discussion rather than to illustrate either effective or ineffective administrative and management practices.

annually, in a market characterized by ever-increasing complexity, changing requirements from customers, and sharp competition. The plant has been struggling with diminishing profits for a number of years, and the plant manager has made many attempts to solve the people side of the problem through training over the past three years. An engineer by training, the plant manager has managed this particular shop for the past 10 years and has worked for Reliance for 19 years.

Historically, the plant manager's management style has been one of very traditional, top-down decision making. He communicates through meetings with the department managers who report to him and has very little direct communication with the frontline employees except when something goes wrong. Over the past five years, the plant manager has embarked on a self-study program to learn how to adapt his approach to management to a more participatory, inclusive style. He now firmly believes that unless the employees are involved in solving the problems at the plant, the problems will not get solved.

Center for Continuous Improvement

The Reliance Electric Control Plant joined the Center for Continuous Improvement at Athens Area Technical Institute in 1991. The mission of the center is to assist charter members and area companies in their transformation into high-performance work cultures. In this effort, the center offers customized training, ongoing consulting, and support through networks that meet monthly. The center is committed to providing meaningful learning opportunities that allow its clients to implement the tenets of total quality management (TQM) in ways that make a difference for their business. For this reason, the center uses a process approach rather than a program approach to training and development. The center was founded by Sherrie Ford as part of her role as vice-president of business and industry services at the institute. She has a working knowledge of TQM, based on interaction with more than 50 manufacturers in northeast Georgia.

Early Involvement

Reliance joined the center to improve quality, lower costs, build teams, and consequently outperform the competition. For three years, Reliance signed on for open workshops, such as "The Changing Role of the Supervisor," and for on-site team training for selected, difficult teams. Goals were not defined specifically in business terms; rather, the assumption was that team and quality training would result in teams and quality.

The center had erred in its assumptions about the expectations Reliance and other companies had, thinking they had requested training out of the conviction that the training was just what the doctor ordered. In retrospect, we see that before making training available, the center should have asked whether the training was specified by an analysis of the work-culture needs. The center had supported Reliance in allowing the company to use the old "training on request" model of planning human resource development interventions. By 1993, however, the center's experience with companies in the middle of failed HRD initiatives pinpointed the lack of effective work-culture assessments as a serious detriment to these companies' successes. Thus, when ISO 9000 Series Standards became a requirement for Reliance in 1993 and the center received a call to help develop a checklist of training to satisfy those requirements, the center was ready to do the right thing.

The recent publication, *Why TQM Fails and What To Do About It,* by Brown, Hitchcock, and Willard (1994) summarizes all too well what we in corporate training and development have been observing in the past few years, but have had a hard time saying out loud. TQM efforts do fail, despite the fury of energy devoted to making them succeed. Or maybe we have been saying this out loud to each other and to clients, even as we sit in the middle of implementation efforts knowing that moving to the empowered work-team culture is the right shift to make. We wonder, "What is eluding us in carrying out what we all know to be fundamental to our survival in the global marketplace?" and "How can we reverse this reactionary trend of withdrawing empowerment goals?" The Center for Continuous Improvement believes that this case study model of interactive assessment, followed by a purely process approach, will ensure that TQM will not fail at Reliance Electric.

Interactive Assessment Using TQM Tools

When the Reliance Electric Control Plant was faced with ISO 9000 requirements and a need to pull together a plan for training, they asked Sherrie Ford for help. On May 7, 1993, she met with the 10 top management staff. The group was made up of engineers, an accountant, a quality manager, a customer service manager, a purchasing manager, and a production manager, with an average length of service of 19 years. In general, the group had been intensely focused on problems as they cropped up, causing Reliance to fall into the trap of crisis management. Also, historically there had been very little interaction between departments, which had caused the typical barriers to clear communication.

The group was expecting to come out of a 30-minute session with a list of topics to schedule in training. By no means were they expecting a three-hour, intensive process focused on changes they anticipated encountering in the next three years and the work culture they desired. Yet there were no complaints that the checklist never evolved; they were too busy comprehending that so much more would be involved in making training decisions. What was Sherrie's rationale for asking top management to detail changes expected as well as the work culture desired?

Try as she might, she could think of no other approach to make a checklist of training meaningful. She needed to know, just for the sake of fulfilling Reliance's request for help, what the managers expected to experience in terms of market, technology, customer demands, competition, organization, and products. Based on these expected changes, she needed to know what people would need to be able to do that they could not or would not already do. In turn, based on the answers about people, she needed to know what training Reliance considered likely to achieve the greatest effects in the desired work culture.

This section of the case study describes what happened at that three-hour meeting. The process yielded an assessment of the work culture, and the assessment told what the culture needed to become a superior workplace. The Reliance case study provided the prototype for this process; Table 1 shows its fine-tuning after additional applications. (Readers interested in learning more about the continuous improvement tools listed in the table—such as structured brainstorming, affinity mapping, and relations diagramming—can find additional information in Brassard, 1989.)

Presentation: "An Overview to Crossroads Faced by American Industry"

This 10-minute presentation illustrated insights about work culture, making the point that the enemies are not drugs, illiteracy, or Japanese government practices, but rather wasted time, variation, and isolation that result from poorly designed systems. Attention was drawn to the responsibility of management to design the systems, develop the people, involve the people, and lead the people. The presentation set the stage for awareness of the magnitude of change sweeping through the country, and through the Reliance Electric Control Plant. ISO 9000 was but one indicator of that change.

Structured Brainstorming, Round One: What Changes Are Expected in the Next Three Years?

The TQM method of structured brainstorming was used to capture the expectations of all people present: plant manager, quality

Table 1. The interactive assessment model for work-culture shift.

	Step 1	Step 2	Step 3	Step 4
What process?	Structured brainstorming, facilitator focus	Structured brainstorming, group focus	Affinity mapping	Relations diagramming
What questions?	"What changes do you expect in the next three years regarding market customer demands, product, technology, competition, and organization?"	"What kind of work culture would it take to accommodate these changes without negative effects?"	"What patterns are emerging in your ideas?"	"What area of concern about the needed work culture is most dominant?"
What steps?	The facilitator captures all answers to the question on flipcharts. Promote hitchhiking on ideas; discourage defending ideas. Continue until all participants "pass."	The facilitator captures each idea on a 3 x 5 card, until all participants "pass." Generate as many cards as possible.	Silently the group members arrange and rearrange 3 x 5 cards until five to seven patterns, or affinities, emerge.	The group compares all possible pairs of affinities to decide which drives the other more. Draw an arrow toward the more affected affinity in each pair. The affinity with the most arrows going out is the driving influence.
Why?	• To use a continuous improvement team method involving everyone present	• To shift the dynamic of equal participation to a process that focuses on the team interaction rather than on looking to the facilitator for directions	• To build on the team interaction established in the previous method • To sort order out of creative chaos captured on the 3 x 5 cards	• To build further on the team interaction established in the two previous methods

Table 1 (continued). The interactive assessment model for work-culture shift.

	Step 1	Step 2	Step 3	Step 4
Why?	• To reveal special knowledge possessed by key functions • To build appreciation and awareness of other functions by hearing their ideas • To "rehearse" the method and prepare for Round Two	• To generate as many ideas as possible about the needed work culture • To identify what the culture needs more of and less of, and what should be preserved • To observe the group's powers of creativity as all participants focus on the future rather than on day-to-day issues	• To allow the common values to emerge as 3 x 5 cards are arranged and rearranged into gradually revealed logical patterns (five to seven). With this silent method, sarcasm, biases, and strong personalities do not have as much chance to get in the way as in traditional debate methods • To allow interpersonal barriers to continue to evaporate, as the overall work culture begins to take on more importance than an individual's role or domain	• To determine which one of the identified affinities influences all others the most • To observe whether the dominant affinity makes any sense, whether it has explainatory power? • To set the stage for strategic organization development based on implications around the driving affinity

manager, purchasing and materials manager, sales order engineering manager, customer service manager, and production manager. Although these managers were accustomed to meeting often—they knew each other well, had habits of interaction, and deferred to the plant manager—they rarely, if ever, had been asked democratically to give opinions about the future in an open-ended format.

Therefore, long silences occurred as they looked to one another or to the facilitator for behavior cues.

All items were written on flipcharts, which gradually filled the wall space. The structured brainstorming continued until everyone had said, "Pass." Then Sherrie pressed for more, deeper-seated ideas. The payoff of following this discipline was that many concepts about change specific to the site were acknowledged simultaneously, comprehensively, and uniquely in one another's presence. For the 45 minutes or so that this step took, differences in job descriptions faded, as did turf protection, the latest crisis in inspection, the usual excuses and finger-pointing for poor performance, and the refusal to share the credit for good things or to support one another across functions.

The managers became focused on the future and what they knew or expected would happen. They were increasingly interested in what they had not realized, as they unwittingly taught each other what the future held. The Reliance Electric Control Plant as a whole became the foreground, not the background that it typically was to the functional manager.

Structured Brainstorming, Round Two: What Kind of Work Culture Would It Take To Accommodate These Changes Without Negative Effects?

Using the same process, but now with greater interest, creativity, and fluency on the part of the participants, the second round of structured brainstorming carried the group to an advanced insight that could not be trained by checklists. The idea of strategy was beginning to emerge. The participants' ideas in this round were also captured on flipcharts for easy analysis in the next step. (However, refinements of this step now suggest that it is best to put all the ideas about the needed work culture on 3-by-5-inch cards for more interactive treatment in the next steps.)

As is typical of top management, the participants centered their thoughts on supervisors and hourly workers rather than on themselves; however, several did express indirectly that it was up to them to create the work culture. Many of the ideas were related to scenes of hostility witnessed on the shop floor—"That's not my job!" "Well, by God, you'd better make it your job!" And everyone concluded that the workforce lacked virtually everything that it would need to survive the next three years of change.

The procedures in Round Two can be summarized as follows:
- If the group is large (over 15) because of shift schedule constraints, it is advisable to break into two groups and work with two facilitators.
- The facilitator should sit at the table and record each idea on a separate 3-by-5-inch card. The ideas the participants volunteer through

structured brainstorming should reflect something their culture needs more of, needs less of, or should keep.

- The guideline for success is to indicate that "when this table is full of cards, we'll stop." This expectation helps curb the participants' tendency to pass too quickly.

Affinity Mapping: What Patterns Appear To Be Emerging in Your Ideas?

Answering this question calls for another TQM tool: affinity mapping. Sorting out the creative chaos resulting from the first two sessions of structured brainstorming means switching off the intuitive, freer side of the mind and switching on the logical, analytical side. Using different colors of magic markers, the managers pointed out which elements of the desired work culture went together. For instance, "more training in personal computers" went with "more vendor training." "Working together more" went with "teamwork." And "problem solving" went with "less machine downtime." Three affinities, or patterns, stood out prominently: attitudes and behavior, knowledge and skills, and performance and results.

(These affinities were acceptable for good post-assessment planning, but in retrospect they appear too easy and perhaps not as revealing of deeper issues as they might have been. In the revised approach, with dozens of 3-by-5-inch cards to be silently manipulated into affinities, far greater depth of analysis is possible. Because the only form of persuasion is moving cards from one emerging affinity to another, people have to think on at least two levels at once: "What do I want to communicate?" and "What are they trying to communicate?" Affinities emerge and are lost as better ideas surface and are accepted.)

Potential users of these methods are no doubt fluent in facilitating structured brainstorming; however, affinity mapping is an intriguing challenge from a facilitator's point of view. The process of affinity mapping can be described as follows:

- The cards from Round Two should be displayed on one table, and a second table should be handy to receive the affinities. Without talking, the group should select any two cards that seem to go together and place them on this second table.
- If the group is large, five people can start this process, spending five minutes mapping affinities. Then another five should take a turn.
- Participants should be encouraged to move the cards around, even to break up someone else's pile and start new piles. In short, the format should be a means of communicating and analyzing.
- All participants must remain vigilant, because the guideline for success at this stage is that no more than seven and no fewer than five

affinities must be determined. The process stops only when all participants have ceased creating categories or moving cards within them.

- The facilitator should check that each person fully ratifies the contents of each affinity. First, the facilitator should ask the group to name the theme of each affinity. Then, he or she should make sure each card within each affinity pile fits the label. If it does not fit, it should be moved to another pile or become a separate one.
- The facilitator should clarify that the labels the participants are giving their piles do not necessarily reflect Webster's dictionary meanings, but rather what the group says the labels mean. For example, "communication" and "training" often show up as labels but mean different things for different groups. A person who was not part of the group that developed a particular affinity might misunderstand a label's significance.
- All cards should be retained with their labels for future reference in defining special meanings. They also become a gold mine of information about perceptions, how people think, and opportunities for improvement that might not have occurred to anyone before.
- The facilitator plays a crucial role in helping management understand these unique differences in meaning.

Relations Diagramming: What Are the Priorities for Next Steps?

The next TQM tool is relations diagramming, whereby the affinities are compared in all possible pairs to determine which influences the other more, until one affinity is identified as the driving influence. In Reliance's case, informal discussion pointed up the greater influence of knowledge and skills over the other two affinities. The rationale was that improved knowledge and skills would directly improve attitudes and behavior and ultimately improve performance and results. Therefore, time, money, and creativity for producing culture shift would best be invested in training in the particular knowledge and skills that would result in the desired behaviors and attitudes (e.g., flexibility, cooperativeness, self-directedness, openness, honesty, and willingness to solve problems).

Probably an unexpected insight was that good attitudes were hindered by the workforce's ignorance about the business: the bottom line, the cost of doing business, the reality of competitors, and the unique demands of customers. We attribute this insight to the managers getting together as a group, essentially for the first time, to talk about the future. They realized how big the "big picture" really is. Later, when employees at nonmanagement levels got together to go through the same interactive process, the insight was equally dramatic.

(Although the process outlined here involved informal discussion in Reliance's case, subsequent applications relying on strict use of TQM tools have produced far superior results. Typically, six to seven affinities emerge, with greater analytical quality and greater potential for strong consensus from managers otherwise in conflict.)

Like affinity mapping, relations diagramming has posed new challenges to the center's staff. Effective pointers on guiding this process include the following:

- Keep in mind that the participants have worked very hard mentally and may be tiring by this point. The facilitator should introduce the next step as the climax of the process: "We're about to find out what organizational priorities will set the stage for the next three years as we set our sites on becoming world class."

- In the middle of a blank flipchart page, draw a circle around a phrase such as "Issues associated with [company name] achieving the needed culture to triumph over change" or "Issues related to having the dream plant by 1997."

- Write all the affinities derived in the previous step around the circle, with plenty of white space between them. Use a different color marker for the affinities than for the circle.

- Ask the group to compare all possible pairs of affinities to see whether there is a relationship between them, no matter how small it might be. If the group agrees that there is a relationship between two affinities, draw a line between them with a marker of a third color.

- For each related pair, ask which of the two affinities influences the other more. Convert the line connecting them into an arrow pointing away from the stronger affinity.

- Continue this process until all possible pairs are connected by arrows. It is possible that some affinities do not have a relationship, but this is rare.

- Evaluate which affinity has the most arrows pointing away to other affinities; this is the driving affinity that, if addressed first with time, money, and human capital, will go the furthest in resolving the remaining issues.

- Evaluate which affinity has the most arrows pointing toward it; this is the ultimate effect for the organization if all affinities are addressed in sequence of descending order of the number of arrows going out.

- If there are five to seven affinities, recommend that the organization address the top three affinities, simultaneously to the degree possible but otherwise in order of priority, and leave the remaining two to four alone. They will, in effect, take care of themselves.

One of the most valuable aspects of facilitating this TQM tool is watching the group members, who had to be silent in the previous step, engage in tentative, less overbearing (or passive, as the case may be) debate about the influences. We have seen previously passive individuals effectively persuade previously dominant individuals to a new way of thinking.

With very few exceptions, the group will want to linger over the "aha!" effect that emerges when the relations diagram, to which they contributed every step of the way as a group, points them in the right direction. We have never seen any participant reject the fruits of this analysis. Virtually without exception, participants hope that this analysis will be the basis for decisions about change in their work culture. If the group has suffered failures of previous TQM programs, they will relate right away to the fact that in the past they may well have jumped into "teams" or "quality" or "communications" programs without analyzing relationships among issues, or even effectively identifying the issues in the first place.

Extending the Assessment to All Levels in the Plant

It was clear to the managers at Reliance that the picture was incomplete without putting the same questions to employees at other levels within the plant. The plant manager had the courage to pioneer new methods and permitted broad use of the interactive process model in his organization; although it was becoming clear that training on certain topics was needed, it was still not time to develop a checklist of courses. Thus, four additional sessions were scheduled to include technical (salaried) personnel, supervisors, and two groups of hourly personnel:

- The technical personnel had jobs that ranged from systems analysis to engineering, drafting, and customer service.
- The supervisors had an average tenure of 21 years. They had traditionally been responsible for making sure that the people got the work out. Although their management styles varied, their time was primarily spent with personnel issues—such as time cards, absenteeism, and vacation schedules—as well as chasing down parts shortages.
- The hourly personnel had an average tenure of 15 years. This stability was a plus, because the employees had an incredible base of practical knowledge. It was also a major hurdle, because the hourly personnel were extremely resistant to change. Two sessions of 25 employees each were held.

In terms of execution, these subsequent sessions were much like the first session with top management except that the number of participants was much higher (25 on average) and the time taken was an hour longer. Otherwise, the same questions were asked, answers were captured democratically on flipcharts, affinities were identified with colored markers, and relationships were discussed. The priority of knowledge and skills development for all levels in the plant was clear.

In addition to the brainstormed ideas, many other comments were captured on flipcharts and were included in the executive summary of the assessment. For example:

● From top management—"[Our hourly employees are] passing on poor quality."
● From technical support—"We seem to fix the same problems over and over."
● From supervisors—"Usually only the supervisor is 'totally involved.'"
● From hourly personnel—"Management doesn't like the answers when they ask questions."

What Top Management Found Out

Overhead transparencies that captured all collected information were prepared, and a time was set for each group that had participated to receive the same feedback. When comparing the responses from the other three levels in the plant with their own, top management found the overall results were counterintuitive. What they themselves sensed as the "feel" of the plant—no cooperation or ownership, complacency about quality and customers—did not square with the message of the assessment process: The other three levels vividly expressed, in specific details, the opposite qualities. Ultimately, top management observed that each level saw itself as the glue holding the organization intact, with little or no help, insight, or sympathy from other levels. Even more surprisingly, top management saw that all four levels arrived at the same conclusions for training and development. There was a longing for harmony, working together, fairness, new technical skills, and superior performance plantwide.

The seemingly massive amount of data that results from structured brainstorming, if not condensed into a manageable form, would leave the top management of any organization bewildered. Mapping data into affinities reduces the dozens of suggestions into a handful. For Reliance, the three areas of knowledge and skills, attitudes and behavior, and performance and results evolved as appropriate categories.

But how do you work on three such all-encompassing fronts at once? It is a big mistake to try! Relations diagramming focuses the analysis on the affinity with the most far-reaching impact. For Reliance, knowledge and skills was the driving affinity. Therefore, training (by internal and external means) was endorsed as significant to the future culture.

But what kind of training was needed? Such an enormous array of topics came under that affinity—everything from literacy to electronics to team skills. The next affinity, attitudes and behavior, pointed to the subject area. Close review of that affinity's definition showed that training in team skills would touch on virtually all features of the desired culture, such as getting along, empowering employees, or being open to new ideas.

Although the managers were at least a year away from knowing strategically or even tactically how they wanted to use teams, it was clear that they were ready to cultivate the team mentality. The recommended sequence of training, adopted by top management, was the following:

- *Work-Style Analysis.* Participants learned individual behavioral tendencies, both under normal conditions and under stress, as a means to learn about themselves and others.
- *Team Dynamics.* With work-style knowledge in place, trainees learned behaviors and attitudes that emphasized listening, valuing differences, building trust, communicating, "zapping" and not "sapping" other people, and managing meetings effectively. These and other topics laid the groundwork for eventual work teams.
- *Problem Solving.* Participants learned step-by-step methods that allow work teams to troubleshoot what is called nonconformance. Though we expected to use basic methods, such as fishbone diagramming and Pareto charting, the primary method became cycle-time reduction analysis, in keeping with emerging issues at the plant.

What Everyone Else in the Organization Found Out

Judging by how difficult it was to clear the conference room at the end of the intensive sessions working through the interactive process, one can safely conclude that technical personnel, supervisors, and hourly personnel relished (perhaps even more than top management) the process. The participants' words matched their deeds; that is, just as the brainstorming brought out the ideas that the future work culture should be characterized by listening, teamwork, quality, and improvement, the participants' behavior right then and there showed the promise that this vision could become a reality. They themselves felt this brief enactment of the future. But they also had a revelation coming. It no longer was viable for any level to claim sole ownership or credit for keeping the company going.

Costs and Benefits

The initial session was offered at no charge. The subsequent four sessions cost $900 per day, the rate for eight hours of service for a member of the Center for Continuous Improvement. Including the hours for interactive assessment and the hours for capturing and analyzing the data and making recommendations for next steps, the cost of the assessment was $5,600, or slightly more than $15 per employee.

The three-year plan of development calls for each employee to have training. Therefore, one benefit of the assessment process is that management has confidence that training dollars and time will no longer be wasted as a result of guesswork. Investing $15 per person to diagnose work-culture needs properly meant that subsequent training dollars would indeed be an investment and not an expense.

Human Resource Interventions Adopted

In short, the assessment showed that
- Training by checklists does not make sense.
- Training without assessment does not make sense; assumptions about other levels, by every level, can be entirely wrong.
- Similar developmental needs are mirrored at every level.
- Every level appeared to have a strong sense of ownership and close identification with the company.
- Every level had the same prescriptions for surviving change.
- Top management's number-one job was to create and communicate focus.
- Top management's other priorities pivoted on learning adaptive behavior.
- All levels should proceed in a development plan that started with understanding self and others, learning team building, and learning basics in problem solving.

The assessment also
- helped participants experience the new "feel" of a consensus-minded organization
- showed participants how to solve a problem using TQM tools
- provided an opportunity to model the new culture
- eliminated barriers founded upon false assumptions
- created a more open mind-set about change
- created, to some extent, an individual awareness of personal needs to change.

So why do TQM efforts fail? In the case of the Reliance Electric Control Plant, it is easy to see that mandated training—because of ISO

9000 standards or any other reason—based on assumptions about other levels in the company leads to training that has unrealistic expectations, is not tailored to the audience, risks being irrelevant, and excludes the top management level. These problems in turn lead to doubts that the company is committed and certainly thwart any attempt to follow through in ensuring that a new culture has taken root (see Brown, Hitchcock, and Willard, 1994). In the case of Reliance before this interactive assessment, not only did people at each level have beliefs, judgments, and ideas that were not confirmed by facts, but a global perspective was missing at all levels. Virtually any training put in motion with this significant barrier would cause training and development objectives to derail.

The plant manager agreed that in order to meet the challenges that the plant was facing in the near future, people at all levels would need to change the way they interacted. Sherrie recommended that top management set aside a day to determine the focus that would guide the three-year process, and a day to decide how to measure progress toward new goals. Further, because a plantwide culture shift was being undertaken, the whole plant (not just a pilot work group or night shift) would participate in work-style analysis, team skills training, and problem solving.

Sherrie brought in Susan Dougherty, a senior consultant with the center. Susan had extensive experience in helping organizations make the shift from a top-down management approach to team-based, participatory management. Reliance was familiar with Susan from two previous training events that were, unfortunately, done outside an assessment process. Susan facilitated the top management group in a day of coming to terms with their past lack of focus and the need to determine one for 1993 through 1996.

Too aggressive a training schedule was initially implemented. The entire plant went through work-style analysis in less than four months, and team skills training began with the salaried workforce while the hourly employees were going through the work-style analysis. It quickly became obvious that the plant could not continue to meet production goals with this much training going on. The cost of this volume of training also became prohibitive.

Therefore, Sherrie met with supervisors and managers to develop quality metrics regarding future training. They needed to define how much could reasonably be done in a month and how well schedules could be communicated in advance. Using these quality metrics as a guide, Reliance adopted a new training schedule, and the team skills training was spread over one year.

Philosophies of Design

From the very beginning, this project was viewed as a process, not a program. The workplace is a living, breathing organism, and the people within it need to be involved in designing changes through highly interactive learning experiences. Susan brought a number of beliefs to the process—for example, all training should be aimed at improving the bottom line. If Reliance is going to use teams, then their focus should be on creatively solving work-related issues and problems rather than just interpersonal issues (though it may be necessary to begin at the interpersonal level). She also believes that the culture change process should be planned strategically by management and that the process should be given a name so that the entire organization can relate to it. At Reliance, management named their process BLAST, which stands for Building Lasting Achievement and Success through Teams. Susan also believes that an organization must be willing to build in follow-up interventions after training, because most learning happens when people try to apply at work what they have learned in a classroom. The plant manager called these follow-up meetings "well-baby checkups." Finally, Susan believes that the process approach is best carried out when every intervention or training activity builds on the previous one. Therefore, the team skills training included opportunities for the participants to further explore and appreciate different work styles learned in the first round of training. Likewise, the problem-solving training emphasized some of the basics that were taught in team skills training.

The managers and supervisors now participate in a monthly day-long meeting to help them become good leaders and facilitators and to discuss next steps for the BLAST process. These well-baby checkups, plus checkups for newly trained teams, mean that this control plant, by remaining in an ever-alert state of assessment, truly is in a work-culture renaissance.

Conclusion

Among companies in Georgia, there is an emerging countermovement that delights in pronouncing the end of the quality management era. These people point up what is seen as the always-doomed efforts to create executive abilities in hourly workers; they admonish managers for taking their eyes off the ball; they decry the team concept (whatever they think "teams" means). Suddenly, after three years or so of quality and team training—or of casual watching what other companies are doing—they are reverting to the old ways of rank-and-file management, and they are struggling with massively demoralized cultures. Union activity has never been busier in the South, as feelings of betrayal run high. Human resource directors are caught holding the bag if they have been associated with trying to redirect work cultures and now are expected to direct those cultures right back to where they started.

At the Reliance Electric Control Plant, because top managers have been able to resist this easy retrenchment, and because they tapped into deep currents of potential leadership throughout the plant prior to creating a training plan mandated by ISO 9000, they have largely enhanced their odds that TQM will succeed. Already on May 7, 1994, concluding the first year of focused work-culture redesign, performance improvements have been dramatic, given the prior state of affairs.

We have discovered that continuing to use and refine this interactive assessment process at all levels in a plant has put the center in a position to help 13 additional clients, several of which are using the results to set up multiyear plans for initial culture transformation. They agree that these three assessment hours have resulted in consensus, alignment, and sheer quality of raw data that might otherwise take a year to accomplish.

Questions for Discussion

1. What are the pros and cons of this approach to needs assessment?
2. How does this approach to needs assessment compare with others you have used or studied?
3. What do you think convinced the plant manager and the other managers to agree to using this assessment approach throughout the organization?
4. How would you use data from this type of needs assessment to design a training intervention or training plan?
5. How are the roles that Sherrie, Susan, and the plant manager played different from the traditional role of consultant, trainer, and plant manager?

The Authors

Sherrie Ford is vice-president of business and industry services at Athens Area Technical Institute, Athens, Georgia. In 1991, at Athens Tech, she founded the Center for Continuous Improvement, which now has more than 20 members. She holds a B.A. and M.A. in English from the University of Southern Mississippi and a Ph.D. in English from the University of Georgia. Ford has presented numerous papers for industrial and academic groups on TQM implementation. She can be contacted at the following address: Athens Area Technical Institute/Center for Continuous Improvement, U.S. Highway 29 North, Athens, GA 30610.

Susan Dougherty is the president of The Center for Effective Power. She has published several articles in journals, including *Lifelong Learning: An Omnibus of Practice and Research, Adult Learning,* and *Association Educator.* She holds a B.S. from Loyola University, M.Ed. from the University of New Orleans, and Ed.D. from the University of Georgia, where she was a Kellogg Fellow from 1987 through 1990.

References

Brassard, M. (1989). *The memory jogger plus +.* Methuen, MA: GOAL/QPC.

Brown, N.G., Hitchcock, D.E., and Willard, M.L. (1994). *Why TQM fails and what to do about it.* Burr Ridge, IL: Irwin Professional Publishing.

Foreman Development Process: First-Line Floor Manager Training

McDonnell Douglas Aerospace-East

Caroline P. Harre

This case illustrates use of a variety of methods, including interviews, input from a steering committee, and focus groups, to obtain internal information. This internal information was combined with external information from trends, best practices, and surveys of other programs. The case also includes a description of how the program was developed after the needs assessment was complete.

Background

As the new vice-president took over the Production Operations Division of McDonnell Douglas Aerospace-East, he observed that not all first-line floor mangers approached their work in the same manner. In addition, the current floor mangers were approaching retirement age, and no replacements were being groomed. Market share in the defense industry was becoming difficult to maintain, companies throughout the industry were downsizing, and more responsibilities were being placed on the first-line floor managers' shoulders. Given all of these circumstances, the need for a development program was evident. The question was, "How do we prepare interested candidates for the position of floor manager and still keep our overhead costs at a reasonable level?"

This company believed in individual development, but had a history of conducting training outside work hours as a means of reducing costs. In addition, training was not always reinforced in the work environment, and some participants did not take training seriously. But times were changing. The company had just introduced a skill-based

This case was prepared to serve as a basis for discussion rather than to illustrate either effective or ineffective administrative and management practices.

performance appraisal system that might be used to add accountability to the training.

The vice-president chartered a steering committee to develop an approach for selecting, training, and evaluating floor managers so that he could be sure all floor managers knew what was expected of them and that floor managers were consistent in their approach to working with the unionized workforce.

Organizational Profile

The organization is one division of McDonnell Douglas Aerospace, a leading aerospace defense contractor. The corporation was founded in 1939 and has grown to employ more than 83,000 people worldwide, divided into three companies. The location discussed in this case study is the manufacturing facility in St. Louis, Missouri, with branches in Florida and Arizona. This company currently employs approximately 26,000 people, 8,500 of whom are unionized.

The corporation had recently reorganized so that all military hardware production would be managed within the same company. This company has a matrix organization in which skilled labor is assigned to a program. The Production Operations Division includes all of the unionized workers responsible for fabricating and assembling the various military aircraft produced. In addition, the division works on sub-assemblies for commercial aircraft.

Industry Profile

The aerospace and defense industry is relatively small and fiercely competitive. Currently there are fewer than 10 companies in the field, and experts predict that there will be only two or three remaining by the early 21st century. Part of the competitive pressure is due to reduced defense spending in the United States and around the world; part is due to increasing global competition. Moreover, in the United States, the industry is highly regulated. These three factors mean that this organization must control costs to maintain or increase its market share. There is a focus on controlling overhead costs, including discretionary expenditures for training and development.

Character Profile

The players associated with this project fall into two categories: sponsors and participants. The sponsors are managers responsible for production and have an average of at least 25 years of experience with the company. Most feel that training might help solve some of the cur-

rent disparities in skills among existing floor managers and help prepare new floor managers to assume line duties.

The participants include current floor managers and candidates
for future floor manager positions. The current floor managers have
seen many changes in the shop environment—reduction in the number
of management levels, increased personal accountability for the floor
managers, changing legal requirements, and changing expectations
from management. Even with all of these changes, however, current
floor managers are somewhat reluctant to embrace training, because
they think either that it is "too theoretical" or that management might
not support these concepts in the workplace.

Floor manager candidates come from both the unionized workforce
and personnel supporting the manufacturing operations. These candidates want to be competitive with existing floor managers and not be
first in line to be laid off if downsizing occurs.

Issues and Events

This project was begun in St. Louis when the vice-president asked
what new floor managers needed to be successful their first week on the
job. Fortunately, one of the executives to whom he posed this question
had been involved in a similar project before the reorganization. He suggested asking the Employee and Organizational Development (E&OD)
Department to make a presentation on the content of previous programs,
including both active programs and proposed programs that had been
put on hold as a result of the reorganization. The presentation was made,
and program directors, a human resource manager, and an E&OD specialist formed a steering committee to develop the Foreman Development
Process (FDP) and define the FDP training content.

The E&OD specialist had been involved in the previous efforts at
defining appropriate floor manager training. There had been two such
efforts. First, the Florida facility had implemented basic supervisory
training with positive results. Then, the St. Louis location had decided
to try to apply the Florida approach, and a comparison of requirements
at the two locations had been undertaken. This second program had
been put on hold after the needs analysis was completed. The specialist
had worked closely with the original analyst from the Florida facility to
define needs in St. Louis, but was concerned about how these previously gathered data could be used without compromising the new committee's support. As in all large organizations, people were not inclined
to accept new ideas imported from the outside, and the managers who
had provided input into the previous assessment were not part of the

current management structure. In addition, training was traditionally seen as a remedial effort rather than a proactive technique that could be used to prepare employees for future assignments.

The biggest asset the committee had on its side was that the company had recently adopted a skill-based approach to performance appraisal in which each employee's performance would be assessed against minimum criteria for successful performance on the job. The content of the previous analyses closely aligned with these criteria, and the steering committee decided that tying training content to these performance criteria was a valid approach.

Target Population

The target audience for the FDP includes first-line floor managers who supervise unionized employees. These floor managers can be housed in either the Production Operations or Quality Assurance divisions. The program is intended to acquaint someone unfamiliar with supervisory responsibilities with skills necessary the first week on the job. It is not intended, however, to teach everything a floor manager will ever need to know to be an effective supervisor. A minimum of two years' experience with the company is assumed; this experience should be directly associated with the manufacture of the product.

Candidates for the FDP can have varying skill levels and backgrounds. They might come from quality, fabrication, assembly, or production support areas. They might be unionized or have no union experience. It is estimated that over the next five years as many as 200 new floor managers may be needed to fill openings due to retirements, attrition, and production growth. This increase would represent approximately one-third of all existing floor managers.

Because the content of the FDP is so closely tied to the performance appraisal system, new floor managers are required to attend. In addition, the program addresses the remedial needs of existing floor managers from all production and production support areas. As specific areas of skill deficiency are identified by the skill-based performance appraisal, appropriate subject matter modules will be made available. Existing floor managers do not have to attend training automatically, but are expected to seek appropriate remedial training if skill deficiencies are identified in their performance appraisals.

Action Items

The assessment included analyses of performance factors and skill dimensions necessary for competent and successful performance in the position of first-line supervisor. The intent was to determine the performance factors that needed to be included in the training program, define the skills and abilities necessary to demonstrate competency in these performance factors, and ensure these factors were included in the performance appraisal system for this position. In an effort to include all relevant performance elements, the steering committee collected data from current literature, contacted organizations of similar size and structure, collected training curricula from industry leaders, consulted local colleges and universities, and worked with the internal human resource management organization.

The E&OD specialist led the effort to collect data from current management, the union, subject matter experts (SMEs), customers, and other interested parties. The committee members began by identifying assumptions and expected outcomes from the process. They asked management to describe the "perfect first-line floor managers" in behavioral terms, assuming no resource constraints. Next, they narrowed the focus by including relevant business conditions (i.e., overhead control and industry downsizing) and asked how management would measure the success of this training effort. To verify assumptions and gather new data, the E&OD specialist conducted focus groups. Participants were selected to represent a cross section of the current floor manager population. Possible content for a new floor manager training program (as determined by management) was presented, and participants were asked to validate that the subject matter was important to a new floor manager. Next, they were asked why the subject matter was important and how one could tell if the job was being performed properly. Data were analyzed using thematic analysis; no objective measures were used except findings of the previous needs analyses. The result was a list of subject matter to be included in the training and rough behavioral objectives for each topic presented.

Findings were presented to appropriate executive and division operations councils, and SMEs were identified to analyze specific needs further and develop appropriate training materials. The SMEs took the basic information developed by focus groups and, using Mager's (1988) criterion-referenced instruction (CRI) approach, identified specific content for training.

For example, one conclusion from the focus groups was that floor managers need to know the company's policies and processes. If floor managers knew and enforced these policies, infractions of company rules would diminish, compliance with government and federal regulations would increase, and audit scores would increase. Along similar lines, the data analysis identified the importance of management competencies in administering discipline, continuous improvement orientation, customer orientation, contracts, monitoring performance, organizational awareness, union and management relations, and valuing diversity. Based on these results, the SMEs decided that the Personnel Issues section of the training module on human resources (HR) should have the objective of providing information to first-line supervisors to enable them to identify potential HR-related problems and become aware of key HR support organizations and the associated services. Subject matter to be discussed in this section included organizational rules, drug and alcohol abuse, ethical behavior, policies relevant to the shop floor, equal opportunity, the link between management's expectations and the company's standards of conduct, the certification process and the training system, emergency contacts and plans, and documentation.

Models and Techniques

Data collected for this project included findings from previous company surveys and structured interviews. Included were surveys conducted by outside consultants to identify appropriate management competencies and the company's relative level of skill in those competencies. A recent job analysis had identified the compensable factors for the first-line floor manager position. Interviews and focus groups verified that these skills were appropriate and identified the rationale for including these skills in the FDP training.

When training development began, the E&OD specialist had a skeleton structure of what was wanted and used Mager's CRI approach to determine the scope of information to be presented. The CRI approach was used because criteria for successful performance had been identified by the performance appraisal process. This approach allowed the SMEs who were developing training materials to conduct performance analysis and develop training objectives that would ensure the effect of training could be measured.

A task team of SMEs was formed and facilitated by the E&OD specialist. Each team member was provided with the rough goals for his or her respective subject matter, as determined by management and the focus groups. The SMEs were also provided with the performance factors for the position of floor manager, as identified in the performance appraisal system. The team met for 10 weeks. Each week the team was asked to perform one step of the CRI analysis to address a specific question. For example, the work began with the question "What do you want to accomplish with this module?" To answer this question, the team was instructed on the tools and techniques to accomplish the task of goal analysis as defined by Mager's CRI. Other questions and the resulting tasks were as follows:

- What indicates that things need to change? What will be the impact of the change? (performance analysis)
- How do you want the student to do the task and accomplish the goal? (task analysis)
- Who are your students? (target population analysis)
- What will you provide for them to learn the task? What will they do? How will they know they have learned enough? (objective analysis)
- How will you (and they) know they are doing the task well enough? (criterion test development)
- What materials will they need to accomplish your goal? (subject matter development).

Materials explaining each step in the CRI program development process were developed and distributed to the SMEs to assist them in answering the questions and developing the training content. Individual assistance was provided when needed. Each SME also identified training aids necessary for instruction and offered recommendations for media and reinforcement exercises.

Cost and Benefits

Although actual costs of the assessment were not tracked, the benefit of analyzing the specific training needs systematically was management's recognition that training was the right answer. Without management's agreement, the time, manpower, and budget necessary for development and on-the-job coaching after training would not have been secured.

Management sees this process not only as preparing new floor managers, but also as a tool to address the performance needs of existing floor managers, thereby increasing performance levels. One last benefit is that management will have floor managers working to a consistent standard across programs and functions—something they have not been able to attain to date.

The business reasons driving this project are projected attrition rates over the next few years and customers' (both internal and government) observations that first-line supervisors might not be consistent in their approach to managing the workforce. In addition to these factors, the company is trying to improve its performance to make itself more competitive in the global environment. To do this, the organization is using the criteria established by the Malcolm Baldrige National Quality Award managed by the U.S. Department of Commerce.

Data Analysis

In the thematic analyses, subject matter themes, or content clusters, were identified. For each subject matter cluster, information to be included and a measurable indicator were developed, based on the performance factors necessary for competent performance as a floor manager. Each such subject matter cluster is called a module, and a module includes two to eight separate sections, or topics. For example, in the Labor Relations section of the People module, the competency Union and Management Relations includes the performance factor "works within the scope and spirit of the contract(s) to solve problems at the lowest level of interaction between union and management officials." The indicator for this behavior is reduced number of formal grievances and increased percentage of complaints settled at the shop floor level.

In the performance analysis, the SMEs were able to determine which factors affected performance. They were also able to determine the approximate cost—in terms of time, downstream effect, cycle time, or observed behavior—of not performing a task in the way it was identified. The data gathered during the performance analysis laid the foundation for development of the evaluation approach using Kirkpatrick's four-level model. Factors identified during the performance analysis were compared with skills identified by the recent job analysis to ensure relevancy.

When deciding what to include and what to defer to other training programs, the steering committee conducted a rank ordering of identified competencies. As a result of the previous job analysis, the company had developed a data base of competencies defined in behavioral terms. These behavioral indicators were structured into competency-related clusters of questions. Each committee member was asked to rank order his or her top 20 performance factors from this data base. These data were then analyzed using an averaged-ranking technique. The committee members were the directors responsible for appraising floor manager performance.

These top 20 competencies were then developed into a multirater assessment instrument to measure a participant's baseline skill levels and indicate movement against that baseline over time. Raters include self, superior, and subordinates. The respondent is asked to rate how effectively the subject demonstrates the identified behavior on a 10-point scale, ranging from "not at all" to "exceptional." The subject (or training participant) is asked to identify his or her immediate supervisor and provide a list of all immediate employees, five of whom are selected randomly to rate the subject. The subject is then provided feedback that compares the self-rating with the ratings of other people. An example scale from this instrument is provided in Figure 1.

Results

The steering committee presented its assumptions, approach, proposed FDP, and milestone schedule to the management teams of the Production Operations and Quality Assurance divisions. The councils that govern training and people-related policies were briefed, as was the union.

The proposed training had four phases: an introduction, modules on basic skills, modules on shop floor skills, and a coaching period. Criterion tests at each module level would be developed from the content of the module.

After the process had gained approval and module development had begun, a short article was written for the company newsletter, and a point of contact was identified for individual employees to receive more information.

Intervention Description

The introductory session begins with an eight-hour presentation delivered by upper management. This session is intended to define expectations and the role of the floor managers, present an overview of the business, and present an overview of shop operations. The first two topics are presented via lecture and group discussion. The last topic is presented via a tour of the work area.

For the modules that make up the second and third phases of training, the primary delivery method is self-paced, programmed instruction. This is followed by instructor-led workshops in which trainees apply their new skills. The instructor is a SME who uses role plays, case studies, simulations, skill practices, or games to demonstrate application of the skills.

The final phase, on-the-job coaching, is designed to ensure maximum training transfer from the learning environment to the work environment. Coaches are schooled in the FDP content and are selected from superintendents, general floor managers, and retired floor managers hired as coaches.

The evaluation strategy incorporates all levels of Kirkpatrick's training evaluation method. Each workshop contains a Level 1 (reaction) evaluation for the workbooks and the workshop. Each workbook contains activities and pre- and posttests for Level 2 evaluation (knowledge and skill). During each workshop, checklists to be used by the

Figure 1. Example of a scale from the multirater assessment instrument.

Monitoring performance	N/A	Not at all	Slight	Moderate	Considerable	Exceptional
Uses statistical information to track customer satisfaction, profitability, quality, schedule, and employee effectiveness						
Works with employees to establish dependable performance measures and tracking systems						
Observes performance in a variety of ways (e.g., attends meetings, reviews status reports, requests customer feedback)						
Evaluates performance in terms of accomplishing specific goals or meeting specific standards						
Monitors performance and provides feedback on a regular basis						
Frequently communicates with employees regarding financial, quality, schedule, and individual performance						

coaches on the floor are distributed. The items on these checklists are the same as the items on the tests and the performance factors against which floor managers are rated. These checklists assess Level 3 (performance and behavior). In addition, the multirater assessment is used prior to training and six months after training is completed to assess behavior change. The E&OD Department is also planning to conduct a longitudinal study on the pilot and control group participants to assess Level 4 (business results). Indices to be tracked include performance appraisal ratings and production performance factors.

Interested candidates will be screened through a selection process that includes math and reading aptitude tests and a behavioral event interview. Upon selection into the program, participants will complete the first three phases (introduction plus 10 modules) over a 12-week period.

Each module includes four to eight hours of reading and exercises, followed by a four-hour workshop designed to apply the principles. All of this training—the programmed instruction and the workshop—will be conducted on the employees' own time. Continuing education units will be accrued through a partnership with the local community college. There is a total of 35 units contained in the 10 modules:

- Basic Skills
  — *Module 1.* Communications: Effective Presentations, Effective Writing Skills, Effective Listening
  — *Module 2.* Employee Job Assignment: Basic Supervision, Coaching
  — *Module 3.* Time Management: Leading Effective Meetings, Responsible Assertion, Goal Setting
  — *Module 4.* Problem Solving: Creative Problem Solving, Stress Management, Conflict Resolution, Ethical Issues in Leadership
- Basic Shop Floor Skills
  — *Module 5.* People: Labor Relations, Administration, Personnel Issues
  — *Module 6.* Quality: Quality Engineering, Inspection, Interchangeability, Corrective Action Process
  — *Module 7.* Cost: Cost/Schedule Control System, Elements of Realization and Standards, Automated Systems
  — *Module 8.* Schedule: Production Control, Requirements and Inventory Management
  — *Module 9.* Procedures: Safety and Medical, Documentation, Procedural Compliance
  — *Module 10.* Support Organizations: Manufacturing Engineering, Methods Engineering, Liaison Engineering, Maintenance, Tooling, Production Procurement, Property Management, Material Operations.

Upon completion of the formal instruction, the participant will be placed as a floor manager and will have a coach assigned for approximately two weeks. The coach will assess the participant against the checklist of behaviors corresponding to items on the criterion tests as well as to factors assessed in the performance appraisal system. The coach will also provide feedback to the participant. This portion of the training is conducted during working hours. The checklists that coaches will use are structured according to four functions:

- communications
- monitoring performance
- supervisory techniques
- job-unique responsibilities.

If an existing floor manager would like to participate in training, he may request the appropriate module, read the material and respond to the exercises, and receive coaching from his or her manager.

There will be three offerings of the full program each year. The number of participants will be determined by the staff forecast in each functional area. In addition, as performance appraisals are conducted each year, existing floor managers will be coached on areas for skill improvement.

Conclusions and Recommendations

The organization considers this effort innovative and a model for development of training in the future. Upper management's support and active involvement in the assessment and in development and delivery of this material are the primary reasons for the program's success. In addition, the company's transition to a skill-based evaluation system allowed this approach to be readily accepted.

It will not be easy, however, for the organization to change its culture and view of training. Some managers and some employees are not yet convinced that management will truly support this process over the long term.

The reaction by management and employees alike is that a training program for floor managers is long overdue, and many people have expressed interest in getting involved—either in delivery or in learning.

One recommendation for future projects of this nature is to get middle managers involved early and keep them involved throughout. In this project, middle managers did not have as much involvement as possible, and this slowed buy-in on the shop floor to a slight degree.

Questions for Discussion

1. How could more quantitative data be collected to validate content, given cost restrictions?

2. Who should provide the inputs for identifying the floor managers' training needs?

3. How should middle management be involved in identifying needs for floor manager training?

4. How should participants who successfully complete training be recognized or rewarded?

5. What would be the consequences of not tying the content of the training program to the expected performance reviewed annually on the performance appraisal?

6. How should the project be communicated to various segments of the population? What should be communicated and when? Consider the following groups: upper management, middle management, current floor managers, potential participants, and the union.

The Author

Caroline P. Harre is an organization development specialist for McDonnell Douglas Aerospace-East. She provides organization development consulting, designs and conducts training, and serves as an evaluation consultant. She has been in the human resource development field for 16 years, having begun her career as a management consultant. Her clients have included Texas Instruments and New York Life Insurance. Harre holds bachelor's degrees in business and psychology and a master's degree in education from the University of Missouri-St. Louis, where she is currently in the doctoral program in behavioral development education. She can be contacted at the following address: 3422 Manhattan Avenue, St. Louis, MO 63143.

Reference

Mager, R.F. (1988). *Making instruction work: Or skillbloomers.* Belmont, CA: David Lake Publishers.

A Training Tool To Promote Organizational Change

Connecticut Department of Labor

Sandra L. Hastings, Ann B. Nichols, Barry G. Sheckley,
and Barry A. Goff

This case shows how a state government agency used a detailed job and task analysis to identify training needs for a planned major change initiative. Three types of documents were used: a job and task analysis worksheet, a detailed job and task analysis document, and a job and task analysis feedback form.

Overview

In June of 1991, the Connecticut Department of Labor (DOL) began a major reorganization to ensure responsiveness to changing customer needs. The agency's leadership recognized that the traditional hierarchical structure was not equipped to deliver the flexible, innovative services required to ensure the employability of Connecticut workers in a global economy. Consequently, a cross section of employees designed a new organizational structure to transform the agency into a customer-oriented, high-performance organization committed to continuous improvement. To improve service delivery, DOL replaced the hierarchical structure—14 layers of responsibility—with a flatter structure—six layers of responsibility. To emphasize the change in business focus, the historic mission was expanded to include five goals related to the reorganization:

- to improve customer service with one-stop shopping
- to reduce the number of interactions each customer has with the DOL staff

This case was prepared to serve as a basis for discussion rather than to illustrate either effective or ineffective administrative and management practices.

- to improve customer support services to meet the needs of internal customers
- to empower frontline workers to make decisions
- to become a model employer and agency.

Finally, the reorganization restructured the job responsibilities of frontline workers to advance the new organizational objectives. The reorganization required workers previously responsible for providing either unemployment insurance services (e.g., processing unemployment insurance benefits) or employment services (e.g., providing career counseling) to combine both client services in a single integrated interview session.

The administration also made several commitments to DOL employees to encourage support for the reorganization. First, the agency promised that there would be no layoffs as a result of the reorganization. In fact, employees were assigned new job responsibilities without a loss of pay even if their new positions were in a lower job classification.

Second, a new job classification system was designed to promote upward mobility and to compensate employees for demonstrating the ability to perform both employment service duties and unemployment insurance duties.

Third, DOL's management team modeled effective labor relations by engaging the union in a partnership to ensure a smooth transition. Employees representing union interests participated actively in the development of the plan for reorganization.

Fourth, DOL management promoted comprehensive cross-training so employees would have the job skills to provide customers with both employment services and unemployment insurance services in a single interview.

Commitment from external sources was also necessary to ensure the success of the reorganization. The deputy commissioner lobbied several key persons extensively to obtain the governmental support needed to implement the plan for reorganization. The U.S. Department of Labor, the governor of Connecticut, the Connecticut General Assembly, the Commission to Effect Government Reorganization, the Office of Policy and Management, and the Department of Administrative Services all supported the reorganization, which allowed DOL to reclassify jobs and institute an innovative evaluation system for assessing individuals' abilities to perform the new jobs. In addition, the establishment of a Labor Management Committee provided the union leadership with a voice in reorganization plans.

Organizational Profile

The historic mission of the Connecticut State DOL is "to protect and to promote the interests of the working men and women of Connecticut." To support this mission, DOL provides individuals with unemployment insurance benefits, job placement assistance, and referral to job training programs, retraining programs, and educational programs, as needed. In addition, DOL ensures job safety for individuals currently employed; provides employers with skilled workers; and collects, analyzes, and disseminates pertinent workforce data. Approximately 1,200 employees are employed in DOL's 19 offices (18 regional job centers plus the central office) to serve Connecticut's workers and employers.

Key Players

The reorganization at the Connecticut DOL was the inspiration of Larry Fox, the deputy commissioner. In fact, the reorganization began because Deputy Commissioner Fox, as a charismatic leader, was able to translate his vision into goals and objectives that agency leaders could implement. Passionate about the reorganization, Fox also frequently engaged in "fireside chats" with employees to share his vision and to listen to employees' fears and concerns about the reorganization. He used the information he gained at these meetings to refine his plans. In addition, Fox employed the University of Connecticut and other consultants to advise him as he crafted the reorganization plan. Because Fox began his career as a union worker, he anticipated union resistance and negotiated with union leadership to gain approval for the proposed changes. He lobbied key political figures tirelessly to eliminate barriers to the reorganization. Fox embodied the reorganization and championed his cause despite the obstacles.

While Fox infused the organization with his vision and gained political support for the reorganization, Bennett Pudlin, the executive director, helped translate the vision into reality. He orchestrated the specific activities that readied the organization for the change. Pudlin guided the design of the new organization, a task that included developing the new organizational structure, job responsibilities, and delivery streams. He worked relentlessly to ensure the effectiveness of the services of the 18 job centers as well as the effectiveness of the central office services. Pudlin's thorough, systematic understanding of the agency's operations enabled him to integrate new practices with current practices for a smooth transition.

Although Fox and Pudlin had been DOL employees for a number of years, the third change agent, Ann Nichols, was hired at the start of the reorganization to help the agency's leaders implement Fox's vision. As director of organizational development, Nichols designed and implemented the participative evaluation process used to hire two levels of new supervisors in the agency. She also designed and delivered supervisory training addressing change management theory, the role of the new managers as sponsors of the reorganization, the national and state trends that drive the agency's new vision, the principles of team building, and the principles of problem solving. Finally, Nichols coordinated the design and delivery of a three-phase, pay-for-skills, cross-training program for 450 frontline workers that incorporated curriculum to standardize procedures and evaluations to test employees' abilities to attain predetermined performance standards.

Rationale for Implementation

A needs assessment was conducted to identify training needed to support the agency's reorganization. Initially, this assessment was utilized to identify the knowledge, skills, and abilities needed to perform the new, integrated jobs designed for the frontline workers. The assessment also provided the information needed to determine the gap between current and required skill levels of frontline staff. Finally, the information gained from the needs assessment was used to develop the comprehensive three-phase training plan to promote the agency's strategic mission. Because formal training for all tasks was impractical, the needs assessment was conducted to identify the core tasks that should be included in a formal training program.

Target Population

The sample for the needs assessment consisted of 410 individuals who worked in the 18 regional job centers. Because employees in the job centers performed a variety of tasks, data were gathered from all staff members to ensure a comprehensive, representative assessment of training needs.

The participants reported a variety of job experiences prior to the needs assessment. About 60 percent of the participants were either job service interviewers or unemployment insurance interviewers. The other 40 percent of the participants held positions as job service counselors, job service local veterans' employment representatives, job service veterans' aides, job service veterans' assistants, unemployment insurance fact finders, or unemployment insurance intermittent interviewers. Finally, the longest length of time reported in the current job was 29 years and nine months, while the least length of time reported in the current job was one month. The average length of time in the current job was eight years and three months.

Project Plan

The director of organizational development determined that a needs assessment was necessary to identify the best way to crosstrain all frontline staff. A 10-person representative committee was formed to design the needs assessment process. Committee members were chosen to represent the three different-sized offices (small, medium, and large) and to ensure the committee had job service expertise, unemployment insurance expertise, and employment and training expertise. In addition, the committee included a job service manager and an unemployment insurance manager. Incumbents were also chosen to represent the union's perspective. To honor the agency's commitment to employee involvement, all 410 individuals affected by the training process also participated in the needs assessment process, which was managed by a consultant from the University of Connecticut and conducted by the staff development unit using the activities outlined in this section. Detailed discussions of the instruments used and the data analysis are presented in the next two sections.

The committee undertook the following tasks:
- develop a job and task analysis worksheet
- develop a job and task analysis document
- develop a job and task analysis feedback form
- complete the job and task analysis worksheet
- gather data using the job and task analysis document and the job and task analysis feedback form
- compile a master list of significant task discrepancies for each job duty, to revise the job and task analysis document and the job and task analysis feedback form
- present the final job and task analysis document to the Labor Management Committee
- use the job and task analysis document to determine which tasks should be included in the first round of crosstraining.

Instruments Used

Three types of instruments were used to collect data for this needs assessment. First, the committee used the job and task analysis worksheet (Figure 1) to collect preliminary data. Next, the committee used the job and task analysis document (Figure 2) to identify the specific job tasks; the performance standards, criticality, and frequency (i.e., how often the duty is performed) of each task; and the best way to learn and demonstrate mastery of each task. Finally, a job and task analysis feedback form (Figure 3) was used to collect additional data from all 410 job incumbents.

Figure 1. Sample job task analysis worksheet.

Job

Community Service Representative I
- List major duty areas in the job
- For each duty area, list all the tasks performed

Duty

Process Unemployment Insurance (UI) claims

Task

Process a partial list
- List the conditions under which the task is performed
- List the standards for task performance
- List all the elements required for task performance
- List skill and knowledge requirements for each element

Conditions

Workspace with two chairs partitioned for privacy, a computer, a telephone, and a printer

Standards

Time Limit: 3-5 minutes (1 claim off list)
Accuracy: 90% with 0 defects
Satisfaction: Claim processed and paid to customer's satisfaction

Steps/Elements

Element	Skill and Knowledge Requirements
Check new claim on system	Knowledge of UI rules, regulations, programs, and procedures
Verify partial claim via last day of work	Knowledge of UI forms Knowledge of screens and stops Knowledge of keyboard, data entry

Figure 2. Sample job task analysis document.

Classification: Community Service Representative I

Task	Criticality	Frequency	Performance standard	Best way to learn	Best way to demonstrate
1. Process new intrastate claim	Extremely important	Hourly	Process a new claim in 8-10 minutes with 90% of the claims having 0 defects; in addition, provide proper information and take claim courteously and professionally	50% classroom training 50% on-the-job training	Supervisory assessment Peer assessment Paper-and-pencil test
2. Process additional claims, reopened claim	Very important	Hourly	Process an additional or reopened claim in 5-7 minutes with 90% of the claims having 0 defects; in addition, provide proper information and take claim courteously and professionally	50% specific classroom training 50% on-the-job training	Supervisory assessment Peer assessment Paper-and-pencil test

Figure 2 (continued). Sample job task analysis document.

Classification: Community Service Representative I

Task	Criticality	Frequency	Performance standard	Best way to learn	Best way to demonstrate
3. Process Eligibility Review Program I form	Very important	Hourly	Perform an Eligibility Review Program I inter- view in 7-10 minutes with 85% having 0 defects; in addition, provide proper information and take claim courteously and professionally; process and pay claim when due	50% on-the-job training with supervisor 25% on-the-job training 15% peer 10% learning network 25% classroom training 15% specific 10% general	Supervisory assessment Peer assessment Assessment of team skills Paper-and-pencil test Paper-and-pencil test
4. Process total continued claim	Extremely important	Hourly	Process a total continued claim in 2-3 minutes with 95% of the claims having 0 defects; in addition, process and pay claim when payment due	50% specific class- room training 50% on-the-job training	Supervisory assessment Peer assessment Paper-and-pencil test

Figure 3. Sample job task analysis feedback form.

Classification: Community Service Representative I

Office Size _____
Classification _____

Task	Criticality	Frequency	Performance standard	Best way to learn	Best way to demonstrate
1. Process new intrastate claim	1 2 3 4 5	1 2 3 4 5 6	Process a new claim in 8-10 minutes with 90% of the claims having 0 defects; in addition, provide proper information and take claim courteously and professionally	1 2 3 4 5 6	1 2 3 4 5
2. Process additional claims, reopened claim	1 2 3 4 5	1 2 3 4 5 6	Process an additional or reopened claim in 5-7 minutes with 90% of the claims having 0 defects; in addition, provide proper information and take claim courteously and professionally	1 2 3 4 5 6	1 2 3 4 5

Figure 3 (continued). Sample job task analysis feedback form.

Classification: Community Service Representative I

Office Size _____
Classification _____

Task	Criticality	Frequency	Performance standard	Best way to learn	Best way to demonstrate
3. Process Eligibility Review Program I form	1 2 3 4 5	1 2 3 4 5 6	Perform an Eligibility Review Program I interview in 7-10 minutes with 85% having 0 defects; in addition, provide proper information and take claim courteously and professionally; process and pay claim when due	1 2 3 4 5 6	1 2 3 4 5

Job and Task Analysis Worksheet

The first step in the design process was to perform a job and task analysis (top of Figure 1) to determine the specific job components. This process was completed by the committee in nine days (two days for the analysis of jobs and duties and seven days for the analysis of tasks). Specifically, the committee identified the job duties for the three jobs (Community Service Representative I, II, and III) performed by frontline workers and compiled a list of critical tasks for each duty. This list was cross-referenced to the list of job tasks outlined in the job classification documents. Based on this assessment, the job classification documents were revised to add three additional tasks.

The committee then listed the minimal requirements needed to perform the job tasks in the "Conditions" section of the worksheet. The next step, defining the performance standards, was the most difficult step for the committee to complete, because performance standards had not previously been established for any of the jobs at DOL. To complete this portion of the worksheet, the committee was instructed to set a minimum and a maximum amount of time that an inexperienced worker would need to complete each task.

In addition, the committee determined that 100 percent accuracy for each task was the ultimate goal, but that this standard was too high for the initial phase of training. The compromise standard (90 percent of each task completed with no defects) was set to accommodate anticipated opposition from the union and from frontline workers. Customer satisfaction was added as the third component of the performance standard, with the expectation that exit surveys would be designed to measure this criterion. A work-flow analysis was created for each job task to guide the identification of all the steps and elements associated with the task. Finally, the skill and knowledge requirements for each step were identified to determine the job competencies that training would need to address.

Job and Task Analysis Document

Once the job and task analysis worksheet was completed, the committee began to develop the job and task analysis document (Figure 2). This phase of the needs assessment was completed in five days. First, the committee created performance standards based on the information in the "Standards" section of the job and task analysis worksheet. Second, the committee created scales to measure criticality and frequency based on working knowledge of the job tasks being assessed. For instance, data on the number of Unemployment Compensation Federal Civilian

Figure 4. Job analysis instruction sheet.

Use the following scales to complete each column on the Job and Task Analysis Feedback form. Your responses will be used to determine the final values for all of the categories.

Criticality
In the column labeled "Criticality," circle one number (from 1 to 5) for each task using the following scale to assess how critical the specific task is in relation to the other duties of the job.

        1 = Not Very Important   4 = Very Important
        2 = Somewhat Important   5 = Extremely Important
        3 = Important

Frequency
In the column labeled "Frequency," circle one number (from 1 to 6) for each task using the following scale to assess how frequently the specific task is performed.

        1 = Yearly   4 = Weekly
        2 = Quarterly   5 = Daily
        3 = Monthly   6 = Hourly

Performance Standard
In the column labeled "Performance Standard," you will notice a time component and a quality component. If you disagree with the standard as written, please record an alternate performance standard on the reverse side of the page. Be sure to identify the corresponding task by number.

Employee claims processed in the previous year were used to determine the appropriate frequency labels. Once criticality and frequency labels were created, each committee member ranked the frequency and criticality for each task. Responses were compared and differences were discussed. Through a facilitated discussion, consensus on the appropriate values for the criticality and frequency of each job task was achieved.

The committee also defined the categories for the best way to learn and the best way to demonstrate job competency, based on a review of the literature describing possible instructional and evaluation methodologies. After determining categories for describing the best way to learn and the best way to demonstrate competency, the committee recommended learning strategies and evaluation strategies for each job task.

Figure 4 (continued). Job analysis instruction sheet.

Best way to learn and best way to demonstrate

The columns labeled "Best way to learn" and "Best way to demonstrate" must be done together. For each "best way to learn" you identify for a task, you must indicate a corresponding "best way to demonstrate." You may identify more than one "best way to learn" and "best way to demonstrate" for each task (see example).

Performance standard	Best way to learn	Best way to demonstrate
Process regular Unemployment Insurance Compensation 280s and correspondence in 5 minutes with 0 defects in 90% of the cases	1 2 3 4 5 6 1 2 3 4 5 6 1 2 3 4 5 6 1 2 3 4 5 6	1 2 3 4 5 1 2 3 4 5 1 2 3 4 5 1 2 3 4 5

Best way to learn

1 = Specific Classroom Training
2 = General Classroom Training
3 = On-the-Job Training with Peer Supervision
4 = On- the-Job Training with Management Supervision
5 = On-the-Job Training in Work Teams/Learning Networks
6 = IIndependent Work with Media Resources

Best way to demonstrate

1 = Peer Assessment of Performance
2 = Supervisory Assessment of Performance
3 = Supervisory Assessment of Team Skills
4 = Supervisory Assessment of Ability to Teach Others
5 = Pencil-and-Paper Test

Job and Task Analysis Feedback Form

Although the job and task analysis document was carefully crafted, it represented the accumulated knowledge of only 10 people. To verify the accuracy of their work, the committee designed the job and task analysis feedback form (Figure 3) to gather the same information from the 410 future training participants. This form was accompanied by an instruction sheet (Figure 4) that explained how to fill it out.

The job and task analysis feedback form was pilot-tested with a group of 60 job incumbents and with the Labor Management Committee (an advisory committee comprising four job center directors, two job incumbents, six union representatives, the director of organizational development, a senior manager, and the University of Connecticut consultant) in a half-day training session. Members from the Staff Development unit were trained in a two-hour session to facilitate this data-gathering process. The pilot group revised the job tasks and performance standards and completed the other sections of the form: criticality, frequency, best way to learn, and best way to demonstrate. After the job and task analysis feedback form was tested, the responses for each category were compared with the committee's responses. Discrepancies were noted and revisions made based on the pilot group's input.

Next, members of the Staff Development unit and members of the needs assessment committee visited each of the job centers to gather data from all of the job incumbents, using the job and task analysis feedback form. First, the job incumbents were instructed to review the job tasks and performance standards listed and to make appropriate revisions based on their job experiences. Second, the job incumbents were asked to indicate, for each task, the criticality, frequency, best way to learn, and best way to demonstrate competency. At each center, after all individuals had completed the feedback forms, Staff Development personnel facilitated a discussion of group rating discrepancies of more than two points. The intent of these discussions was to identify the rationale for the ratings and to try to gain group consensus. Needs assessment committee members acted as scribes, recording the ratings and the rationale for the discrepancies. Once the data had been collected from the 18 job centers, the committee analyzed the data and made revisions to the job and task analysis document.

The data-gathering phase of the needs assessment process was completed in four weeks. The data analysis and subsequent revision of the job and task analysis document were also completed in four weeks.

Data Analysis

Both quantitative and qualitative data were analyzed to determine the final list of tasks, the final list of standards, and the final ratings for criticality, frequency, best way to learn, and best way to demonstrate competency. First, the mean frequencies for each scale item for the criticality and frequency variables were calculated. Second, data related to the performance standards were analyzed. Specifically, the number of participants agreeing with the amount of time needed to perform each job task and the number of participants agreeing with the amount of accuracy needed to perform each job task were calculated. Third, the mean scores of participants' first and second choices for the best way to learn and the corresponding best way to demonstrate competency were calculated. Because responses showed no significant differences related to office size, the overall data were used to determine the final lists and ratings. In addition, the qualitative data collected during the discussions at each job center were grouped by theme, with the number of times each theme emerged recorded.

To determine the final values for the job and task analysis document, the ratings assigned by the participants were compared with the ratings assigned by the committee. If the assessments of the two groups were different, the committee used the qualitative data to consider the validity of the participants' responses. For example, if the committee determined a task was "extremely important," but the job incumbents determined it was "important," qualitative data were examined to identify the rationale job incumbents used to justify their rating. If the committee considered the rationale valid, the criticality label was changed to reflect the incumbents' perspective. In other instances, the label was changed to reflect a compromise between the rating assigned by the committee and the rating assigned by the job incumbents. In this way, the committee arrived at a final list or label for each of the six variables.

Results

The final version of the job and task analysis document was presented to the Labor Management Committee for review. In addition, an overall three-year training plan was outlined. Finally, a specific, detailed training plan for Phase One of the training was highlighted. The most critical, most frequently performed job tasks for the Community Service Representative I job were included in this training design. The most critical, most frequently performed job tasks for the Community Service Representative II job would be taught in Phase Two of the training. And the most critical, most frequently performed job tasks for the Community Service Representative III job would be taught in Phase Three of the training. The latter two phases were designed to build on the application of knowledge, skills, and abilities learned in Phase One training. All job tasks not included in the formal training plan would be learned on the job as frontline workers performed their new jobs. The three-phase training plan was also explained to a group of senior managers before implementation of the training plan began.

Members of the Labor Management Committee and the designated senior managers were instructed to explain the training plan to staff in each of the job centers. Focus groups were also convened to share with job incumbents drafts of the curriculum and the evaluation methodologies. The design process relied on the involvement of all levels of staff to ensure commitment and buy-in to the training process and the redesign of jobs.

Phase One Training

To support the goals of DOL's reorganization, crosstraining was necessary to teach frontline staff how to integrate job service tasks and unemployment insurance tasks in a single job interview. Phase One training was designed to reduce the number of interactions a customer must have with DOL staff and to improve customer service by teaching participants how to perform basic job service and unemployment insurance tasks with uniform procedures. Upon successful completion of Phase One training, participants were promoted to a higher job classification based on their abilities to conduct an integrated interview session with the agency's customers. Phase One training began seven months after the needs assessment was conducted.

Phase One training included three training modules: Customer Service, Job Service, and Unemployment Insurance. Upon completion of each training module, participants were required to complete an evaluation. Each module, therefore, consisted of four days of training, a half day of study time, and a half-day evaluation to assess learning and ability to perform job simulations.

The Customer Service module included only classroom training. The Job Service module and the Unemployment Insurance module had on-the-job training as well as classroom training. The classroom training was offered off site simultaneously in six regional locations. In contrast, the on-the-job training was offered simultaneously in all 18 job centers. The three-week training was repeated three times to train and evaluate all 410 job center staff members.

Based on principles of adult learning and participants' input on the job and task analysis document, Phase One training incorporated several distinct delivery techniques. The classroom training incorporated presentation and discussion, interactive video and discussion, role plays, demonstration, and simulations. For example, the Customer Service classroom training incorporated role plays and demonstration to teach participants how to improve face-to-face and telephone interactions with DOL's customers. The Job Service and Unemployment Insurance classroom training, in contrast, combined presentation and discussion with a variety of simulations to teach the technical skills needed to perform the job.

The on-the-job training incorporated presentation and discussion, role plays, demonstration, simulations, and computer-based instruction. Access to computers allowed participants to practice what they learned in the classroom phase.

Peer training was a critical element of both classroom and on-the-job training. Trainees with complementary skills (i.e., one person with Job Service expertise and one with Unemployment Insurance expertise) were paired at the start of the training and worked together during the three weeks to learn from each other. These pairings were especially useful during the computer application portions of the training, because partners could coach one another while the trainers rotated among job stations.

Team teaching was also an essential component of this training. Staff Development trainers were paired with supervisors to ensure effective delivery of the training. This pairing was necessary because Staff Development trainers had training expertise but did not have the technical skills needed to provide credible training to the front-line workers; the supervisors had the technical skills but lacked the presentation skills of professional trainers. Working together, the professional trainers and the supervisors combined their expertise to effectively deliver general Customer Service training and technical Job Service and Unemployment Insurance training. Finally, the pairing of the trainers and the supervisors enhanced the skills of both groups. Supervisors learned presentation skills in a formal train-the-trainer session and practiced the new skills as they delivered the training. Staff Development trainers developed technical skills as they worked with supervisors to deliver the technical portions of the training.

Conclusions and Recommendations

Collaboration with the union and the involvement of job incumbents in the needs assessment process were effective strategies that signaled a real change in the agency's business operations. The majority of the job incumbents were delighted that they had been asked to help design the performance standards, to suggest best ways to learn their new jobs, and to suggest best ways to be evaluated. Participants were optimistic that the subsequent training would provide them with the skills they needed to perform new job duties successfully. Similarly, the union welcomed the opportunity to be a partner with management in the reorganization effort. In fact, changes made in the job and task analysis document based on data gathered during the needs assessment process impressed skeptical job incumbents and skeptical union members. Skeptical managers, however, were not convinced that staff input would be used to modify the training plans, because managers' involvement in the process was limited. To correct this limitation, managers could have been asked to work with Staff Development personnel to explain the needs assessment process to their employees and to gather the data.

The reaction to Phase One training was less favorable and more difficult to assess because the training's formal evaluation presented some risk for the participants. Although union members and training participants contributed to the design and implementation of Phase One training, and despite the enthusiastic endorsement of the training by DOL executives, resistance to the process was still evident—at the organizational, work-group, and individual levels.

Participants' feedback suggests that two significant organizational barriers limited the effectiveness of the training intervention. First, participants perceived that senior managers' sponsorship of the training was weak. For example, senior managers heralded the training as the single most important agency initiative, yet they did not allocate additional resources to support the training effort. Second, as change agents, senior managers were criticized for not integrating the goals of the reorganization with daily work operations.

Work-group barriers also emerged because the training significantly altered work operations. Consequently, many participants were less than enthusiastic about participating in these change efforts. In fact, work groups often adopted a "don't rock the boat" posture, which may have restricted participants' commitment to learning new skills during the training.

Finally, individual factors may have also impeded full participation in Phase One training activities. For example, some employees stated that they were nervous about participating in a training session with an evaluation component. Data gathered to assess the effectiveness of the training also suggest that motivation, self-efficacy, and age may have influenced the effectiveness of the interventions. Individuals who were motivated to improve their job performance and believed in their own abilities to learn new job duties were probably actively engaged in Phase One training activities. Conversely, individuals who were not motivated to improve their job performance because they did not believe in their own abilities to learn new job duties were probably not actively engaged in Phase One training activities.

Based on the data gathered from Phase One training, the plans for Phase Two training and Phase Three training have been revised. To reduce the organizational barriers that emerged in this case study, a formal strategy to increase the visible involvement of senior managers and supervisors in the training process has been developed.

In fact, a strategic quality training model will be used to augment training for both job incumbents (task training) and managers (leadership training). Classroom training will be supplemented with structured on-the-job training. Senior managers and supervisors will define the skills and subsequent training they need to support each training intervention for frontline workers.

The effectiveness of the training will be evaluated for both job incumbents and supervisors immediately after the training (reaction evaluations and learning evaluations) and again after both groups have had the opportunity to apply the training in the workplace (behavior change evaluations and organizational results evaluations). The ultimate goal is to improve the job performance of both groups to improve customer service.

The director of organizational development has also worked consistently with the senior managers to help them translate the reorganization goals into specific activities for each job center.

In addition, the director of staff development has worked with the supervisors to reduce work-group barriers as well as individual barriers that limited the effectiveness of training. For example, changes were made in the evaluation procedures to reduce test anxiety. Performance evaluation procedures have also been revised to link the training to the compensation package for the Community Service Representative II job classification.

Finally, Phase Three training will use competency-based training strategies to allow individuals to demonstrate mastery of key competencies over time.

In summary, this needs assessment and the subsequent Phase One training were the first steps in a five-year plan to reorganize the DOL into a more efficient, customer-driven public agency. Based on the analysis of data gathered in the needs assessment, the Staff Development unit designed and delivered training to initiate and sustain behavior change that will improve the agency's delivery of services. Future needs assessments and subsequent human resource development interventions at DOL will focus on helping participants apply classroom theory to solve workplace problems.

Questions for Discussion

1. To accomplish the goals of the reorganization, the commitment of all employees was needed. Identify the key groups of employees that had to be committed to the reorganization. For each group of employees, identify strategies that could have been used to gain their support.

2. How would you design the needs assessment process to promote the goals of the reorganization—specifically, to improve customer support service and to empower frontline workers? Determine who you would involve in the design of the needs assessment, define your target population for the needs assessment, and outline the overall process you would use to collect the necessary data.

3. Based on this case study, list some of the benefits of a management-union partnership in implementing a needs assessment and subsequent training for an organization that is undergoing significant change.

4. List specific examples of "good practice" that DOL built into its needs assessment process and subsequent training process.

5. What changes could DOL incorporate in future needs assessments and future training efforts to continue to promote the goals of the agency's reorganization?

The Authors

Sandra L. Hastings, Ph.D., is the director of staff development at the Connecticut State Department of Labor. She is responsible for the design and delivery of training to promote continuous learning and transfer of training for all staff. She is also an adjunct faculty member in the Adult Education Department at the University of Connecticut. Hastings can be contacted at the following address: Connecticut State Department of Labor, 200 Folly Brook Boulevard, Wethersfield, CT 06109.

Ann B. Nichols, a certified change management consultant, is the director of organizational development at the Connecticut State Department of Labor. As an internal consultant to the agency's leadership team, she is responsible for institutionalizing change management to support the agency's reorganization.

Barry G. Sheckley, Ph.D., is section head and associate professor of adult education at the University of Connecticut. His numerous publications include the recent book *Employability in a High-Performance Economy* (Council for Adult and Experiential Learning, 1992). In his research, he is exploring how the adult and experiential learning process can be harnessed to transform work settings into learning environments.

Barry A. Goff, Ph.D., is an organizational consultant specializing in the evaluation and monitoring of training, technological innovation, and business restructuring. He also assists businesses and government agencies in developing total performance measurement systems. Currently, he is working with the Connecticut State Department of Labor to institutionalize a performance measurement system for the new One-Stop Career Centers.

An Action Research Approach

General Electric Aircraft Engines

Sharon J. Korth

This case involves a training needs assessment of engineering and technical staff. Action research methodology was used collaboratively with clients to collect data, report back to them the information gathered, and have them use it to make decisions.

Overview

This needs assessment process was developed for the engineering division of General Electric Aircraft Engines, a large manufacturer of gas turbines and other industrial equipment. The facilitators utilized action research methodology, an organization development approach developed by Kurt Lewin (1946). Action research is a collaborative, client-consultant inquiry consisting of data collection, feedback of the data to the clients, and action planning based on the data (French and Bell, 1984). This approach was used because of the scope and complexity of the situation. Although the project was initiated as a "training" project, organization development in the form of team building, collaboration, and creation of a vision was necessary for the project to be successful. The overall process included some of the traditional techniques used in assessing training needs—such as interviews, focus groups, and questionnaires—but they were all integrated into a broader action research process. The clients and consultants collaboratively designed the assessment process, analyzed the data, and developed the action plan based on the results.

One feature of the needs assessment was the use of the team process model—interlocking layers of teams with different roles and responsibilities participated in the process. Another feature was the use

This case was prepared to serve as a basis for discussion rather than to illustrate either effective or ineffective administrative and management practices.

of training process logic to link business objectives, job behaviors, and the skills and knowledge learned in training. Qualitative data were collected at various levels in the organization, and several techniques were used to compare, consolidate, prioritize, and align the data with key organizational objectives and strategies. Some of this work was done via video-conference meetings.

This needs assessment process was designed jointly by the facilitators and the top engineering managers. Although the process was very time-consuming and did not involve statistical analyses, it resulted in tremendous buy-in by engineering personnel throughout the organization. Several training projects that were launched had potentially high payoffs for the organization. The process also served as a team-building function for the top engineering managers and provided education on the role of training in improving organizational effectiveness.

Background

At the time of the assessment, engineering employees were already participating in numerous human resource development (HRD) activities, including training on leadership, communication, information systems, and continuous improvement. The majority of newly hired engineers participated in two other development programs as well, one involving job rotations and the other leading to a graduate engineering degree. In addition, informal on-the-job training occurred in some parts of the organization, along with orientation and mentoring programs. Although readily available, these programs were not well integrated and did not address technical training issues.

Three years prior to the engineering-wide needs assessment, an HRD position had been created within one of the 10 engineering departments, and an extensive technical training program had been developed within that department. This program included forming a training advisory board, conducting a comprehensive needs assessment, developing 70 new courses and seminars, and publishing a curriculum guide that served as an individual development and career-planning tool for employees and their managers. A second engineering department developed a similar program soon after. Once these programs and processes were established, questions were raised about the need for and the feasibility of expanding the programs across the eight other engineering departments.

Target Population

The engineering division comprised approximately 7,000 employees. The majority were engineers involved in the design of gas turbines and other industrial equipment. The organization was divided by functional areas and operated in a matrix format along product lines. Although engineering employees were scattered at several locations, most were located at the main Midwest location, and about 1,000 worked at a plant in New England. The department in New England was responsible for designing small gas turbines, whereas the nine other departments designed the larger products.

The engineering organization was headed by a vice-president. Reporting to him were 10 department managers—one from the New England location and nine others from the Midwest location—and two staff engineers. The target population of the assessment was defined as all people in the engineering division who did technical work, at all experience and skill levels. This group included more than 6,000 employees.

Character Profile

Several key individuals were involved in this HRD needs assessment process. As the engineering training manager, I had worked in HRD positions within the company for eight years and had developed the original department-wide technical training program. I believed that buy-in, involvement, and support from top management were critical. Because this was a political endeavor and had the potential to be an important, unifying organization development opportunity for the division, I enlisted the help of two other people, and we became the facilitation team.

The second member of the facilitation team, Eric Young, had 35 years of systems engineering and management experience with the company. At the time, he was an internal total quality management consultant for new product development. He had credibility with the top engineering managers, had conducted the study that identified the need to create the original HRD position, and was interested in helping with this effort. Young was involved with other organizational initiatives and was able to help align the training effort to the business objectives and strategies.

The team's third member was an outside consultant, Jan Salzmann, an organization development specialist and partner of Change and Development Consultants. She brought expertise in team building, effective communication, and process improvement. In addition to having extensive experience with other companies, Jan had been involved with a major team-related initiative within the engineering division, so she was known and respected within the division and was aware of the cultural and political issues.

Other key players in the assessment included the manager of the centralized HRD organization and the human resource manager in engineering. They were both important contacts for integrating the program with other HRD efforts involving engineering personnel, because most of the other programs came under their control.

The most important players in this assessment, however, were the vice-president of engineering and his staff. They were the primary stakeholders, because the purpose was to improve the effectiveness of their organization.

Issues and Events

Although many issues and events led to the decision to conduct a needs assessment, there were two major instigating factors. The first factor was inconsistency across the division. Two departments had programs and the others did not. This had raised many questions.

The second factor was the imminent formation of training councils across the entire business. The manager of the centralized HRD organization was forming the Training Guidance Council of Vice-Presidents (which would set the overall training strategy) as well as divisional training councils (which would address needs specific to their organizations).

The formation of the engineering division training council would provide an excellent opportunity to address the consistency and integration issues that had surfaced over the previous years. It was critical at this time, however, to determine the level of interest and support from the vice-president of engineering and the other department-level managers. This is where the needs assessment started.

Action Items

The facilitators utilized action research methodology for the needs assessment, working collaboratively with the clients to collect data, report back to them about the information gathered, and have them use it to make decisions. Phase One involved making the decision to form an engineering training council; Phase Two involved determining the training needs; and Phase Three involved detailed planning for the HRD interventions. This section focuses on Phase Two, because some unique models and techniques were employed during that phase.

Phase One

The decision to form an engineering training council came after a series of steps. First, the facilitation team gathered information from the department managers and their staffs, asking the following types of questions: What are the technical training needs of your employees? How similar are your needs to the needs of other departments in the division? How different are your needs? Should engineering technical training for different departments be managed separately, integrated, or centralized? Then the team analyzed the data and summarized the findings on several charts that showed the range of responses across the division.

In accordance with the action research process, these charts and others served as discussion vehicles for further meetings. The facilitators met first with the engineering vice-president and then with his staff. The vice-president was supportive and insisted that the project involve both the Midwest and the New England locations. At the staff meeting, 10 people volunteered to participate in a subgroup to decide how to move ahead with this project. This group became known as the Training Interest Group and served as the training council originally requested by the central HRD manager. The interest group would decide when to report back or involve the engineering staff as a whole.

Phase Two

In Phase Two of the needs assessment process, the interest group worked on determining technical training needs. Establishing the mission for the division-wide initiative and the process by which to determine the training needs became very complex and difficult. The interest group members had difficulty distinguishing how this project would be different from all of the other development efforts available for employees. They debated the definitions of *technical, training*, and *education*. Some thought that separating out the technical aspects of the job was a violation of systems thinking. Others felt that they needed to have some programs specifically focusing on technical expertise, because that was the core of the engineering business. To help with the discussion, the facilitators developed the graphic in Figure 1, which displayed all of the development efforts available to engineers.

The chart, in illustrating the number and breadth of HRD programs, raised awareness that there were many available programs being administered independently by various individuals throughout the organization. It sparked discussion, during which the interest group members realized that no one had responsibility for division-wide technical skill development, nor for prioritizing and integrating all the HRD programs for engineering personnel. The interest group members determined that they could not expect someone else to do that and that they would not want someone else to make those decisions for them. They felt that it was their responsibility to provide for technical skill development, ensure that all programs were aligned with their

Figure 1. Development opportunities supporting the vision of the engineering division.

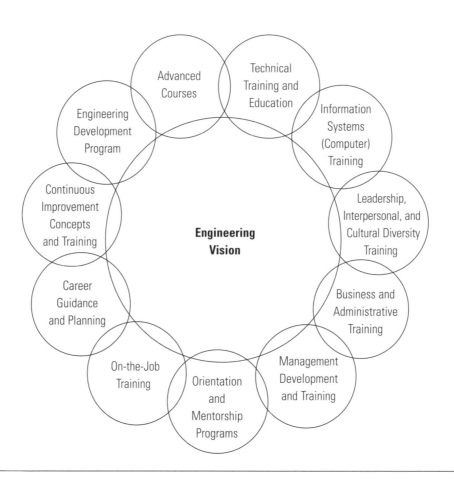

vision and mission, and make decisions about the priority of programs.

Over the course of two or three challenging meetings, the interest group made some key decisions. They decided to use the combined term "training and education" because they could not come to a consensus on the definitions of the words separately, and they also decided to focus on technical training and education because it was the missing piece in the HRD efforts. Without avail, the facilitators tried several techniques to help them define *technical*, including posing topics and deciding if they were technical or not. For example, the engineering managers agreed that conducting a stress analysis was technical, and writing a memo was not technical, but could not agree if project management techniques were technical or not. They finally decided to move ahead; if any skills they had not defined as technical were found lacking, those skills could be added to this initiative or other employee development efforts later.

From these discussions, the interest group members also developed the mission statement for technical training and education, making the statement broad enough to cover these unresolved issues. The mission was expressed as follows:

- provide training and education that will enable engineering employees to support business objectives
- accelerate the growth of inexperienced engineering personnel into technical leadership positions
- expand the capability of functionally experienced engineering personnel
- integrate employee development efforts to make more efficient use of resources.

Another important issue that surfaced at this time concerned the engineering vision. The facilitators were planning to use the training and education process logic as a model for linking the training needs to the organization's vision, and discussed this model with the interest group. This model, illustrated in Figure 2, was adapted from the impact

Figure 2. The training and education process logic model.

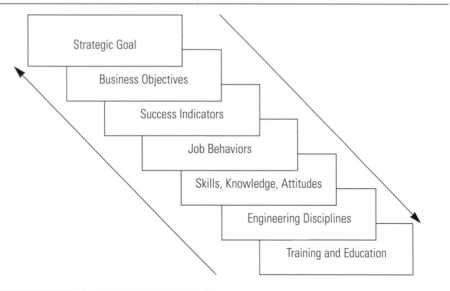

map concept developed by Robert Brinkerhoff and Stephen Gill (Brinkerhoff, 1987; Brinkerhoff and Gill, 1994). Underlying this model is the connection between organizational goals and objectives, indicators of successful performance on the job, and skills and knowledge learned in training. This logic also sets up a framework for the four levels of evaluation defined by Don Kirkpatrick (1975).

The group was very interested in this model and wanted to use it as part of the needs assessment process. To create the process logic, the interest group members turned to existing documents to provide the facilitators with information for the strategic goal and business objectives categories. However, when the facilitators asked the interest group members about information regarding the job behaviors that would help achieve those objectives and how they would measure the success of those behaviors, they were at a loss.

In order to create the additional categories in the model, the facilitators asked the interest group members for written responses to questions such as these: If the organization were operating successfully, what would be happening? What would not be happening? What skills were needed to create the desired state?

The facilitators separated the responses from the first two questions into process results (which they categorized as success indicators) and process descriptions (which fell into the job behaviors category). Answers to the third question went on a list of skills, knowledge, and attitudes. The facilitators sent the compiled lists back to the interest group members, asking them to look over the lists for similarities and points needing clarification. In preparation for a subsequent meeting, the facilitators put each response on an 8.5-by-11-inch card. At the meeting, each success indicator card was discussed, clarified if needed, and then placed randomly on the wall. After changes, combinations, and additions, the interest group members went to the wall and categorized the cards. They then developed titles or headings for the different groupings. The same process was repeated for the job behaviors cards and the skills, knowledge, and attitudes cards. To categorize engineers in terms of common needs for skills and knowledge, and therefore common training needs, the interest group members first brainstormed a list of technical work done in the organization and then grouped items in the list into categories of similar work. These categories were the "engineering disciplines" in the model in Figure 2.

Input was also solicited from the rest of the engineering staff and the vice-president. The resulting document became a unifying tool for the division and part of the strategic planning activities. It also set the stage for the development of very detailed impact maps after the specific training needs were identified.

Another important decision made by the interest group was that they wanted to identify the high-priority technical training issues rather than to conduct full-blown, detailed task analyses of the numerous job categories in the division. The rationale was that the high-priority approach could be completed within a few months, would identify high-impact items, and would serve a unifying and integrating function across the division. The more detailed task analysis approach, which would lead to the development of job-specific curricula across the division, was postponed because it would be very tedious and time-consuming, and would not serve the same unifying function.

The interest group decided to collect information on the factors that affected the engineering personnel in the technical aspects of their jobs, including both existing problems and future opportunities. These factors might be at the organizational level (e.g., clear communication of standards), at the task level (e.g., availability of equipment and tools), or at the person level (e.g., motivation or lack of skill or knowledge). Not all of the factors would indicate a training need. Some would require another form of intervention.

As the needs assessment process was being formulated, the interest group members acknowledged that they did not know the detailed issues related to the technical aspects of the work done in their organization. They also thought that people who were too close to the work might not have a big-picture, integrative perspective. Therefore, the facilitators developed the team process model for involving the appropriate people in the many decisions that needed to be made. The team process model consisted of three interlocking layers of teams: the interest group, a steering committee, and the discipline-related subgroup teams (see Figure 3). The roles and responsibilities of each team were clearly delineated throughout the start-up, needs assessment, and implementation phases of the process.

The teams included members from both major business locations, as the engineering vice-president required. In addition, the discipline-related subgroup teams were developed around similarity of work, rather than around location in the organizational structure. This helped break down territorial barriers at the department level and clustered people who would have similar training needs. Team members in each layer were recommended by people in the layer just above, but participation was voluntary.

Figure 3. The team process model.

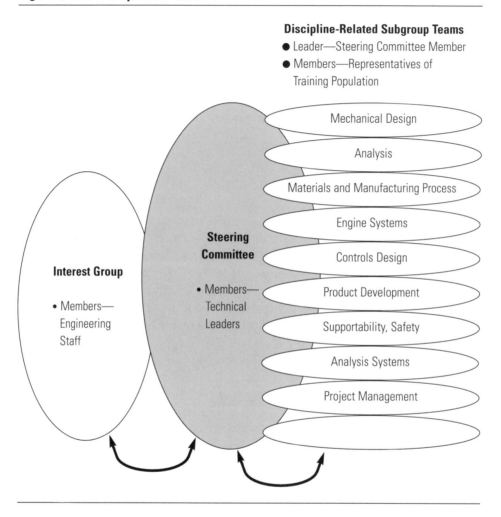

Based on this process model, the interest group and facilitators developed the needs assessment process. The collaborative development of this action research process was important; top managers acknowledged that they could not make sound decisions without information from other people, they agreed to have the facilitators collect the information, and they wanted to be involved in making the decisions from the data collected. The facilitators played a central role in this process, planning and conducting all of the meetings and communicating information between teams. The process became totally consuming for several months: Eleven teams, each with members at two locations, worked with huge amounts of data and held 18 video-conference meetings. However, the assessment did result, as planned, with the identification of the top technical training issues across the division.

Phase Three

After the top issues were identified in Phase Two, Phase Three involved the detailed planning for the HRD interventions. This planning included some additional assessment as well as program design and development. Phase Three is discussed in more detail in the results section.

Costs and Benefits of the Assessment

The cost of the first two phases of the assessment was an important issue. Although not literally spelled out in dollars, costs included the time spent by the engineering training manager, the internal facilitator, an administrative associate who scheduled meetings and compiled data, and all of the team members. Each team member spent eight hours on the needs assessment, including time spent on homework and at meetings. Steering committee members each spent six additional hours. The interest group met for two to three hours each quarter and completed some homework between meetings. Additional costs included the cost of hiring the external consultant, one trip to the New England location by the engineering training manager, and the 18 video-conference meetings.

Data Analysis

Several strategies were used to analyze the qualitative data collected in this assessment. The original information in Phase Two was collected via worksheets and answer sheets. Members of the discipline-related subgroup teams provided answers to two questions: "What problems or issues get in the way of your being able to perform the technical aspects of your job?" and "What do you see as the future technical needs in your area?" They sorted their answers into those that indicated a training need (i.e., a lack of skill or knowledge) and those that were nontraining issues. (See Korth, Salzmann, and Young, 1994, for copies of the forms.)

Following action research methodology, the facilitators compiled the training issues for each team and utilized them for discussion and decision making at the video-conference meetings. (Video-conference meetings allowed for balanced participation from both business locations.) The facilitators first clarified the issues and had the team members compare items and combine similar ones into clusters. Once the list was consolidated, the team members voted individually on the items they felt would result in the greatest payoff to the organization and had the greatest urgency. Points were tallied (3 points for each first-place vote, 2 points for each second-place vote, and 1 point for each third-place vote). If there was not a clear delineation of the top five to seven items, the lowest items were dropped and the team members voted on the reduced list. When the list was reduced to five to seven items, each item was designated on a criteria matrix as high, medium, or low for potential payoff and for degree of urgency. This process led to a discussion and, eventually, consensus on the top three training issues for each of the groups.

After the facilitators and the steering committee members analyzed the 27 training topics (9 teams times 3 topics per team) for similarities or themes, the interest group used an interactive alignment process to help select the training topics. Prior to the meeting, the interest group had identified what they thought were the top technical issues for which training could be part of the solution. For the meeting, the facilitators prepared a wall with cards identifying the organizational objectives, strategies, and technical training issues, as defined by the interest group members. As the 27 training topics from the other teams were described, the interest group members placed cards on which these themes were written where they aligned with the top technical issues the interest group had identified. The manipulation of cards on the wall helped the interest group members establish their priorities and shape their plans.

Results

The assessment resulted in the interest group launching seven training projects. Phase Three of the process, the detailed planning for the training interventions, involved forming seven Training Project Teams. Each team, with an interest group member as a champion, developed a detailed training map using the training process logic, as well as a project plan (which included costs, needed resources, and a timeline for development and implementation). These plans were presented to the interest group and the entire engineering staff for approval. After this approval, the development of the seven programs began.

HRD Intervention

Each of the seven training initiatives was unique. Whereas some took a traditional course structure, one project took a team learning format. This project involved a cross-functional group that worked on a particular component of the product (a total of 25 to 30 people), including people in engineering, manufacturing, materials procurement, and field support. The objective of the training was to enhance the concurrent engineering process already under way and improve the long-term quality, timeliness, and cost of the product. Their "training" would involve informal sessions at which group members would explain to each other the nature of their work, discuss their common goals, and determine how they could share data and streamline the process. The sessions would be facilitated by a process consultant, but responsibility for leading the sessions would rotate from one function and one team member to another.

Conclusions and Recommendations

One unexpected outcome of this project was the enthusiasm of and participation by the top managers. The interest group grew as the project progressed, and people who were reluctant in the beginning joined in as time went on.

One possible factor was the action research process itself, which was quite compelling. People will not argue with their own data and want to be part of decisions that affect them. Furthermore, the facilitators made very efficient use of the top managers' time.

In addition, several of the teams grew larger than recommended, because people wanted to be involved in the process. Even though the large teams created a challenge for the facilitators, especially in the video-conference meetings, it was encouraging to see so much interest. The active involvement of the top managers and the finite commitment (eight hours per team member) for the needs assessment process were two factors that contributed to the widespread involvement.

An extra benefit from this process was the communication, through the video-conference meetings, between people who worked in similar disciplines. Coming from different departments and locations, some of these people had corresponded over the years by letters or over the telephone, but had not ever met face-to-face. Some worked near each other but had never realized the similarity in their work.

Additionally, top managers were pleasantly surprised that the organizational issues they identified were almost identical to the training issues that surfaced in the teams. This agreement indicated an effective communication process in the organization.

The issues that were forwarded to the top managers tended to be broad issues. Using criteria of payoff to the organization and urgency meant that some of the more focused, localized needs fell off the list. Localized needs are important; there is much more work to be done to develop a comprehensive, integrated HRD system for all engineering personnel. However, this assessment was designed to uncover some of the more complex, cross-functional technical issues—which it did. Several of the team members commented that the process made them think more broadly and consider how their discipline both integrated with others and contributed to the total organization. Top-level managers were pleased with this result.

Finally, an important benefit was that people became more aware of the role of training in increasing organizational effectiveness. Training is often targeted as the solution for any problem, and then training is blamed when the problem is not corrected. Participants in this process had to distinguish between training and nontraining issues, which educated them about the relationship between training and organization development and provided some insight on what training can and cannot do. The collaborative nature of the action research process helped develop insights as well as ownership.

Questions for Discussion

1. What are the advantages and disadvantages of an action research approach?
2. What are the strengths and limitations of the team process model?
3. What are additional uses of the impact map (training process logic) concept?
4. What are the limitations of the qualitative nature of the data? How might more quantitative methods be incorporated into the process?

The Author

Sharon J. Korth is an assistant professor in the Executive Human Resource Development Graduate Program at Xavier University in Cincinnati, Ohio. Created with working adults in mind, the program utilizes a cohort, weekend format, which allows for an integrated curriculum, provides a classroom laboratory for ongoing learning, and emphasizes community growth and development. Korth joined Xavier University in 1993, after 10 years with General Electric Aircraft Engines (GEAE), also in Cincinnati. While at GEAE, she worked as an instructional designer and also as the engineering training manager, responsible for the technical training needs of more than 6,000 engineering employees. She can be contacted at the following address: Xavier University, Executive Human Resource Development Graduate Program, 3800 Victory Parkway, Cincinnati, OH 45207-6521.

References

Brinkerhoff, R.O. (1987). *Achieving results from training: How to evaluate human resource development to strengthen programs and increase impact.* San Francisco: Jossey-Bass.

Brinkerhoff, R.O., and Gill, S.J. (1994). *The learning alliance: Systems thinking in human resource development.* San Francisco: Jossey-Bass.

French, W.L., and Bell, C.H. (1984). *Organization development: Behavioral science interventions for organization improvement* (3d ed.). Englewood Cliffs, NJ: Prentice-Hall.

Kirkpatrick, D. (1975). *Evaluating training programs.* Madison, WI: American Society for Training and Development.

Korth, S., Salzmann, J., and Young, E. (1994). G.E. Aircraft Engines. In J. Wilcox (Ed.) *ASTD trainer's toolkit: More needs assessment instruments* (pp. 75-84). Alexandria, VA: American Society for Training and Development.

Lewin, K. (1946). Action research and minority problems. *Journal of Social Issues, 2*(4), 34-46.

Team Leader Performance Analysis

AT&T Universal Card Services

Lisa C. LeVerrier and Michele K. Stevens

This case shows the use of a wide range of assessment methodologies to determine the training needs of team leaders in the customer service function. Surveys, interviews, training histories, focus groups, human resource data, and content analysis were all used to determine specific training needs.

Background

In July 1993, Universal Card University (UCU), the training department within AT&T Universal Card Services (UCS), initiated a performance analysis of Customer Services team leaders. The study was in response to several sources of information indicating that line supervisors (i.e., team leaders) in Customer Services Operations were experiencing performance problems. Early data indicated that team leaders were having difficulty in providing career development for their team members, administering company policies fairly and consistently, and relating with team members on an interpersonal level.

One major cause of performance problems among the team leaders was a lack of depth of previous management experience. Because of the rapid growth of the company, many Customer Services associates were promoted very quickly into team leader positions. Although these associates had gained mastery over the technical aspects of customer service delivery, they had little opportunity to develop managerial skills.

A second major cause of performance problems was related to the extent and effectiveness of training provided to newly promoted team leaders. During the early stage of the company's development, a generic curriculum of supervisory and soft skills training was established for

This case was prepared to serve as a basis for discussion rather than to illustrate either effective or ineffective administrative and management practices.

team leaders. Courses in the curriculum were, for the most part, purchased from external vendors or imported from AT&T's corporate training organization. The initial curriculum for team leaders was encouraged but not required and, therefore, was attended unevenly by the team leader population. Reasons for the low participation in the curriculum included the high volume of work during the start-up phase of UCS and inconsistent organizational support for attending. These gaps in training caused some team leaders to learn mostly by trial and error on the job, resulting in the performance problems already mentioned.

Organizational Profile

UCS is a wholly owned subsidiary of the AT&T corporation. UCS was launched on March 29, 1990, to market a combination credit card and long-distance calling card. Headquarters are in Jacksonville, Florida, and satellite sites include the Statement Processing Center in Columbus, Georgia, and the Customer Service Center in Salt Lake City, Utah. Currently, UCS employs approximately 3,000 associates. In just four years of operation, it has become the second largest issuer of bank credit cards.

The main product is a combination long-distance calling card and credit card that is either a Visa or a MasterCard. The organization's top priority is providing preeminent world-class customer service to its cardholders. In 1992, UCS was awarded the prestigious Malcolm Baldrige National Quality Award by the U.S. Department of Commerce.

UCS is organized into the following functional areas:
- Corporate and Consumer Affairs
- Credit Policy
- Customer Services
- Finance
- Human Resources
- Information Technology Services
- Legal
- Marketing.

UCS's main environmental challenge is the increasing level of competition within the credit card industry. The marketplace has become increasingly complex, with multiple fees, interest rates, and incentive programs competing for market share—a trend started in large part by the entry of UCS into the market.

Industry Profile

The credit card industry is a very competitive one, and the companies that make a concerted effort to get to know their customers and meet their customers' needs are the only ones that will prosper. During the early 1990s, the industry experienced major changes as several strong nonbank competitors—such as AT&T, General Motors, Shell Oil, and General Electric—entered the market. These entrants joined major issuing banks, smaller niche players, and others to produce a level of competition that was unprecedented in the credit card industry.

Bank credit card issuers make their profits on interest rates paid by card members. Therefore, each issuer attempts to ensure its card is the one used most by consumers. The high level of competition has led to issuers increasing the overall value of their cards so that consumers find them more attractive. For example, over the past couple of years, issuers have eliminated most annual fees, lowered interest rates, and initiated special programs that reward card members for using particular cards.

Most experts agree that there is plenty of room for growth in the credit card industry for those issuers that recognize how the credit card business has changed, and what is necessary to meet customers' needs. Entry into the market is now more difficult than it was; consumers are more savvy and have many more choices.

Key Players

Lisa LeVerrier, course developer and instructor, conducted the performance analysis, wrote the summary report, made recommendations for training and nontraining solutions, and was involved in reporting results to the client organization. She was the key instructor and developer for the resulting curriculum. LeVerrier is an instructional design specialist and joined UCS in 1993.

Michele Stevens, curriculum manager at UCU, managed the performance analysis and secured and allocated resources for the development and delivery of the resulting curriculum. With management responsibility for the entire project, Stevens established and maintained relationships with the client organization. She had more than a dozen years of service with AT&T, many in the field of training and development, when she joined UCS in 1992. She is responsible for managing UCU's Quality and Professional Skills curricula.

Bob O'Neal, dean at UCU, has approximately 10 years of experience with AT&T in the field of training and development. He joined UCS at its start-up in 1990 and was responsible for creating UCU. O'Neal formerly served as organizational leader for training and development at UCS and is a strong supporter of systematic training development and performance analysis. He is also very active in engaging the support of Customer Services senior management for implementing the recommendations resulting from the study.

Many other UCU staff members were involved in the subsequent development, delivery, and administration of the team leader curriculum.

Jerry Hines, executive vice-president and chief operating officer (COO), began his AT&T career in 1970 and joined UCS in 1993. He served as a catalyst for the performance analysis by examining the team leader role, as well as the training the team leaders received. Hines was also a decision maker for carrying out the resulting recommendations and curriculum.

Other key contacts in Customer Services included vice-presidents and senior managers who gave their support to data collection efforts and the resulting curriculum, as well as team leaders and senior team leaders who participated in data collection.

Finally, associate relations (AR) representatives serve as human resource representatives within the various UCS organizations. They help to resolve issues between team leaders and associates, and also ensure that AT&T and legal requirements (e.g., concerning administration of benefits, or the attendance policy) are met. These individuals have daily contact with team leaders and associates and, therefore, were an important source of information for the study.

Issues and Events

As mentioned earlier, the project was initiated by UCU to study performance difficulties being experienced by team leaders in Customer Services. UCU had the resources to complete the study, which was given top priority within UCU. Customer Services employs most of the associates who work at UCS, and these associates are the primary contact for UCS customers. Team leaders directly supervise this entire associate population. Thus, the potential return on investment for identifying and addressing performance gaps within this functional area has tremendous potential impact on UCS's product and, therefore, business success.

The initiation of a performance analysis and needs assessment was triggered by the following events:

- UCS experienced a change in a key leadership position, the COO, during early 1993. Shortly after the new COO assumed his position at UCS, he began to examine the role of the team leader, including the training received and the scope of responsibilities.
- A manager from the Human Resources Benefits group asked UCU to design a course on UCS policies and procedures to be delivered to line supervisors. Inconsistencies regarding the administration of

these policies drove this request.

In addition, each year an annual Associate Opinion Survey (AOS) is conducted at UCS. The results of this survey are taken very seriously by senior management; typically, results help determine the direction of key initiatives for the next calendar year. Results from the AOS conducted in fall 1993 showed below-target scores for quality of supervision, development of associates, and communication. These results confirmed the need for the performance analysis, which was already under way.

Interestingly, it was the training organization (UCU) that proactively initiated this study. During the study, UCU sought buy-in from the Customer Services organization when it became clear that significant organizational commitment would be required to close performance gaps. The triggering events mentioned, combined with an inherent culture of continuous improvement, drove the decision to conduct this needs assessment. Client buy-in and support were sought during the study, and the Customer Services senior management team was kept informed of findings throughout the process.

Target Population

Team leaders in the Customer Services area were the target population of this study. At the time of the study, the location of the performers included Jacksonville, Florida; Columbus, Georgia; and Salt Lake City, Utah.

The target population included approximately 185 people. Data would be collected from a sample of this population. Most of the people contacted would be asked to respond to a survey, and a smaller number would be interviewed.

Learner Characteristics

Nearly half (44 percent) of the team leaders had completed a bachelor's degree, had attended graduate school, or had completed their master's degree. About a tenth (11.8 percent) had not gone beyond a General Equivalency Diploma or a high school diploma. The remainder had some college experience or had obtained an associate of arts degree.

Team leaders ranged from 22 to 54 years of age. The median age was 34 years; 41.6 percent of the team leaders were between 20 and 30 years old. Most of the team leaders (72.7 percent) had been at UCS for at least three years.

Most team leaders (79 percent) who responded to the survey indicated they had had supervisory experience prior to working at UCS.

However, only a small percentage of the team leaders had previous supervisory experience within AT&T. Therefore, the level of experience with administering AT&T policies and procedures was low. Supervising within an empowered environment such as UCS also provided a new challenge for many of the team leaders.

The majority of the team leaders (69 percent) had been promoted from the Customer Services associate position. Length of time served as an associate prior to promotion ranged from three months to more than three years. One unique issue affecting the target population was the early business success and sustained rapid growth rate of UCS. This led to rapid promotions into the team leader ranks by individuals holding entry-level Customer Services associate positions. During this time, there was little emphasis on training these new team leaders, and performance problems resulted from gaps in the leadership and supervisory skills of the team leader population.

Action Items

The main goal of the assessment was to collect data on team leader performance to determine how skill and knowledge levels, motivational issues, or environmental factors might be enhancing or inhibiting organizational performance.

One key action item that requires some explanation is the process used to present the assessment results to the client organization. The following steps helped UCU gain client buy-in, obtain funding for the project, and communicate the results and implementation strategy to UCS:

- Shortly after the leadership changed in Customer Services, the UCU team met with the new COO to discuss work in progress that would affect the Customer Services organization. At that time, a status report on this study was presented.
- Once the study was completed and a report summarizing the results of the study was created, the head of UCU, the curriculum manager, and a course developer-instructor met with the senior managers within Customer Services to present the specific results and to provide each of them with a copy of the report. Personal visits or one-on-one debriefings were conducted with all vice-presidents and senior managers who were unable to attend this meeting. All the vice-presidents and senior managers supported the results of the study and the recommendations made by UCU.
- The head of UCU and the curriculum manager went directly to the COO to present the results of the study and to gain support for the recommendations made.

- The COO then called a meeting with all of his team members to ask for their support for the training recommendations. A formal decision was made to support the recommended curriculum. This meant that the new 12-day curriculum proposed by UCU would be mandatory for all existing team leaders and for all newly hired or promoted team leaders on an ongoing basis.
- The COO asked for a business case to justify the investment needed to develop and deliver the revised team leader training that was being proposed. Shortly after the business case was prepared, funding was allocated for the project.
- UCU then met with the Employee Communications Department to create a communications plan so that all associates could understand why the initial needs assessment was conducted and what the training implementation plan entailed.

Models and Techniques

Data were collected via the following sources:
- surveys
- interviews
- training histories
- focus group
- Human Resources demographic and employment data
- content analysis.

Surveys

To begin this study, a survey was administered to 62 team leaders. The survey asked them to verify job tasks identified as critical to the team leader position in a previous needs assessment conducted during 1991. The job task categories utilized in the survey were
- leadership
- job-specific knowledge
- supervision
- development of associates
- interviewing and selection of job candidates
- communication
- administration
- special projects
- business knowledge.

Each category had been operationally defined and broken down into individual tasks by interviewing team leaders during the prior needs assessment. In the current survey, team leaders were asked whether each task applied or did not apply to their job.

A task was considered to be of questionable applicability if five or more of the 34 team leaders who returned the survey indicated it did not apply to their job (5 ÷ 34 = approximately 15 percent). Because UCS is a high-performance organization, cutoff points for surveys tend to be high. The task the fewest respondents said was applicable was interviewing and selection of job candidates: Fifteen of the 34 team leaders (44 percent) found this task inapplicable because their managers (i.e., senior team leaders) typically handled that responsibility.

Interviews

One-on-one interviews were conducted according to structured guidelines. Thirteen interviews were conducted with Human Resources Benefits managers and UCS team leaders and staff from the following departments:

- Telephone Relationships
- Customer Assistance (i.e., collections)
- Credit Relationships
- Billing Assistance
- Data Entry and Remittance Processing
- Loss Prevention
- Claims.

Eleven team leaders and two Human Resources Benefits managers were interviewed. Previous performance appraisal data were used to select team leaders across the range of performance quality. Of the 11 team leaders, four were in the excellent-very good range (model performers), four were in the good range (average performers), and three were in the needs-improvement category (below-average performers).

The structured interview protocol initially asked team leaders to rate themselves on the nine job task categories (i.e., leadership, job-specific knowledge, etc.) on a scale from 1 to 5, where 1 is poor and 5 is excellent. Each category was operationally defined with examples of individual job tasks in that category. Table 1 lists the interview questions that were asked following completion of this self-assessment.

For nine of the 11 team leaders, downward and upward feedback was obtained by interviewing their managers and the associates they supervised.

Training Histories

Training histories were examined to determine when team leaders received training and the types of training they received.

Table 1. Interview questions asked following self-assessment.

1. How long have you been in the team leader job?

2. Generally, on a scale from 1 to 10, how do you rate yourself in the quality of your performance of this job? (1 is low, 10 is high)

3. In general, how satisfied are you in your current job? (1 is low, 10 is high)

4. What problems have you had during your job as a team leader? What would you attribute these problems to, and what do you think is necessary to help resolve them?

5. When you moved into the team leader position, how did you meet the responsibilities of your job? Was there training available? If so, what were the courses and modules? What books were used? When did you participate in training?

6. What could have made your transition easier (i.e., what was missing)? Specifically, what courses, programs, or training aids do you think you need to help you do this job even better than you are now doing it?

7. What are your performance standards? What are you specifically measured on (i.e., quality indicators, administrative duties, team productivity)?

8. Were you ever shown the team leader curriculum training path by your manager?

9. What have you done during your career as a team leader to develop yourself personally and professionally?

10. How were your personal and professional development programs chosen? Were they simply chosen by you? Did your manager make suggestions based on your performance review? based on a career development discussion?

11. What characteristics do you think make someone an effective team leader? How would you define someone who has expertise in the team leader job?

12. Describe a typical day as a team leader.

Focus Group

Six AR representatives participated in a focus group on their perspectives of UCS team leaders and job performance issues. Because the AR representatives interact with team leaders daily, they are a good source of information regarding team leader performance.

The focus group took place in a conference room, so issues could be discussed in a private setting. The purpose of the meeting was communicated clearly: to get the representatives' input regarding ways in which the team leader role could be improved.

The AR representatives were introduced to the nine job function areas and their associated job tasks. Table 2 shows the questions that were used to guide the focus group session.

Table 2. Questions used to guide the focus group session.

1. Which tasks of the team leader job do you think need improvement or skill building? Which tasks do you have to take responsibility for if the team leaders cannot or will not perform them correctly?

2. What would you attribute these performance problems to, and what do you think is necessary to help resolve them?

3. Based on your experience, what is the frequency of each problem? If you were to rank the performance gaps from most common to least common, how would you rank them?

4. The key question we are after is what the team leaders are measured on (i.e., quality indicators, administrative duties, team results). What are the performance standards? How do they know how well they are doing?

5. I'd like to interview representatives from the team leader job. Could you help me identify team leaders over the range of the performance spectrum? I'd like representation from each of these categories: model performers (excellent-very good), average performers (good), and below-average performers.

Human Resources Data

Additional information was captured using the Human Resources Data Base. Among the variables investigated were team leaders' tenures at UCS, tenures at AT&T, and ages.

Content Analysis

Several other records and studies within UCS served as additional sources of data on performance deficiencies. A content analysis of these records and studies was conducted, and relevant data were summarized to corroborate the findings of this assessment. Examples of the types of documents analyzed included time sheets and attendance records.

The following UCS surveys were examined for evidence of team leader performance trends:

- *Upward Feedback.* Team members provided written ratings of their team leaders on various management competencies.
- *Fear of Reprisal Report.* This report was prepared by a continuous improvement team that was charged with uncovering the root causes of fear of reprisal, which surfaced as an issue within certain pockets of the organization.
- *The 1993 Human Resources Client Satisfaction Survey.* This survey was designed to assess UCS employees' satisfaction with the products and services of the Human Resources Department. A key area was how accessible managers were to assist associates in career development planning.

Cost and Benefits

The cost of the needs assessment was limited to salary dollars. One course developer spent approximately three months conducting the study.

Although a formal cost-benefit analysis was not conducted prior to beginning this study, it was assumed that any improvement in team leader performance would have a positive influence on the Customer Services associates, and ultimately on the customers.

Data regarding the effects of the training and nontraining solutions implemented will be collected as part of the evaluation strategy.

Data Analysis

Qualitative data obtained via surveys and verbatim comments were examined to discover issues and trends. Qualitative data were also obtained via team members' and managers' ratings of the team leaders on various aspects of their jobs (on a scale from 1 to 5, with 5 being excellent).

Ratings from the team leaders themselves, their team members, and their managers were averaged across performance appraisal categories. Any score below 4.0 (80 percent) was considered an opportunity for improvement. This cutoff point was selected to mirror cutoff points used for previous company reports. In addition, high-performance norms for survey data typically show similar cutoff points.

Recommendations were made based on how frequently issues were mentioned, and whether performance deficiencies were related to a lack of skill and knowledge (or experience), a lack of rewards or incentives, or an organizational barrier to improved performance. Each of the nine job skill areas was analyzed using all available data to make both training and nontraining recommendations. In the nontraining recommendations, environmental and motivational barriers were identified, and recommendations were made to address these issues.

Results

A detailed report communicated the study results. The report included an executive summary, a detailed explanation of data sources and data collection strategies, a profile of the target population, a report of findings, and recommendations and solutions.

Recommendations and solutions were separated into training and nontraining categories, based on whether the findings were related to skill and knowledge gaps or to motivational and environmental issues.

The recommendations were summarized in chart form, as illustrated in Figure 1.

Figure 1. Example of an action items matrix.

Action item	Training solution	Nontraining solution	Group responsible
Leadership: employ training course such as *Principle-Centered Leadership*	✓		Universal Card University
Leadership: provide frequent feedback for below-average performers		✓	Human Resources Performance Management Customer Services
Job-specific knowledge: develop checklist of competencies		✓	Customer Services Universal Card University
Job-specific knowledge: provide frequent feedback for below-average performers		✓	Human Resources Performance Management Customer Services

Figure 1 (continued). Example of an action items matrix.

Action item	Training solution	Nontraining solution	Group responsible
Supervision: design training	✓		Universal Card University Customer Services Human Resources Employment and Staffing Benefits
Supervision: develop decision-support tools		✓	Universal Card University Customer Services Human Resources Employment and Staffing
Supervision: provide backup support for AR representatives		✓	Human Resources Employment and Staffing
Development: Have team leaders attend developmental manager training	✓		Universal Card University
Development: certify team leaders as developmental managers		✓	Universal Card University Customer Services
Development: provide training on coaching for performance	✓		Universal Card University
Development: pair model performers with team leaders as on-the-job coaches		✓	Customer Services

Intervention Description

As the direct result of this study, a 12-day training curriculum was implemented for all team leaders. This training is expected to close performance gaps in supervision and administration, communication skills, and the development of associates. The sequence of courses is shown in Figure 2.

Figure 2. Recommended team leader curriculum path. (Numbers in parentheses indicate how many days of training were recommended.)

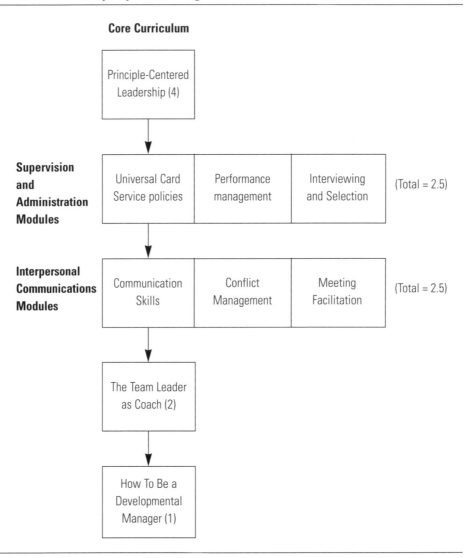

Core Curriculum

Principle-Centered Leadership (4)

Supervision and Administration Modules

| Universal Card Service policies | Performance management | Interviewing and Selection | (Total = 2.5) |

Interpersonal Communications Modules

| Communication Skills | Conflict Management | Meeting Facilitation | (Total = 2.5) |

The Team Leader as Coach (2)

How To Be a Developmental Manager (1)

Most of the courses in the team leader curriculum are primarily led by instructors. Several courses have required follow-up activities for students to complete. These follow-up activities were designed to reinforce the skills that the team leaders learn in class, and to help provide evaluation data regarding the impact of the curriculum on team leader performance.

For the initial delivery of the new curriculum, the 185 existing team leaders were grouped into "tracks" of approximately 30 participants each. Members of each track completed the training together and served as peer coaches for one another throughout the curriculum.

Conclusions and Recommendations

This needs assessment confirmed performance gaps in three major areas: administration, development of associates, and communications. In addition to a lack of skill and knowledge in these areas, several environmental and motivational causes contributed to the performance gaps. As a result, the recommendations included a wide range of nontraining solutions, as the example in Figure 1 illustrates.

The 12-day training curriculum was custom-developed to meet the specific needs of the team leaders. The curriculum was approved by the senior management of the Customer Services department and is now required for existing and future team leaders. Most existing team leaders have now completed the entire curriculum.

Some of the nontraining recommendations have been implemented quickly and easily, whereas others are still works-in-progress. Span of control, for example, was examined and reduced. Each team leader currently has no more than 20 associates reporting to him or her. Formerly, team size was as large as 35.

Lessons Learned

Formal summaries of the study were presented to senior management, and the team leaders themselves were given a brief overview of the findings. They were also given access to the completed study during one of their training classes. In hindsight, a formal and detailed presentation to team leaders may have been a better approach. Better communication up front may have helped to allay the resistance to training that emerged.

Because both training and nontraining solutions are being implemented at the same time, it is difficult to attribute any specific changes in performance to training. Many factors are currently influencing the team leaders' performance environment, including organizational changes, policy changes, and developmental activities. Therefore, evaluators should not credit training for all positive change that occurs.

UCU realized early on that the team leaders needed training that was customized to their role and environment. Generic soft skills training was not relevant. The assessment involved team leaders and senior team leaders as subject matter experts and reviewers for designing the courses. Also, role plays, case studies, and exercises for the training came directly from the performance environment. The result was training that receives extremely high marks for job impact and relevance.

Questions for Discussion

1. What measures or procedures would you use to evaluate the success of the training curriculum?

2. What action would you take to increase team leaders' acceptance of the curriculum?

3. Would you use any different or additional data collection strategies?

The Authors

Lisa C. LeVerrier is an instructor and course developer for AT&T Universal Card Services in Jacksonville, Florida. Her main duties include conducting performance and training needs analyses and designing and delivering training for management employees. She holds a B.S. in psychology and an M.S. in instructional systems design from Florida State University, and an M.A. in psychology from Wake Forest University. She is involved in the local chapter of the American Society for Training and Development, the North Florida Chapter of the National Speakers' Association, and the National Society for Performance and Instruction. LeVerrier can be contacted at the following address: AT&T Universal Card Services, 8787 Baypine Road 1-2-120S, Jacksonville, FL 32256.

Michele K. Stevens is a curriculum manager of professional skills and quality training for AT&T Universal Card Services. Over the past 10 years, she has held various training positions within AT&T; her responsibilities have included delivering courses on instructional design and instructor skills. She holds a bachelor's degree in English and education from Miami University and a master's degree in education from Eastern Michigan University. She is a national member of the American Society for Training and Development and the National Society for Performance and Instruction.

Pride in Public Service

Oregon Department of Transportation

Frank J. Navran and Donald E. Forbes

This assessment used interviews and focus groups, coupled with a comprehensive written survey, to determine training needs for all employees as part of an ethics enhancement project. The case explores a variety of issues that show how a unique project is developed and implemented in an organization.

Background

In December of 1991, the Oregon Department of Transportation (ODOT) solicited proposals for an ethics enhancement project from a number of ethics consulting companies. The Request for Proposals (RFP) clearly sought bids for specific ethics management tools that would help ODOT's management "enhance their individual ethical effectiveness and that of their organization."

The RFP outlined a series of specific objectives or outcomes:

- tools for dealing with the ethical implications of strategic change
- tools for demonstrating values-based management
- mechanisms for assessing management accountability and commitment
- tools for making values-based management resistant to "erosion"
- tools to reinforce the importance of and commitment to ethical conduct
- mechanisms for ensuring ethical decision making by employees
- ethics-based tools for managing organizational change
- strategies and mechanisms to encourage employee participation in the program
- training on ethical decision-making processes, including policies and laws
- pre- and posttests for evaluating the program's effectiveness.

This case was prepared to serve as a basis for discussion rather than to illustrate either effective or ineffective administrative and management practices.

The RFP emphasized that ODOT was in the process of reorganizing in an effort to decentralize, while embracing the concepts of shared leadership, teams, and empowered employees. In addition, its mission was being redefined as transportation, rather than highway construction and maintenance. Whatever process was proposed to address the ethics agenda would have to demonstrate ODOT's commitment to these other strategic initiatives as well.

It was clear that a front-end needs assessment was necessary. It was also clear that the needs assessment should be viewed as a pretest and should form a natural basis for the required posttest. The needs assessment would both drive the project and provide baseline data for assessing the project's impact and effectiveness.

What follows is a review of the processes used in the needs assessment, a description of how that needs assessment contributed to the success of the overall project, and a discussion of lessons learned through the experience.

Please note that this description is presented from two points of view. Most of the sections are written from the perspective of the consultants leading the project. But several sections (i.e., those with the word "Director" in the heading) express the thoughts of the chief executive officer of the client organization.

Why and How the Director Sought an Ethics Consultant

At the time we elected to embark on an organizational ethics program, ODOT was several years into an extensive restructuring effort. ODOT had not changed in any meaningful way in at least several decades. It was best characterized as having a rigid hierarchy with narrow spans of control that left decision-making authority in the hands of a few managers. Few people, including senior managers, understood our mission. For the most part, employees had no say in the operations of the department, nor were they even encouraged to participate by making suggestions. A formalized employee suggestion program yielded some outstanding suggestions, but few of the nearly 5,000 employees bothered to submit ideas.

Our efforts to change the department were widespread and affected virtually all aspects of the business. Not only were we revising the formal organizational structure by eliminating managerial layers and broadening the managerial span of control, we were also building a department-wide performance measurement process. One of our earliest restructuring endeavors was to provide team training for all employees. This team training was first pilot-tested in the highway division and later extended to the rest of the department.

We recognized that if we were going to decentralize the decision-making process, we had to empower managers and employees. Because nearly everyone in the department already worked in crews or groups, it made sense that empowerment should occur in these work units. It was not until we had spent several years on team training with crews that we realized we had missed an important ingredient—an ethical context for decisions. Our recognition of this error coincided with a very serious chain of events.

Independently of our team development efforts, we were trying to strengthen our outreach efforts with employees. We conducted meetings across the state with representatives of all crews. The intent of the meetings was to learn from employees what they perceived to be going well and what needed fixing. These meetings were small and informal. They were hosted by senior managers. After one such meeting, employees came up to the senior manager and expressed concerns with what they believed was inappropriate actions by another employee.

Subsequent investigations indicated that at least several people were stealing from the department, and others might be involved. At that point, we elected to call in the state police, who conducted a year-long investigation. Less than 20 employees were found to be involved, but through the course of the investigation, it became clear that most employees did not know how to handle ambiguous situations. Clearly, they knew that stealing was wrong, but less obvious situations, like the personal use of materials from scrap piles, left employees feeling afraid to do anything for fear that the state police would investigate them.

This uncertainty alone could have been enough to prompt us to provide employees with an ethics training module. As we were beginning to learn through our team development efforts, successfully decentralizing decision making requires an ethical context for decisions. It was at this point that we decided to marry the two ideas and include an ethics component in our department-wide restructuring effort. The ethics package would include training on basic ethical responsibilities of public employees and discussions about the types of ethical situations they might encounter.

A second element of the package would be to provide people with the ethical decision-making skills that would help them make more solid decisions within their teams. This element would provide the context for, or draw a fence around the limits of, acceptable decisions that would be supported by senior management. This "managerial insurance policy" would help ensure that a decision made by a team in one part of the state would likely be consistent with decisions made elsewhere in the state.

Although we had learned enough to state our needs broadly, we did not know how to proceed—the perfect situation in which to seek the advice of a consultant. During our restructuring, we had acknowledged that there would be situations that we as leaders in ODOT would not have the particular expertise to address efficiently. If given enough time, we could become expert enough to guide the organization through such situations, but time was of the essence. In those instances, we chose instead to hire subject matter experts to advise us. We had one caveat that guided us in each instance: We would not become dependent on the consultant. At the end of each such situation, we would be left with a level of competence enabling us to manage that particular area successfully in the future.

In our search for an ethics consultant, we were guided by one other caveat: We did not want a one-time training effort for employees. We wanted ethical principles to be woven into the fabric of our organization so all training, from employee introductory training to senior manager training, would have an ethical component.

We chose our ethics consultant competitively, based on candidates' proposed courses of action to address our issues. The consultants we selected took a customized approach. Although they had considerable experience in helping other organizations set up ethics initiatives, they did not suggest a cookie-cutter program based on that experience. For example, the consultants suggested that we really needed a systematic needs analysis of managers' and employees' attitudes about and understandings of ethical issues before we could successfully craft either initial training or the long-term training modules.

The Consultants' Agenda

Foremost on our agenda was the need to prepare a successful proposal. The proposal had to be specific enough to demonstrate that we could meet or exceed every requirement of the project and be flexible enough to allow us to meet unforeseen needs. The balance between specific commitments and flexibility was reflected in all aspects of the proposal.

The process for achieving that balance was heavy reliance on the needs assessment phase of the project to drive the specific content of later phases. The needs assessment would determine the desired outcomes, and those would form the basis for determining the client's and our mutual success.

We also knew that once we were awarded the contract, we were bound by our explicit performance guarantees, which promised ODOT that if all requirements of the RFP were not met, ODOT need not pay for the services. By limiting those promises to needs assessment processes and a commitment to address the assessment's findings, we avoided making promises that we would be unable to keep.

We have a philosophy, borrowed from the medical profession, that prescription without diagnosis is malpractice. We would have insisted on a front-end assessment even if one had not been specified in the RFP. The fact that a needs assessment was prescribed made it easier to propose that it be the driver of the processes and content to follow.

Finally, we were committed to moving the project beyond the limits presented in the RFP, ensuring that the project would be done right. By relying on a needs assessment as the project driver, we were confident that we would be able to deal with the issues and their causes, not just symptoms or superficial remedies.

The project as defined in the RFP was for a fixed price. Anything we added to the project's scope, whether or not dictated by the findings of the needs assessment, would not add to that price. Therefore, by suggesting a more extensive process, we were not trying to increase the price but to ensure that the project was done right. This project represented one of those rare opportunities to do the right thing the right way. The client was very willing to accept added value, as long as all of the RFP's requirements were met. For us, this was an opportunity to test some of our newer products and services under fire.

The Proposed Approach

We proposed a paper-and-pencil survey of 15 percent of the organization's 4,700 employees. The number was somewhat arbitrary. It was large enough to provide for some credibility in the analysis, although there would be no sophisticated statistical analyses of responses. We preferred an intuitive analysis based on our experience in interpreting data, rather than reliance on rigorous statistical processes.

The prime consideration in selecting the sample size was to ensure that even small organizational units had enough representation to allow for respondents' anonymity, despite the expectation that the data would be broken down by organizational entity and respondents' levels and work locations.

Specific details—such as what questions were to be asked, how the sample was to be selected, and how the survey was to be administered—would await input from the agency's director and his immediate employees.

The Model Used To Design the Needs Assessment Strategy

We were preparing to propose a series of interviews with all of the senior managers. This group, called the management team in ODOT, consisted of the director, the deputy director, five region engineers, and a number of branch managers—a total of about 14 members.

The interviews were to be based on Nadler's organization performance model (OPM) (Nadler, Tushman, and Hatvany, 1982). This model is built on a view of organizations as systems and uses the concept of congruence to describe the equilibrium of an organizational system in which the various subsystems interconnect in ways that optimize the system's overall effectiveness.

The OPM systematically describes an organization's processes from four perspectives:

- Inputs are those strategic elements that determine what the work of the organization should be, such as environment, resources, history, mission, vision, values, strategic goals, and strategic plans.
- The transformation process is the operational side of the organization, those processes that transform the strategic inputs into the organization's outputs or results. The four elements of the transformation process are the work that is performed, the people who perform it, the formal systems that govern how the work is performed, and the behaviors of management that influence the other three elements.
- Output examines the desired or expected results and compares them with actual results at three levels: strategic, operational, and individual.
- Feedback is the process for monitoring the effectiveness of the transformation process and the quality of the outputs so that the organization can determine what is working and not working, and thereby learn how to be more effective.

Each of these elements is further broken down and refined in the fully developed model.

The real strength of the model is its power as a diagnostic tool. According to the OPM, when a system is not optimally effective—when the actual outcomes of the system are different from those that are desired or expected (i.e., when there is a problem)—investigating the areas of congruence and incongruence among the system's components will lead the investigator to an understanding of the causes of the problem. In the 12 years that we had used the OPM, it had proven to be a powerful needs assessment model that accurately identified issues and recommended effective remedies.

The ODOT management team had little or no appreciation of organizational systems theory and no familiarity with Nadler's model.

Therefore, we needed an opportunity to convince the team of the value of a systemic approach to needs assessment (and, subsequently, a systemic approach to intervention). That opportunity presented itself in the introductory meeting.

The Introductory Meeting

Our first meeting with the management team provided the opportunity to "sell" the group on the overall approach and the need for a systemic, Nadler-based needs analysis rather than a limited assessment confined to the ethics issues (as laid out in the RFP) or top management's perception of the need. Ostensibly, the meeting was a chance for us all to meet and build rapport. In reality, it was our best chance to obtain approval for the preferred process while at the same time planting the seeds needed to redefine the project's parameters and, consequently, its potential effect on the client organization.

The meeting started with a formal presentation. Titled "Why Ethics? Why Now?" the presentation was an opportunity to enlighten the team members on reasons why other organizations were paying so much attention to ethics, to demonstrate our expertise in the field, and to search for each management team member's "hot button." The presentation included a review of the four reasons to care about the ethics enhancement project:

- *the moral imperative*—doing the right thing because it is the right thing to do
- *the legal imperative*—doing the right thing because there are penalties for doing the wrong thing
- *the pragmatic imperative*—doing the right thing because it is good business to do the right thing
- *the perceptual imperative*—doing the right thing to earn the trust of critical stockholders.

The search for hot buttons was our attempt to answer some questions that were critical to the project's success. What in this project was seen as being of value to each of these key managers? How could we engage them in the process? How could we earn their support for and commitment to the project that was needed, not just the project that was defined in the RFP? How could we continue to redefine the project so that the necessary goals would be met?

Our best estimate following the presentation was that six or seven of the management team members were hooked by one or more of the imperatives. Three were just hanging on until retirement, and the rest were skeptical but willing to go along with the program because the director seemed to want the project to proceed.

The final point raised in the introductory meeting was a strategic gamble. In an effort to increase the client's trust in our motives. we proposed the needs assessment as the first phase of the total project. We suggested that the needs assessment be the only step funded and approved by the management team at this time. They were advised not to release the funds for the full project until after the needs assessment had been conducted, the data had been analyzed, and the findings and recommendations had been presented for their consideration. Then, if the outcomes and recommendations were acceptable, they could approve our participation in the remainder of the project and release the remainder of the approved funds. The team agreed to begin the assessment with a series of one-on-one interviews.

Challenges From Within: The Director's Perspective

One of the first hurdles we encountered was my own management team. I manage some aspects of the department's business with 14 senior line and staff managers. Although it is hard to maintain efficiency with such a large team, it accurately reflects our business issues, and I have found that change occurs faster if all 14 are at the table when key decisions are made. In retrospect, the management team being a hurdle should not have been surprising. On the one hand, ODOT was in the midst of an extensive restructuring. Managers were asked to do their normal work as well as guide the change effort. In other words, they had been pushed very hard and were wearing out. The last thing they wanted was another change initiative to manage. On the other hand, they reflected the organization they were leading; that is, their understanding of ethics was very similar to the understanding of most employees and lower level managers. They were largely ambivalent about ethics and questioned the value of doing much more than superficial training. The attitude is best expressed as "I know stealing is wrong. I don't need a class to tell me that."

The Management Team Interviews

Following the initial meeting, the series of interviews was set up. The interviews were part of an overall strategy for identifying management team members' degree of support for the needs assessment and for earning their support if it was lacking. It was both an information-gathering process and an inclusionary process.

It was evident during the first meeting that several key managers felt that this ethics project was being foisted upon them by virtue of the director's belief that the organization needed it. He was a relative newcomer to the position, and these seasoned senior managers would support the project only if they were given their proper respect. Although no one was overtly threatening to sabotage the project, a lack of support for what was essentially a cultural change was tantamount to covert sabotage.

Ultimately, the long-term success of the project demanded the wholehearted support of this management team. They needed to be converted into true supporters because the eventual success of the project depended on their actions as role models and motivators. The management team interviews were a first step. These interviews were then supplemented with an additional 25 interviews with some of the management team's immediate employees. The added interviews would be valuable in substantiating the opinions and perceptions raised in the first round.

The interviews, built around Nadler's OPM, sought key leaders' input on several critical needs assessment issues, especially how the survey should be designed and administered. The content of the needs assessment survey was fairly well defined. It would attempt to articulate employees' perceptions of the

- organization's explicit values
- organization's implicit values
- importance of the organization's values in decision making
- relative importance of each of the identified values
- effectiveness of supervisors in applying the organization's values
- effectiveness of senior management in applying the organization's values
- understandability and fairness of existing ethics policies
- credibility of senior management's change agenda.

Although these interviews were highly structured, the tone of the questions was conversational. We probed for indicators of explicit and implicit values in a number of questions:

- *Question 2.* There has been a lot of discussion leading up to this project. In your opinion, why is ODOT going ahead with an Ethics/Pride in Public Service project?
- *Question 10.* Irrespective of the press coverage, how important do you think your employees believe the ethics issues are to ODOT? to themselves?

Some questions reflected our "Nadlerized" approach:

- *Question 14.* Sometimes an organization's policies and procedures encourage unethical behavior. For example, the punishment for being tardy may be more severe than the punishment for being absent. That might encourage an employee to lie and call in sick rather than be late to work. Or an employee might be encouraged to take quality or safety shortcuts to meet productivity standards. What inappropriate behaviors do you see that may be resulting from policies, procedures, measurements, or other formal systems?

- *Question 15.* In many organizations, there are different priorities or requirements depending on who one's immediate supervisor is. In your organization, which priorities or requirements are likely to vary depending on who is supervising?

The interviews were needed to refine the assessment processes to be used. The results were even better than expected. Not only did all the senior managers have an opportunity to be listened to, but they candidly discussed several concerns about how the assessment should be conducted.

The managers were asked for their concerns and, perhaps more important, for their perspectives. How would they like the results to be presented? How might the data be broken down to be of optimal value to them? How might the sample be selected? What questions were they particularly keen on? How would they like the survey to be administered? Were there any additional questions that they believed should be added to the survey?

Issues of Survey Administration

In the course of these interviews, the senior managers raised a serious issue that dramatically altered the needs assessment's basic structure. As many as 25 percent of ODOT's frontline employees and 10 percent of frontline supervisors could not read at the eighth-grade level at which the survey was written. Any survey that addressed perceptions of the importance and effectiveness of various ethical principles, policies, and mechanisms as applied in the organization would be beyond the grasp of that group. We needed to supplement the proposed paper-and-pencil survey with another mechanism that would be able to reach this subpopulation, and do so in a way that respected them as people and valued their opinions as employees.

The final decision was to supplement the employee surveys with a series of focus groups so that the needs assessment would include the employees who could not read the written survey. The focus groups would be facilitated by trained team leaders who had some facilitation skills. The same survey being given to the rest of the sample population would be the basis for discussion. Participants would complete the written survey in a group setting, with the facilitator clarifying questions and offering assistance with the response scales, and then the facilitators would conduct group discussions around the open-ended questions in the survey for the purpose of collecting anecdotal support for the more objective ratings.

It was agreed that the survey population would be randomly selected. Employees were chosen based on the appearance of random numbers among the last two digits of the employees' social security numbers.

The entire employee population was advised before the fact that the needs assessment was coming. Letters to employees, notices in the in-house newsletter, and discussion of the needs assessment in a monthly in-house video would ensure that everyone knew what was afoot.

Any employee volunteering to be part of the survey sample would be provided with a survey and invited to participate. It was also made clear that employees selected through the random process were free not to participate. Instructions in the invitation letter suggested that any employee who was concerned that participation was being monitored could simply return a blank survey in the envelope provided.

Participants could choose to attend any of the more than 20 open focus groups if they preferred that setting to the paper-and-pencil format. No records of focus group attendance were to be maintained, nor would there be any differentiation between individual and focus group-based surveys when the data were collected and analyzed.

All completed surveys, plus focus group facilitators' notes, would be forwarded via U.S. mail, rather than company mail, to the consultants' main office for data entry.

The requested demographic data were limited to region or branch (i.e., organizational unit), level or function, age range, and seniority range. We also asked if the respondent was located in the city of Salem, because there was a common belief that employees in Salem (the headquarters city) were different.

Nine hundred employees were invited to participate in the survey. That population included a random cross section of the entire ODOT population. The hope was that we would wind up with a sample size of no less than 10 percent (470) and perhaps as many as 15 percent (705).

The management team and all senior managers, a subpopulation of approximately 100, were invited to participate as well. The survey they completed contained all the same items as the employee survey, but asked the questions from a slightly different perspective. In Section 1 of the survey, where employees were asked to assess the effectiveness of their immediate managers, senior managers were asked to assess the effectiveness of the employees reporting directly to them. The open-ended questions were also worded differently for senior managers.

A total of 606 people (almost 13 percent of the total employee body) completed surveys, participated in focus groups, or both.

The Survey

The survey consisted of three sections. Each section included structured responses and several open-ended questions with space for write-in responses.

Section 1

This section listed 33 items. Each item was a statement representing a critical element of ODOT's values, mission, policies, and principles. Respondents were asked to provide three responses to each of the 33 items, using a scale from 1 to 7. Following are several example items referring to values:

- *Customer Service.* Our customers are the public. We value our customers and are committed to providing quality service and customer satisfaction.
- *Listening to Others.* We honor the right of every individual to be heard and to be taken seriously, to have an open and honest exchange of viewpoints while being treated fairly and politely.

The three responses asked:

- How important is this item to you personally?
- How well does your supervisor manage this item? (for senior managers: How well do your employees manage this item?)
- How good a job does ODOT do managing this item?

The higher the number, the more positive the response. In this case, the result was a total of 99 responses.

Section 1 also included four open-ended questions that asked respondents how knowing these items was helpful and what changes would contribute positively to their perceptions of ODOT and of being an ODOT employee.

Section 2

For each of 19 specific issues addressed in two key ethics policies, this section asked the respondents two questions, using a 7-point response scale similar to the one for Section 1. Thus, this section asked for 38 additional responses. The questions asked for each issue were these:

- How clearly do you understand ODOT's policies in this area?
- How fair is ODOT's policy in this area?

Six open-ended questions in this section asked how employees dealt with uncertainty, what changes they would like in the ethics policies, and how they felt about ODOT's position that public employees were held to a higher standard than employees in the private sector. Respondents also were asked to use the space to communicate with the management team about anything relating to ODOT ethics.

Section 3

This section was aimed at prioritizing 10 operational values, such as staying within budget, following procedures, being productive, and serving the customer. Each of the 10 operational values was paired with each of the others, for a total of 45 pairings. Employees were asked which operational value they were more likely to choose when the two values in each pair were in conflict.

Also, four open-ended questions asked how the management team could help employees deal with these types of values-based conflicts and whether the respondent believed the survey would produce beneficial results. A final question was intended to identify response biases; respondents were asked how they thought they would answer if a question seemed unclear or if they had no strong opinion. Would they lean to a negative, positive, or neutral score?

The total survey contained 182 items answerable with either a number or a check mark and 15 open-ended questions that required a written, narrative response.

The survey was tested with three pilot populations. In groups of about 12, personnel officers, union stewards, and focus group facilitators completed the survey and discussed the open-ended questions. Their comments and observations were useful in fine-tuning several of the instructions printed in both the survey and the focus group leaders' guide and in rewording some of the demographic questions. This input did not result in changes to any of the questions in the body of the assessment survey. Survey responses and written comments from the pilot groups were included in the total data set.

Managing the Data

Survey responses and focus group facilitators' notes were forwarded to our main office in Atlanta, Georgia. As each survey came in, it was assigned a sequential number indicating the order in which it was received. Envelopes or attachments indicating geographic location, date of completion, or postmarks were disassociated from the surveys and discarded.

Raw numerical data—responses to the 182 items answerable with a number or check mark—were entered into a data base management program. Each response was associated with the appropriate sequential number to facilitate cross-checking accuracy of data entry.

Narrative responses to the 15 open-ended questions were transcribed into a word processing program. Once a transcription's accuracy was verified, the tracking number was removed from the file and the narrative data disassociated from the numerical data, as a further protection of the respondent's anonymity.

Graphical Data

Once all raw data were in the system, 15 sets of graphs were generated, one for each identified unit or subunit of the organization. Each set contained six graphs, one each for the responses concerning

- The importance and effectiveness of
  — ODOT's values
  — ODOT's mission
  — ODOT's ethics policies
  — ODOT's ethical principles
- The clarity and fairness of ODOT's ethics policies
- The relative importance of ODOT's operational values.

The 15 sets of graphs addressed various segments of the total sample population:

- ODOT overall ($n = 606$)
- management team members ($n = 10$)
- senior managers ($n = 37$)
- other managers and supervisors ($n = 145$)
- professional technical employees ($n = 262$)
- nonmanagement and professional nontechnical employees ($n = 142$)
- specific organizational branches and regions.

In addition, 22 partial sets of the data (Sections 1 and 2 only) were graphed based on geographic location, length of service, branch or unit affiliation, and (in the Technical Services Branch) identification with maintenance or construction functions. Unit-specific data were provided to the director, the deputy director, and the manager of that particular unit.

All told, 158 pages of graphs were generated. One example is shown as Figure 1. (To protect the sensitivity of the data, the questions are listed by number only.)

Figure 1. Survey responses concerning the Oregon Department of Transportation's mission.

Respondents rated personal importance (PI), management effectiveness (ME), and ODOT's effectiveness (OE), using a 7-point scale (the higher the number, the more effective or important). Each question (Q11, Q12, Q13, Q14) identified a different element of the mission.

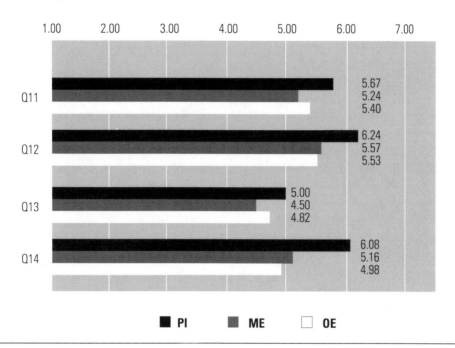

Narrative Data

The narrative data consisted of the verbatim responses of all survey respondents plus the notes from the focus group facilitators. These responses were separated, by question, into two categories: senior management, and all other employees. Management team narrative responses were excluded from this set of data.

Within each category, all narrative data were listed by question, but in no particular sequence within each question. In other words, all the responses to Question 1 were listed together, but the order was randomized to prevent anyone from associating responses to different questions in an attempt to identify which employee said what. Exact duplicate answers and answers that were not responsive to the question being asked were then eliminated.

If the efforts to prevent management from identifying individual respondents' responses seem overdone, it is because the organization was frightened by the issues being addressed in the needs assessment. We intentionally created added protections of anonymity as one way of encouraging candid participation in the face of widespread distrust and fear.

A total of 50 pages of verbatim responses was generated, with 25 pages on senior management and 25 pages on all other employees.

The Final Report

The completed written report contained 15 sections:
- a three-page executive summary
- a 20-page narrative report
- six sections of graphs (as described earlier)
- two sections of verbatim responses (as described earlier)
- two sample surveys, one for senior management and one for employees
- a copy of the focus group leaders' guide
- supplemental graphical data (by geographic location, seniority, department, and function)
- data unique to the particular organizational entity whose manager would receive the report.

Key Findings

After thoroughly reviewing the data and the hundreds of individual findings that emerged, we boiled down the findings to eight that were critical to the project:
- Neither individual supervisors nor ODOT overall was viewed as even marginally effective in managing according to the values, mission, ethics policies, or ethical principles addressed in the survey.
- ODOT's ethics policies were impossible to understand and apply routinely, and because they could not be understood, they were, by definition, unfair.
- Employees relied on their immediate supervisors to clarify a policy and provide guidance when they were in doubt as to what the policy allowed or required. The good news was that this was the correct procedure for employees to follow. The bad news was that the policies were as much a mystery to the supervisors as they were to the employees seeking help.
- There was general agreement as to which of ODOT's operational values were most important. Safety, excellence, and customer service were the top three values in the view of a vast majority of the assessment participants. That was also good news because the management team agreed that these should be the top three, although there was no agreement as to the relative ranking within this group of three.

- The formal mission statement, which had existed for several years, was unknown to a large number of the respondents. Because it was largely unknown, it was useless in guiding most frontline employees in their decision making.
- Communications, in every form and fashion, was roundly criticized. People said information from the top down was inconsistent and unevenly distributed. Information from the bottom up was routinely blocked before reaching the people who needed to hear it. For example, ODOT's mission was unknown to about one fourth of the people responding to the survey.
- Employees believed that there was a double standard regarding key issues such as accountability. For example, the ethics investigation resulted in discipline for the frontline employees who acted improperly, but not for the supervisors who condoned or encouraged that behavior.
- Employees were skeptical that the management team was committed to creating an ODOT that was principle based. They flatly accused management team members of being hypocrites who consistently made promises and then ignored them. They felt the team was unworthy of the leadership position it held and were disrespectful of that group's "best intentions."

The Feedback Meeting

The feedback meeting was the culminating event of the needs assessment. This was the forum for presenting the final report to the members of the management team and guiding them through three critical stages.

The first stage was to review the information contained in the report to ensure that each manager understood the data and what the implications were for the effectiveness of the organization and themselves, individually. The second stage was to work through the resistance, denial, anger, and political jockeying that the data were certain to stimulate. The third stage was to interpret the data in terms suggesting actions that were responsive to the issues raised and that had a high probability of helping the organization address the issues and achieve the desired results of the project as initially proposed.

Two days were set aside for the meeting. Day 1 was for presenting the findings and beginning to diffuse the negative responses. Day 2 was for assessing the managers' conviction and helping them develop responses to the findings.

It was the last two findings, the double standard and the vote of no confidence, that got the management team's attention. Denial and anger were full-blown and clearly expressed, along with a fair share of rationalizing and self-justifying during Day 1 of the meeting. The attitude was captured in the not-quite-facetious remark that the project had "obviously randomly sampled the wrong 600 people. We need to go back and randomly survey a different 600 employees who have better attitudes."

Our best hope for working through the senior managers' resistance was to make the data more real to them. We had to break through their desire to deny. They had to be willing to accept that what we were saying was both real and important. The best available tool was that the survey itself was laced with open-ended questions. Employees had a chance to speak to the group on the importance of the issues in their own words, not just through the sterile graphs. Our task was to get the group to read the nearly 50 pages of single-spaced text that captured the emotions, pain, anger, and frustration of the employees.

Therefore, we gave the team a homework assignment at the end of Day 1. Half of the group was to read the 25 pages of employee responses to the open-ended questions. The other half would read the 25 pages from the supervisors and managers. The first task the next morning would be to identify the highest priority concerns they gleaned from their readings, and to compare and contrast the employees' and managers' responses.

It was not until the members of the management team had the opportunity to read those verbatim responses that they judged the findings valid and believed that their task was to address the findings and act in ways that would earn the trust and respect of their employees. The validity of the employees' own words was undeniable.

The Director's View of the Feedback Meeting

I had hoped that the outcome of the needs assessment would alter the management team's ambivalence and convey a sense of urgency. The assessment identified deep-seated cynicism about how ODOT was managed and revealed large gaps in understanding how to approach real-life work situations. In some instances, employees understood the universal ethical principles well and pointed out glaring dichotomies between the principles and existing departmental policies. The assessment pointed out that generally ODOT staff could handle black-and-white situations, but situations with shades of gray were very discomforting. The solutions that people sought in those instances were lists of do's and don't's. Clearly, this assessment indicated to me that we also had a real problem in implementing our teams concept successfully within the department.

When I witnessed the denial of the evidence the consultants presented and the lack of enthusiasm from management team members to move the ethics agenda forward, I took immediate action. Immediately following the feedback meeting, I let all the members of the management team know that they were failing in their responsibility to help me manage the department. Their membership on the team was provisional for six months. Improved performance during that period would result in their reinstatement, but continued lack of performance at any time would result in their removal from the team. Their reaction was gratifying. Although several members were annoyed at me, most took my action as a wake-up call and picked up their level of effort immediately. Now that we are several years down the road, I believe this action may have been the pivotal event that coalesced the management team and secured the entire change effort—not just the ethics initiative.

Developing Action Plans

Based on the data and the emotions the data expressed, the members of the management team eventually concluded that they needed to accept the reported perceptions as accurate, understandable, and unacceptable. The ultimate objective of the ethics enhancement project was expanded to include building confidence in the department's leadership through demonstrated commitment to the high priority of ethical principles and values.

One mechanism for building employee trust and confidence in the organization's leadership was for each management team member to manage at least one of the tasks the team agreed needed to be undertaken. The list of actions suggested by the findings was long. It included
- redefining the organization's values and priorities
- rewriting the organization's ethics policies
- creating an ethics oversight committee
- creating an ombudsman's office
- developing an ethics hot line
- initiating whistle-blower protections
- creating a decision-making process usable by and useful to all employees irrespective of educational or reading level
- developing communications and education strategies, including
  — articles in the in-house newsletter
  — a videotaped introduction to the action items by the department's director
  — targeted visits by senior management to demonstrate commitment to the project

— executive training
— senior management training
— supervisor training
— employee training
— integration of ethics modules into the existing management development curriculum

(Total training was on the order of 6,000 person-days over a 20-month period.)

- using a training follow-up strategy to reinforce transfer of training and to evaluate the training's effectiveness in causing the desired behavioral changes
- developing feedback mechanisms to facilitate organizational learning
- using a project posttest (scheduled for 1995), based on the initial needs assessment survey instrument, to assess the long-term effectiveness of the earlier interventions and to identify new, emerging issues.

The Director's View of How the Plans Are Being Implemented

We are well on the way to implementing all aspects of the action plans:

- The safe-haven process—the ombudsman's office and the ethics hot line—is in place, providing a mechanism for employees to obtain authoritative guidance and policy interpretations.
- The ethics policy revisions have been completed and, pending completion of the employee training, will be looked at again.
- Initial executive, senior manager, manager, and supervisor training was completed early in 1994.
- Employee training is nearly completed.
- We are in the process of developing training modules for integration into our other training efforts to ensure that ethics training is not a one-time phenomenon.

No one on the management team would suggest turning back. All have come to believe in the importance of the program. All use what has become its cornerstone—the Decision PLUS model, a tool ensuring that ethical components will be addressed in decision making.

Lessons Learned

The ultimate objective for the organization and the consultants was to move the organization from where it was to where it wanted and needed to be. Along the way, there were several lessons that both parties learned or relearned.

What the Director and ODOT Learned

In general, the ethics initiative has progressed as expected. Many people are skeptical before they become involved. After the initial training, most are very supportive. The organization as a whole is considerably more aware of the ethical issues that confront it. The Decision PLUS model is being widely used by upper level managers. Time will tell whether frontline employees will embrace it as openly as managers. We are in the middle of employee training.

From my perspective, the most significant midcourse correction that we have made is in the employee training. We started with class sizes that were too large, and there was too much reliance on the consultant-trainer, with too little involvement by senior managers. Employee feedback indicates that reducing class sizes and including senior managers in the training discussions has been beneficial.

The only significant change I would make with the entire effort would be to start sooner. The benefit of 20/20 hindsight has shown me that the most important shift necessary in decentralizing decision making in an organization is converting the rules-based culture to a values-based culture.

Ethics initiatives such as ours provide employees with the skills necessary to identify and evaluate the competing values that are inherent in nearly all business decisions. When employees and managers are adept at values-based decision making, the potential benefits of decentralized decision making will be realized.

What the Consultants Learned

There were three lessons learned anew.

The first was to trust the process. The value of a systematic and systemic needs analysis cannot be overstated. Once again, Nadler's OPM proved its strength as a conceptual framework for needs assessment and diagnosis. It defined the problems and suggested the solutions.

The second lesson was the value of flexibility. When selling a client on an approach as complex as this, do not overspecify the steps. Allow the needs assessment to drive the specifics.

The third lesson was that the needs assessment not only drives the process, but also defines the status quo at the beginning of the project. Needs assessment findings become the baseline data needed for assessing the project's impact and effectiveness over time. The needs assessment, because it defines the desired state as well as the current state, becomes the posttest as well.

Questions for Discussion

1. In this case, the consultant and client did not always appear to have the same agenda. How can a client or consultant ensure that all parties are operating from a common set of goals and objectives?

2. This needs assessment included responses from a significant portion of the employee body who, because of a relatively high rate of functional illiteracy, could not be expected to respond to a detailed paper-and-pencil survey. Focus groups were used to supplement the surveys. What other approaches could have been utilized to ensure that all employees could voice their opinions?

3. This was an organization in the midst of several change initiatives. What might the client and consultant have done to overcome employees' resistance to more change—the "here we go again" reaction?

4. This survey required 182 quantitative and 15 narrative responses. Most participants took at least an hour to complete it, yet there were no complaints about its length. Common wisdom suggests that an hour is too long for a survey. What alternative strategies might be used when complex data are being sought, but it is not feasible to give each of 600 employees an hour of work time to complete a survey?

5. During the feedback meeting, the narrative data convinced the senior management team that the findings were valid, but this did not happen until the evening of the first day. If you have only a half-day to present your findings, with no time for the clients to read and digest the narrative data, how else might you get them to accept that the findings are valid?

6. In this organization, the director took a very strong position, essentially putting each member of his senior team on probation for six months. How else might the director and the consultant have dealt with the reluctance of the senior managers to embrace the director's agenda?

The Authors

Founder and president of Navran Associates, Frank J. Navran has focused his consulting practice on three interrelated aspects of leadership: employee empowerment, quality and customer service, and business ethics. He has successfully brought a number of clients through the transition from traditional leader-centered employee practices and structures to more contemporary—that is, participative and employee-centered—leadership modes. Navran is the author of *Feeding the Hog* (Navran, Levine, and Brown, 1993), *The Desktop Guide to Total Ethics Management* (Navran Associates, 1994), and *Truth & Trust: The First Two Victims of Downsizing* (Navran Associates, 1995). He was the architect for *The Ethics Effectiveness Quick-Test* (Navran Associates, 1990) and *The Ethics Inventory* (Navran Associates, 1991). He has developed more than 50 training programs and consulting processes. Most recently, he has produced *Managing and Caring for the Survivors of Downsizing* (Navran Associates, 1995), the first video-based seminar for the classroom or individual learner on this topic. Navran can be contacted at the following address: Navran Associates, 3037 Wembley Ridge, Atlanta, GA 30340-4716.

Donald E. Forbes's appointment as director of the 4,700-person Oregon Department of Transportation became effective July 1, 1991. The department is responsible for licensing drivers and pilots, building and maintaining the state highway system, supporting public transit, and promoting traffic safety. In Forbes's previous position, he served as head of the State Highway Division—the first person in the 75-year history of the division to be named to the top management job from outside the agency. Before joining ODOT, Forbes managed civil and structural engineering for transportation projects at the Portland engineering firm CH2M Hill. He had worked in the Corvallis and Portland offices of CH2M Hill since 1979. Before that, he worked as a design engineer in Colorado. Forbes, a registered civil engineer, holds a B.S. in aeronautical engineering from the U.S. Air Force Academy, an M.S. in structural engineering from the University of Colorado, and an M.B.A. from Pacific Lutheran University.

Reference

Nadler, D.A., Tushman, M.L., and Hatvany, N.G. (1982). *Managing organizations: Readings and cases.* Glenview, IL: Scott, Foresman.

Overcoming Resistance to a Successful Diversity Effort

Nestlé Beverage Company

Tina Rasmussen

This case shows how one-on-one interviews yielded a very successful needs assessment for a diversity program for all employees.

Overview

Workforce diversity is an issue that addresses not only skills but also people's long-held values. Because of this, "canned" or off-the-shelf diversity strategies and workshops often fail to generate the buy-in and commitment required for success. However, one company has had initial success, in part because of the needs assessment that was a cornerstone for designing the overall diversity change process and associated training.

In preparation for its diversity effort, Nestlé Beverage Company (NBC) conducted qualitative one-on-one interviews with employees from all levels and departments. The purpose of the study was to take a "snapshot" of the current corporate climate, which helped focus efforts on the issues critical to achieving the company's diversity goals. As NBC's training and organizational development manager, I felt that without an accurate understanding of people's perceptions, NBC might waste a great deal of energy on issues with a small payoff.

The interview data produced six themes that helped focus diversity efforts on areas that would be of the greatest benefit to the company. The data also helped determine how to generate true commitment from the majority of employees, while minimizing the often-found

This case was prepared to serve as a basis for discussion rather than to illustrate either effective or ineffective administrative and management practices.

white male backlash. An unexpected benefit of the study was discovery of key values the company could build upon in helping the diversity effort succeed.

The resulting large-scale change and education effort has been labeled a success by employees and management alike. Subsequently, a quantitative survey validated the findings of the original study and provided additional insights on demographic differences.

Most recently, the benefits of the needs assessment and change effort were seen in NBC's companywide reengineering. The concept of needs assessment was embraced, and the results of the assessment became a foundation for the human resource aspects of the reengineering. In addition, many items identified in the original needs assessment were integrated into NBC's new vision and values, which served as the core of the reengineering effort.

Organizational Profile

NBC is a division of Nestlé USA, which is a division of Nestlé SA, the world's largest food company. NBC has about 2,500 employees nationwide in its headquarters, six factories, and regional sales offices. More than 400 employees are located at the corporate office in San Francisco, where this needs assessment was conducted.

NBC's 1993 net sales were $1.5 billion, making it the second largest of five Nestlé USA divisions, with 21 percent of total sales. If NBC were its own company, it would rank 274th in the Fortune 500. Nestlé USA had 1993 net sales of $7.2 billion, with 22,000 U.S. employees. Nestlé SA, the Swiss parent company, had worldwide sales of $38 billion in 1993, making it one of the world's 50 largest companies in any industry.

NBC's corporate culture and senior management come predominantly from Hills Bros, a 120-year-old, family-owned firm. Until 1991, Hills Bros was a 500-person company. When it was acquired by Nestlé, Hills Bros became the foundation of NBC and added several other companies, including MJB Coffee, Chase & Sanborn Coffee, Carnation Beverages, and Libby's Juices. The resulting corporate culture was largely undefined, except for Hills Bros' age-old traditions and ways of doing business.

Products offered by NBC include Hills Bros Coffee, Taster's Choice Freeze-Dried Coffee, Coffeemate Non-Dairy Creamer, Nestea, Nestlé Quik, Carnation Hot Cocoa Mix, and Libby's Juicy Juice. In six of its nine product categories, NBC holds the number-one or -two market position. The company's mission is to be the premier diversified beverage company in the United States.

The food industry has experienced dramatic change in recent years. In the past, products were brought to market primarily from a manufacturer "push" standpoint; that is, a manufacturer produced a new product, provided incentives for retailers to put it on the shelves with promotions, and encouraged consumers to buy it with price specials. Now, consumers are demanding greater variety and higher quality, and the market is more segmented by various demographic groups.

In addition, retailers (who are NBC's direct customers) have become much more sophisticated in their use of information technology. In the old days, inventories and ordering were done manually. Now, when an item is scanned for checkout, the information goes directly into a data base for use in reordering and monitoring purchasing patterns. Grocery, club, and drug store retailers are making greater demands of manufacturers. They want business partners, not just suppliers, and they form alliances with companies that can provide data and ideas on how to merchandise more effectively.

Finally, more women now populate the food industry, once almost exclusively the province of men.

Deciding To Conduct the Needs Assessment

NBC's Diversity Advisory Board was formed in mid-1992. Its charge was to find out how changes in the American workforce and consumer population would affect the business, and to implement strategies to adapt to those changes. The board originally comprised nine people: four vice-presidents, three directors, and two managers. The member with the most seniority was Barry Reis, executive vice-president of divisions, to whom more than half of the company reported. The senior vice-president of purchasing, Dick Thompson, was also a member.

Later, Claudia Horty, vice-president of human resources and my manager, added herself, an additional director, and me to the Diversity Advisory Board, for a total of 11 members, all from the corporate office. Until that time, the director of employee relations, Phil Ray, had maintained leadership of the group, which then transferred to me. The board had just completed a first draft of the diversity strategy.

As a new member, I observed that everyone seemed to care about the effort and was committed in spirit. Darryl Sudduth, purchasing manager, noted, however, that the group seemed to be a bit adrift and needed a clearer focus and direction.

I proposed that the group undertake a needs assessment to gain insights about and determine the needs of other people in the company. The results might help the group focus and determine the company's current position relative to diversity. The board agreed, and I drafted a proposal for a full-blown needs assessment. I took the draft to Horty and Ray for their review.

Because the company was in the midst of many changes, and because of a previous employee opinion survey that raised some issues the company could not address immediately, Horty and Ray had some concerns about doing a large-scale survey at that point. Instead, they decided to start small, with qualitative interviews of about 30 people, all anonymous. The results would be reported only to the Diversity Advisory Board, the Officers' Committee, and the interview participants. This approach would provide valuable input and lay the groundwork for possibly conducting a quantitative survey with a larger sampling of employees later.

Conducting the Needs Assessment

Conducting the needs assessment consisted of several steps:
- selecting methods
- planning
- conducting interviews
- analyzing the data.

A few comments on objectivity in research are in order. Historically, the research community attempted to create simulations in which the researcher would be able to be as objective as possible. To this end, clinical experiments became more highly revered than "subjective" research such as interviews. In the past 20 years, however, numerous studies have shown that even objective clinical researchers filter data through their own "lenses" as human beings—in effect, making the data subjective. As a result, subjective types of data have come to be regarded as more "scientific" than previously thought. The bottom line is that researchers need to acknowledge that they have biases, and to make the research audience aware of the circumstances and filters under which the data were gathered. Because I conducted this needs assessment, my situation at the time is an important consideration. In addition to my work at Nestlé, I was completing my Ph.D. in human and organizational systems at the Fielding Institute, and a few aspects of my studies were directly relevant to this project.

First, I had just completed a class on conducting qualitative research, which added to my previous needs assessment experience. Also, during the three months of the needs assessment, I read more than 80 books and articles on diversity, which prompted me to reflect on my own biases. How did I really feel about diversity? What influence did my own upbringing and experiences have on my views? I found that I very much wanted to become an active champion of human rights.

Selecting Methods

The first step in conducting the needs assessment was to determine the overall purpose and set specific goals. The purpose of the assessment was to obtain an understanding of the current situation before implementing interventions designed to meet corporate goals and achieve the company's diversity strategy. The specific goals of the research are listed in Table 1.

Table 1. Goals of the diversity needs assessment.

Main goals	Additional goals
● To define the current climate in key areas that affect the valuing of diversity	● To help people be comfortable with needs assessment
● To define the current climate in key areas that affect the managing of diversity	● To demonstrate that needs assessment can be a useful tool
● To understand the critical areas for improvement in implementing the company's diversity strategy	● To create a process of two-way communication about difficult issues
● To understand the critical roadblocks to implementing the diversity strategy	
● To understand the current reality for most employees, so that this information can be used in making the learning effort realistic and applicable	
● To understand differences in specific areas of the company, so that the learning effort will be flexible enough to be used in areas with specific needs	

The assessment would involve qualitative one-on-one interviews, sampling employees at all levels of the corporate administrative, sales, and plant staffs. This method was chosen for many reasons.

First, this type of needs assessment is very different from assessments that are task or skills based. Because the issue of diversity is so grounded in people's deepest values and even subliminal programming from childhood, the issues can be more difficult to uncover than a person's ability to work through a sales process or put together a printed circuit board. Second, it was important to research the organizational issues that surrounded diversity, rather than the obvious issues of diversity itself. Third, I did not want to superimpose my own preconceived ideas of what the roadblocks to diversity were. I wanted people to have their own voice to shape any questions that might appear later in a quantitative survey. Fourth, I wondered whether some people would resist or even sabotage the diversity effort if they felt pressured or at risk, and I wanted to explore that possibility. The only way to address these four issues was through interviews.

Creating the list of interview questions was a laborious process. Every diversity instrument available at the time was reviewed and considered. Few could be found, and none had been validated or subjected to any rigorous scientific scrutiny. Eventually, I developed questions from the existing instruments and my own ideas. Most questions were not related specifically to diversity, but were designed to reveal underlying diversity-related issues the company might need to face. The interview would begin with generic questions and gradually lead to questions that were obviously about diversity.

Two of the more helpful resources were *The Questions of Diversity* by George Simons (1990) and the Avon Interview Guide found in Roosevelt Thomas's classic book *Beyond Race and Gender* (1991). The final list of questions appears in Table 2.

Planning

Planning included deciding who would be interviewed, for how long, when, and where. Why to conduct the interviews and what to ask had already been determined.

To determine the "who," NBC's human resource data base specialist randomly created a list of about 60 people who were a representative sampling of ages, ethnic backgrounds, lengths of service, levels within the company, departments, and gender. At the time, the Diversity Advisory Board was unsure how the diversity effort would be implemented for the field sales force and the plants, so these areas of the company were represented primarily through their corporate management.

The list of participants contained twice as many names as needed to ensure anonymity of participants. I did not want anyone but myself to know who the final participants were, and this was accomplished (except when participants voluntarily told someone themselves). In this situation, people needed strong reassurance and specifics about confidentiality, and were promised they would receive a copy of the same report the officers received. With these guarantees, I hoped people would be willing to respond honestly and openly.

Table 2. Questions asked in the needs assessment interview.

Work environment

1. How long have you been with Nestlé Beverage Company (NBC)? Briefly describe your job.
2. What attracted you to NBC?
3. How well has the company met your expectations?
4. What kinds of things have encouraged you to stay here?
5. What does it take to be successful here?
6. Are there any norms—unwritten rules—people need to follow to be successful?
7. How clear are your job expectations?
8. What kind of feedback do you get? How do you know how you're doing?
9. If you could change one thing so you could be more productive, what would it be?

Management

10. Describe the supervision you've had here.
11. What does management pay attention to?
12. What does management do when something goes wrong?

13. What does management do when something goes right?
14. What are managers rewarded for? Are they rewarded for developing people?

Opportunity

15. How do you think NBC is doing at providing an environment where everyone has the same chance to succeed, based on merit? What have you seen that makes you think that?
16. Are there any obstacles for "nontraditional employees" (women, people of color, etc.)?
17. What do people think about female managers?
18. Have you ever witnessed or heard about behaviors exhibiting bias here? What were they?
19. Do you think other people would answer these questions the same way you did?

Appointments were scheduled by telephone. The initial contact was carefully scripted to put people at ease as soon as possible. First, I explained who I was and the purpose of the interview. I described the study as taking a snapshot of the current corporate climate. Participants were also told how the results would be used, that the interview would take 30 to 60 minutes, that it was entirely confidential, and—most important—that it was totally voluntary. Once participants agreed to be interviewed, they selected the time and location most comfortable for them. Everyone who was asked wanted to participate.

Conducting Interviews

Twenty-eight people were interviewed, including 18 managers and officers and 10 nonexempt, professional employees. About 50 percent were male and 50 percent female, with an age range from 24 to 50. Length of service ranged from two to 27 years, the average being 8.8 years. Eighteen participants were white, six were Asian, four were Hispanic, and one was African American; (one participant fell into two categories).

I asked people questions from the prepared list. If a respondent brought up an issue outside the list, I asked additional questions to delve further into that topic. Having the ability to discover unexpected areas of importance was an advantage of conducting interviews rather than a quantitative survey.

The interviews began, as had the initial telephone contacts, with an introduction designed to put respondents at ease and begin to build trust. Again, they were told the purpose, how the results would be used, what my role was, and that their responses would be totally anonymous. They also had the opportunity to ask questions. I asked if it was all right to take notes, explaining that I wanted to capture their thoughts accurately. People were also assured that there were no right or wrong answers, that being frank and honest would help most, and that if they did not have a response, it was okay to say so.

The first questions were easy for people to answer, and served as warm-ups. Then came the "big picture" questions, which revealed valuable data regarding the corporate culture. Next were the specific questions about diversity. Finally, people reflected on whether other employees would have the same views. This question helped determine whether they saw themselves as mainstream or radical.

It was important during the interviews that I refrain from showing emotion or stating judgments about responses. I did give nonverbal and verbal cues to encourage elaboration, and allowed silence while respondents were thinking about answers, rather than filling the gaps with follow-up questions.

Generally, participants opened up and disclosed quite a bit of information, some of it personal and potentially risky. Several participants commented that they had "said a lot more than they intended to." Many people said they were glad the company was undertaking this assessment and that they had been selected. Some even expressed thanks. It always amazes me how much people like to participate in interviews once they feel comfortable. People generally feel good that the company cares enough to ask for their opinions. Only two participants seemed to hold back; both indicated that they had been given a high level of opportunity by the company, possibly beyond that of their peers.

Analyzing the Data

Analyzing the data was an arduous process of reviewing more than 100 pages of handwritten notes. As I explained earlier, it is important for researchers to focus on what a respondent says, rather than the researchers' own preconceived ideas of what will emerge. Researchers need to define and acknowledge their own biases before beginning analysis. Qualitative research can be highly valid if researchers acknowledge their own lenses.

After reviewing my own biases and preconceived ideas about what the interviews would uncover, my first step was to obtain an overview of the data. I started by reading all the material at one sitting to gain a general impression of what people said. Doing this enabled me to begin identifying broad categories of common statements. When I was finished reading, I jotted down topics that seemed to come up frequently. Each topic was summarized in a two- to five-word statement that captured the essence of what people conveyed in the interviews.

In the next pass of the data, I went back through all the handwritten notes and tallied how many times each of these topics was mentioned. I also made a mark next to each handwritten note that was tallied. This process confirmed which topics were indeed important; those not mentioned frequently were removed from the list.

When this step was completed, I reviewed the handwritten notes again for ideas that had not been included in the broad categories. A few concepts recurred frequently enough to be included on the list of predominant topics. There were also many comments that were made by only one person. I compiled these comments in a separate list and reviewed them to see if any might be consolidated to warrant a new topic area.

An additional aspect of qualitative research that can add richness to the results (but requires researcher sophistication) is determining when an item that does not occur frequently is important enough to be included in the final summary. For example, what if only one respondent says that he or she has been subjected to sexual harassment? Should this be mentioned, or saved for a study of a wider scope? Should it be written off as an isolated incident, or discounted as being untrue? Or what if a respondent tells a story of the president showing favoritism to his or her personal friends, and then later the researcher hears the same story confirmed through the grapevine? Should the comment then be considered accurate? There are no easy answers to these questions. Regardless of whether any of the stories respondents tell are based in fact, however, they do represent what people believe, and in that alone they are meaningful.

Determining the final trends in a qualitative data analysis requires judgment, discretion, and experience. It is helpful to remember that frequency is only one measure of whether an idea should be included; importance to the respondents is another.

But how does one know what is frequent enough or important enough to warrant a new topic area? When should two topics be consolidated into one, and when should they be left separate? How can topic areas be named to reflect what respondents really meant? Unfortunately, these questions cannot be answered within the scope of this case study.

(Many excellent books have been written on qualitative research. The ones I used most were *Analyzing Social Settings* by John and Lyn Lofland (1984) and *Naturalistic Inquiry* by Yvonna Lincoln and Egon Guba (1985).)

Through an iterative process of consolidating the trends, reviewing the handwritten notes, entering partial sentences and relevant words into the computer, letting the material sit for a few days, and starting again, a final list of about 20 topics emerged. I was eventually able to omit "stragglers" or work them into the main categories, rather than weakening the analysis by having too many items.

At this point, I went back and reviewed the original interview questions, as a prompt for thinking about the data further. Note that the predominant themes were not organized according to the interview questions; rather, I let the results emerge in a manner that reflected the way participants expressed their views.

By continuing the back-and-forth process of reviewing the data and recalling people's intentions, not just their statements, I was able to reveal interconnections between topics and consolidate them into six all-encompassing themes that revealed the predominant aspects of the company's culture, values, norms, and behaviors as they related to the issue of diversity.

I then went back to the handwritten notes to discern subtle nuances within each theme and to extract statements that captured the flavor of people's responses. This final review also enabled me to ask myself whether these six final themes truly embodied the bulk of respondents' statements.

Summarizing and Presenting the Results

The six themes, descriptions, and quotations were summarized in a nine-page report. It went through several drafts, during which the descriptions were honed, edited for clarity and conciseness, and sometimes toned down. I deleted a few inflammatory quotations in order to increase the chances that the information would be accepted. Even the sequence of the themes was strategically planned to start with easy ones and work up to the more difficult.

The introduction was important. Again, it indicated the results were a snapshot that would help the company focus its efforts on the critical issues. It emphasized that the contents were not necessarily facts, but were people's perceptions. Words such as "perceived" and "believed" were used frequently to reinforce that these were opinions, not necessarily facts. The quotations brought the report to life and had a tremendous effect on readers.

The report also led to the finalization of NBC's diversity strategy, shown in Figure 1.

Figure 1. Nestlé Beverage Company's diversity strategy.

The diversity goal is that Nestlé Beverage Company will compete in an increasingly diverse and rapidly changing marketplace by enabling managers and employees to create highly productive work environments that naturally encourage innovation, open communication, flexibility, and teamwork for everyone.

The comprehensive diversity strategy has been designed to address not only interpersonal diversity issues, but also the cornerstones of structural inequality that may exist. The plan includes

● recruiting
● performance management
● compensation and benefits
● communication and events
● training and education.

The Diversity Advisory Board recommended that the diversity strategy and needs assessment results be presented at the next officers' meeting, held in July 1993. Prior to the meeting, the report was also mailed (in a "confidential" envelope, both for security and to increase people's level of interest) to the officers, interview participants, and human resource managers.

The board's goal for the meeting was not only to ask the officers for their commitment to the strategy and to having a one-day workshop for all employees, but also to participate in the workshop themselves along with the other managers. Two vice-presidents who were on the Diversity Advisory Board had agreed to initiate support and approval of all three items. Ray was to present an overview, and Sudduth the strategy. I would present the needs assessment.

The needs assessment results were to be presented as a review, because the officers already had read the full report. As shown in Table 3, data were divided into two categories: strengths to build on and potential obstacles. Presenting strengths would make the results less threatening and put the focus on the positive as much as the negative.

Table 3. Interviewees' perceptions about the organizational climate at Nestlé Beverage.

Strengths to build on	Potential obstacles
● Management's caring about people	● Key role of politics
● Importance of people skills for success	● Good-old-boy network
● Value placed on teamwork	● Lack of feedback
● Value placed on innovation	● Backlash
● Growth opportunities	● Opportunity not open to everyone

The presentations went well; the officers were interested and supportive, asking many questions and engaging in considerable discussion of the results. NBC President Paul Miller wanted specifics and explanations of several items. By the end of the presentation, the strategy and training were approved, and the officers had decided they wanted to participate in the workshops, too.

The officers' meeting had many positive outcomes. It initiated a process of discussing sensitive issues productively, by considering strengths to build on as well as potential obstacles. People saw the value of taking time to gain an understanding of employees' perceptions, and found the snapshot idea was much less judgmental than an "evaluation."

Although the company made a strong commitment to the diversity strategy and change effort, some issues identified in the needs assessment were not addressed. As high as the level of receptivity was, there was still a tendency to gloss over some things and assume they had fixed themselves. Even so, approval was given for the results of the interviews to be communicated and a quantitative survey to be given to all employees as part of the diversity workshop.

Resulting Interventions

The diversity effort then proceeded with vigor and enthusiasm. The needs assessment pointed to approaches that would be most likely to generate true commitment from employees at all levels. The discovery of the key values the company could build upon to help the diversity effort to succeed was an unexpected bonus.

As time went on and development of the workshop began, the most important discovery in the needs assessment became apparent: the concerns of people who might resist and even sabotage the effort if they felt pressured or at risk. Based on the interviews, I believed that the standard approach to cultural diversity, which often places blame on the white male, would backfire at NBC. If the white males who constituted most of the power structure saw no benefit—or even a disadvantage—to supporting the effort, it was doomed to failure. Because of this, the Diversity Advisory Board decided to create a customized program.

Thus, the perceptions disclosed in the needs assessment were used to make the diversity effort acceptable to the white males who were so crucial in making the effort a success. Instead of being labeled a cultural diversity effort, the concept was expanded to include all dimensions of differences, including personality and communication style. This extended the concept to include everyone and to benefit everyone—including white males. The effort also focused on concrete business benefits that would come from understanding the diversity of the consumer base. The diversity strategy included several interventions:

- Recruiting practices included a renewed emphasis on hiring and promoting employees based on competence, rather than ability to fit into the traditional mold. Applicants were recruited from a wider variety of places, including nontraditional colleges. Reliance on word of mouth or the "good old boy" network decreased. Managers were counseled to consider a variety of applicants, and to disregard preconceived ideas about what women and people of color can and cannot do.

- A new performance management process, which included task goals as well as eight core competencies people use to reach their goals, was designed. One core competency was "respect for others." All employees would be responsible and accountable for placing a value on diversity. Eventually, feedback from other people would contribute directly to a person's performance summary.

- NBC also examined compensation companywide and found no preferential treatment based on race or gender. New, progressive benefits were also reviewed, and some were adopted.

An unexpected groundswell of support, energy, and momentum occurred almost spontaneously. As a kickoff, the company sponsored "The Six Weeks of Diversity," a series of events held six Fridays in a row from 11 a.m. to 1 p.m., plus activities throughout the weeks. These events were designed to educate employees while being fun as well. The initial event featured foods from around the world and artwork from a variety of artists. Events thereafter were sponsored by one of the following groups of employees from within the company: women, Asian Americans, African Americans, Native Americans, gays and lesbians, and Hispanics. The groups were led by people at all levels, from director to receptionist. For weeks, hallways were decorated and people were excited; at least 350 of the 500 employees attended every event. These events created a momentum that made diversity a topic everyone was interested in.

The most visible of all the diversity strategies was training and education. All 500 corporate employees, including the officers, participated in the one-day Valuing Diversity workshop. Managers also participated in a segment on Managing Diversity. Prior to the workshop, each individual spent two hours reading and thinking about his or her own background, perceptions, and attitudes. The session included short lectures, group discussions, videos, and experiential learning activities. People had an opportunity to share and learn from each other about the benefits of valuing diversity, both for working as a team and for understanding customers and consumers to stay competitive in the marketplace. The program was then scheduled to be offered to the other 2,000 employees in the plants and field sales force.

The involvement of the officers was a key aspect of the workshops. Every Managing Diversity workshop contained at least one officer. An officer also kicked off each session with a short presentation on why diversity was important both to the company and to him- or herself personally. Beforehand, the officers were coached on how to fill this role effectively and given a brief outline. The importance of their preparation was emphasized, and they were ready for the instructors to turn to them for support of the company's commitment. NBC's president attended one of the first sessions, and word spread rapidly of his enthusiasm—and the fact that he had completed all the reading and introspection required before the session.

Workshop participants were asked to fill out a quantitative diversity survey. In addition, reaction sheets were collected after each session. Many comments were positive: "I'm glad to see the company is doing this. I support it 100 percent." Other participants said, "I'll believe we're committed when I see it in management's actions." The most surprising feedback was the word of mouth. Conservative, longtime employees who had complained about going to the workshop went back to their co-workers and said, "It wasn't what I expected. It was good. I can see that diversity relates to me as much as anyone. The company needs to pay attention to this." The positive response from potential backlash candidates was an indication to the Diversity Advisory Board that the time spent researching the best way to handle the diversity effort was a key to its success.

Round Two: Results of the Quantitative Needs Assessment

In January 1994, NBC began preparing to implement its reengineered customer and consumer processes. The company formed a People Development Team (which included me) to determine how to help employees be successful in the new, reengineered environment.

At the start of the effort, the team considered conducting a needs assessment for this reengineering. A few team members thought the officers might not be open to the idea, but when it was presented to the Reengineering Steering Committee (which included Diversity Advisory Board members Reis, Thompson, and Horty), the needs assessment was readily approved. The results, though difficult to face, became the foundation for the human resource aspects of the reengineering.

At the same time the team was conducting the reengineering needs assessment, the quantitative diversity surveys (containing questions similar to those used in the interviews) were being collected during Valuing Diversity workshops. The People Development Team had the 337 responses tabulated for their own use. The findings validated the results of the original qualitative study and provided additional insights on demographic differences.

Using qualitative and quantitative methods together affirmed the validity of both approaches and solidified the accuracy of the findings in people's minds. Each method also provided valuable data that the other did not. The interviews provided the rich perceptual information with which to finalize the diversity strategy and ensure it would be supported by the majority of employees. The survey provided statistical data on differences between various demographic groups.

The survey showed that there was a higher percentage of white males in management than nonmanagement levels, and managements' ratings of satisfaction with the work environment were slightly higher than those of nonmanagement. Minorities and women were a higher percentage of nonmanagement than management levels. They tended to rate the quality of work life lower than management did; they also gave lower ratings for the degree of respect they received and their opportunity for advancement. A summary of strengths and areas for improvement identified through the diversity survey is in Table 4.

Table 4. Summary of results of the diversity survey.

Strengths	Areas for improvement
● Communicating what is expected of employees	● Importance of unwritten rules for getting ahead
● Offering a good-quality work life	● Quality of supervision
● Treating employees with respect	● Rewarding competence rather than playing politics
● Teamwork in the department	● Tapping employee potential
● Usefulness of manager feedback	● Reducing the amount of biased behavior

Finally, the results of the original needs assessment and subsequent change efforts could be seen at the heart of the reengineering effort. The value of diversity was integrated into company thinking so that corporate advertising and marketing teams were assigned to research diversity of consumers rather than assuming consumers were homogeneous.

Furthermore, many of the values and issues identified in the original diversity needs assessment were integrated into the new vision and values that served as the foundation of the reengineered NBC.

Conclusion

The diversity needs assessment revealed key obstacles to a successful intervention in an area that is "soft," values-laden, and the site of many failures. The results helped create a meaningful, multifaceted organizational change process that has been labeled a success by the majority of stakeholders. The effort, which began in 1993, has now had active employee and senior management commitment for over a year. In addition, during NBC's subsequent reengineering effort, senior management incorporated diversity as one of the organization's core values.

This project was not perfect by any means, and it would be an overstatement to suggest that all the issues that were uncovered have been addressed. Still, most of them are in the process of being addressed. Solutions to foundational issues such as these take years, energy, and persistence to implement, but people see the value of beginning with effective needs assessment that allows for open dialogue and mutual understanding. They also see that human resource development can be a strategic partner by establishing a foundation from which to address the organization's realities.

Questions for Discussion

1. How were concerns about conducting the needs assessment addressed? What compromises had to be made, and what were the benefits and drawbacks of doing so?

2. What were the advantages of choosing qualitative one-on-one interviews as the methodology? What were the disadvantages?

3. What do you think was the most useful information discovered in the needs assessment? Why?

4. How did the results of the qualitative needs assessment and quantitative questionnaire relate to one another? In general, what are the advantages and disadvantages of using a combined approach or either methodology alone?

5. How did the needs assessment contribute to establishing human resource development as a strategic business partner?

The Author

Tina Rasmussen is the founder of Advantage Consulting. Her background includes more than 10 years of training and organization development experience in the high-tech, retail, financial services, and consumer products industries. Her mission is to help people discover practical tools and methods with which to tap into their own and others' abilities and aspirations. Her specialty is working with senior executives to translate their visions and goals into tangible processes resulting in lasting, large-scale change. Rasmussen is also a contributing author of two recent books on leadership, and is completing her Ph.D. at the Fielding Institute. She can be contacted at the following address: Advantage Consulting, P.O. Box 363, Moraga, CA 94556.

References

Lincoln, Y., and Guba, E. (1985). *Naturalistic inquiry.* Newbury Park, CA: Sage Publications.

Lofland, J., and Lofland, L. (1984). *Analyzing social settings.* Belmont, CA: Wadsworth Publishing.

Simons, G. (1990). *The questions of diversity.* Santa Cruz, CA: LMA.

Thomas, R. (1991). *Beyond race and gender.* New York: Amacom.

Acknowledgment

Dr. Stephen Brookfield of the University of Minnesota provided helpful ideas on formulating the interview questions used in this needs assessment.

Quality Skills Needs Assessment

AER Inc.

Lilanthi P. Ravishankar and Darlene F. Russ-Eft

This case illustrates the use of standardized questionnaires focusing on job competencies for managers and supervisors. The needs assessment was part of a quality initiative.

Background

In response to the positive pressure of quality and the negative pressure of foreign competition, organizations such as Western Energy Corporation (WestCo) decided that they had to do business differently. WestCo decided that implementing quality was a new and better way to do business.

In response to the growing push for a quality environment throughout the entire organization, AER Inc., a business unit of WestCo, conducted an executive conference in 1990. A quality plan, a new mission, and a core values statement for the unit were developed during this meeting. A major feature of the quality plan was the decision to provide employees throughout the business unit with basic skills to enable an effective implementation of the quality vision. As a result of this decision, AER, in conjunction with our company (which specializes in effecting organizational change) conducted some needs assessment studies in 1990. The main objective of the assessment was to determine the skill needs of the organization, especially in relation to quality and quality awareness.

The decision to conduct a needs assessment was partly influenced by the fact that another division of WestCo had already conducted a

This case was prepared to serve as a basis for discussion rather than to illustrate either effective or ineffective administrative and management practices. All names, dates, places, and organizations have been disguised at the request of the organization involved or the case author.

successful quality needs assessment. The quality coordinator responsible for the needs assessment at the other location was also responsible for the needs assessment process at AER.

Organizational Profile

WestCo enjoys the position of being one of the United States' major energy production companies. The corporation has approximately 20,000 employees worldwide. AER Inc. is a division of the Alternate Energy and Resources Department of WestCo. AER has approximately 100 employees.

AER provides electric power to utilities that sell to approximately one million homes in the United States. In addition, the company also serves its internal customer, WestCo, with the energy needed for producing and refining oil. AER has facilities operating in California, Washington, and Nevada.

AER's business units are Cogeneration Development and Cogeneration Operations. Cogeneration refers to the simultaneous production of two energy streams—electricity and steam—from a single fuel source. Cogeneration is a proven and efficient dual energy production process that has become a leading technology in the independent generation of electric power. By burning a single fuel to produce electricity and thermal energy, cogeneration is more effective than the separate production of thermal energy and electricity. AER grew out of WestCo's experience in generating energy and steam for its own production and refinery operations. Today, AER is a significant business unit of the Alternate Energy and Resources Department, providing significant earnings and cost savings for WestCo's production and refining divisions. AER's charter is to pursue and operate profitable and environmentally sound cogeneration opportunities throughout the world.

The organization is structured hierarchically, with several layers of management. For the most part, the managers are "grown" in the organization, with many of them rising in the ranks through the years. Thus, many of the managers are longtime employees of AER.

Industry Profile

The organization is in the power and fuel production industry. Competitors are U.S. Generating, DESTEC, AES, and ENRON. Some major success factors in this industry are access to cheap fuel and the ability to generate power. Another important measure of success is reliability, which measures the percentage of time that a facility is in operation versus the time it is scheduled for operation. The key to growth in this industry is to expand the business continuously by investigating new growth areas and developing new projects.

Key Players

Several key individuals were involved in the needs assessment. The president of the organization, who had approximately 30 years of experience in the industry, became the champion for the needs assessment process. He wanted to identify the skills that managers needed to move from a hierarchically structured organization to a more team-oriented organization.

The vice-president of operations and vice-president of business development helped implement the needs assessment. Each of these individuals had more than 25 years of experience in the industry.

Finally, key managers formed the target group for the needs assessment. The rationale for assessing these managers first was that they were to become the champions of the later training efforts to be implemented throughout the organization. Thus, managers needed these skills the most in order to support the training that was to occur later at all levels of the organization.

Issues and Events

The decision to conduct a training needs assessment was made after top management at WestCo decided to launch a quality initiative in response to concerns about competitiveness and market share. AER decided to follow in the parent organization's footsteps. The president and other key managers formed a quality council at AER to champion and implement this vision throughout the unit. Members of the council decided to implement a large-scale training effort at all levels of the organization, because they believed that the entire organization needed extensive training to ensure that the quality vision would take hold.

The quality council and the quality coordinator thought that a needs assessment would help pinpoint high-priority skills needed within the context of a phased and lengthy implementation of quality skills training. Because the needs assessment process had proved very successful in another division of WestCo (and had pointed out clear training needs) AER decided to follow the same process. Based on a recommendation, the organization asked our research division to help. A needs assessment questionnaire related to key quality management competencies had been developed by our company several years earlier. Our division was responsible for the implementation, data analysis, and interpretation of the needs assessment at AER.

Target Population

The initial target population for the quality needs assessment at AER included 10 middle managers and supervisors. For the most part, they were veterans of the organization, having risen through the ranks to managerial positions.

These managers were highly skilled in their technical areas of expertise, with extensive experience in the organization. However, they were accustomed to a hierarchical style of management. Changes desired by the organization required a more empowering and participative style of management. Buy-in from middle management was essential for the success of the quality initiative. Therefore, middle managers occupied a critical role in the training effort.

Managers in the target group averaged about 25 years of experience in the oil and gas industry. Most of these individuals had been involved in starting up the organization's power generation business.

Participation in the needs assessment was mandatory for the managers, because they were expected to be champions of the quality initiative at AER.

Action Items

Several factors led to the decision to conduct a needs assessment. After deciding to implement a quality initiative, the human resource department felt it necessary to identify training needs. Given limited resources, it was essential to find out what the true needs for training were.

Another reason for initiating a needs assessment revolved around establishing training priorities. A needs assessment would help to uncover the level of needs in different areas so that the greatest needs could be addressed first.

The human resource group also hoped to define the scope of the needs in the organization in order to determine appropriate levels of spending. Because the implementation of a quality initiative was the driving force for change within the organization, resources needed to be allocated for training that was specifically tied to the success of this initiative.

Finally, another goal of the needs assessment was to create buy-in for the training solutions from senior management. Even though senior managers mandated the quality initiative within the organization, they would support the training solutions more actively if data substantiated the training recommendations.

Models and Techniques

The needs assessment questionnaires, which were standardized instruments developed several years earlier, focused on job competencies that managers and supervisors need.

Instrument Development

The original development of the questionnaires required several separate research efforts. First, based on our clients' feedback about critical on-the-job behaviors, as well as a review of the literature, we created a large pool of survey items focusing on skills of managers-supervisors and nonmanagerial contributors. Next, we conducted three critical incident studies. By analyzing effective and ineffective job performance behaviors in the critical incidents, we developed lists of job competencies required for managers-supervisors and nonmanagerial contributors. We then categorized items from the survey pool according to the various competencies. If the items did not form a comprehensive picture of a competency, we developed additional items directly from the critical incidents. Finally, we field-tested and revised questionnaire items and instructions to ensure clarity and completeness.

As a part of these research projects, research in job and functional competencies and approaches to needs assessment were reviewed exhaustively. From these sources as well as from individuals participating in the research, thousands of incidents of effective and ineffective performance behaviors were collected.

SUBJECTS AND PROCEDURES. The subjects for the first critical incident study were employed at two separate organizations—a manufacturing plant and a bank. There were 135 managers-supervisors (85 from the plant and 50 from the bank) and 394 nonmanagerial contributors (84 from the plant and 310 from the bank). The second study involved 46 managers and 219 nonmanagerial contributors from a pharmaceutical company. The third study collected critical incidents from 77 managers and 383 nonmanagerial contributors in a manufacturing organization.

Managers-supervisors and nonmanagerial contributors both received two separate critical incident questionnaires. The form regarding managers-supervisors included the following questions:

- Think of a time when a supervisor or manager has shown good leadership—the type of action that points out the effective supervisor or manager.
  — What did the person do that showed his or her effectiveness?
  — What was the result of that behavior?

- Think of a time when a supervisor or manager has shown poor leadership—the type of action that points out the ineffective supervisor or manager.
  — What did the person do that showed his or her ineffectiveness?
  — What was the result of that behavior?

The second form had similar questions focusing on the behaviors of nonmanagerial contributors:

- Think of a recent time when an individual contributor has shown good on-the-job skills—the type of action that points out the effective contributor.
  — What did the person do that showed effectiveness?
  — What was the result of that behavior?
- Think of a recent time when an individual contributor has shown poor on-the-job skills—the type of action that points out the ineffective contributor.
  — What did the person do that showed ineffectiveness?
  — What was the result of that behavior?

In small-group sessions, subjects received the two critical incident forms, along with a rating form designed to measure needs for training. The forms were completed anonymously and returned to the administrator.

ANALYSIS. Each response was placed on a separate card, along with information identifying the characteristics of the participant who made the response. Each incident identified as critical by the participant, or judged by the analyst as so intended, was considered as a separate event. If a response included more than one incident, a duplicate of the entire response was placed on a separate card for each incident. This procedure permitted the analyst to physically separate the different incidents for classification purposes, while still being able to identify the entire response.

A total of 1,158 usable critical incidents on managers-supervisors was obtained from the sample, and 1,273 usable critical incidents were obtained on nonmanagerial contributors. The only responses not used in the analysis were those that were clearly not about incidents or were uninterpretable.

The analysis of the incidents followed the guidelines set forth by Flanagan (1954, 1974). The steps included the following:

- *Step 1.* Select a general frame of reference.
- *Step 2.* Sort a sample of incidents into a few piles in accordance with the selected frame of reference.
- *Step 3.* Formulate tentative headings for these major areas.

- *Step 4.* Sort additional incidents into these major areas, setting up new subcategories as necessary. (All incidents that were so similar that they would probably remain together regardless of changes in category definitions were clipped together and treated as one unit.)
- *Step 5.* Prepare tentative definitions for major headings and generalized statements for the main categories of incidents.
- *Step 6.* Make a tentative selection of the level of specificity to be used in reporting definitions.
- *Step 7.* Redefine major areas and subcategories as necessary while incidents are being classified.
- *Step 8.* Review definitions (after all incidents are classified) and revise as necessary.
- *Step 9.* Record the classification of each incident on the back of the card.
- *Step 10.* Have an independent check made on the classification of all incidents.

In this previous study, identifying critical behaviors within manager and employee competency areas was to be the foundation for assessing training needs and designing training programs. In addition, identifying examples of effective behavior would be useful in developing a performance appraisal instrument. And, because the critical incident technique can be used to develop general competency areas, tests for selection purposes could be developed based on the competency categories that indicate successful employees in the same or similar jobs.

RESULTS. This research indicated that the following competency areas define essential skills for managers and supervisors:
- leadership
  - organization's goals
  - commitment to quality
  - innovation, change
  - results orientation, productivity
  - leading other people
- relationships
  - relationships with upper managers
  - employee performance and development
  - team building, organization climate
  - peer relationships
  - customer or client orientation
- personal skills
  - technical competence

— cognitive abilities

— administrative skills.

In addition, the critical incidents identified specific items that fell into each of these categories.

CONTINUING VALIDATION. Several years after the needs assessment instrument was standardized, a final critical incident analysis was undertaken to validate the items. In 1991, 2,100 critical incidents were collected from 1,080 managers in 13 different organizations. The analysis validated the job competencies and items in the managers' needs assessment survey.

AER Needs Assessment Instrument

The instrument for the needs assessment at AER used the competencies identified previously. The instrument gathered ratings of skill levels as well as ratings of the importance of those skills for the designated jobs. Ratings used two separate scales: a 7-point Likert-type scale, with 1 representing not at all skilled and 7 representing very skilled; and a 7-point Likert-type rating scale, with 1 representing not at all important and 7 representing very important.

Assessment Design

Ten key middle managers were the initial target group chosen for the needs assessment effort at AER Inc. The managers completed questionnaires rating themselves. In addition, their managers ($n = 10$) and immediate employees ($n = 87$) completed questionnaires. Each respondent rated the current skill levels of the target group, as well as the importance of these skills to the managers' jobs.

In addition to the group results, the 10 target managers received individual feedback (or 360-feedback) reports. The human resource department used the group report to determine the kinds of training needed by these managers. The individual feedback reports provided the individual managers with information to use in setting training goals during their performance appraisals.

Administration of Questionnaires

We sent quality needs assessment questionnaires to the quality coordinator at AER. The targeted managers, their managers, and their immediate employees completed questionnaires in separate group sessions. The individuals being assessed were instructed to write in their own names on the questionnaire. The managers and employees of the target individuals wrote in the name of the individual being rated. Raters also indicated their work relationship to the target individual.

Participants were assured that their responses were confidential and that the data would be seen in its individual form only by an external firm. To ensure confidentiality, we provided self-addressed envelopes so that the survey participants could give sealed envelopes to the quality coordinator.

The sealed envelopes were collected by the quality coordinator, bundled according to the various groups (i.e., immediate employees, managers, and target group), and sent back to us for compilation.

Costs and Benefits

The key managers who drove the quality initiative at AER were convinced of the need for a quality needs assessment to determine precise training needs. The cost of the needs assessment totaled approximately $10,000. The key organizational players considered this money well spent, because the cost of the training, including the time spent by managers and other employees in the training classes, was well over $300,000. The quality coordinator for the organization also highly recommended a needs assessment to ensure that the training money targeted the critical needs. The rationale was that if the quality initiative was to be at all successful, it would be essential to provide the appropriate and needed training. Thus, the key change agents within the organization were resolute in their belief that a needs assessment would provide important data that would help them maximize their training dollars.

Data Analysis

From the responses of the target group of 10 managers, we obtained the mean skill rating for each of the 128 items on the questionnaire. Also, we grouped these items into the 13 competency areas that had been determined in the previous research and obtained a mean value for each of these competencies. This process was repeated for the responses of the other two rating groups. These three sets of ratings were compared using bar graphs (see Figure 1).

The same process was repeated for the groups' ratings on the importance of the skills to the managers' jobs. These results are presented in Figure 2. The mean importance ratings on both the items and the competencies were compared across groups to get a sense of the discrepancies or agreement among the various organizational levels with regard to the target group's training needs.

Figure 1. Mean ratings of the target group's skill levels, by target group members, their managers, and their immediate employees.

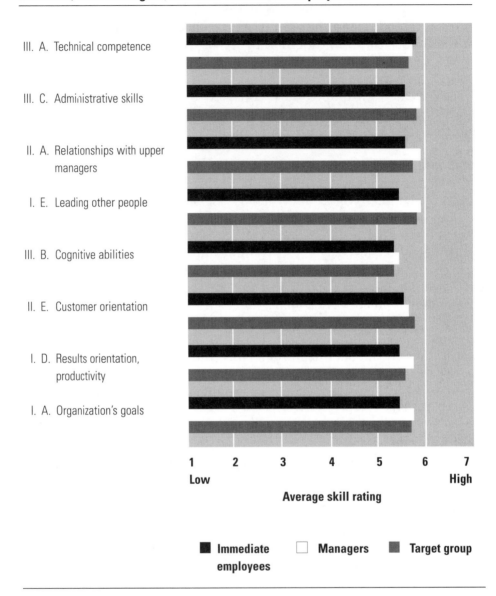

Finally, the skill and importance scores were mathematically combined into a "level of need" index. The level of need was calculated as follows:

● Determine the discrepancy between the ideal skill rating (i.e., a rating of 7) and the actual skill rating. This can be considered a skill gap.

Figure 1 (continued). Mean ratings of the target group's skill levels, by target group members, their managers, and their immediate employees.

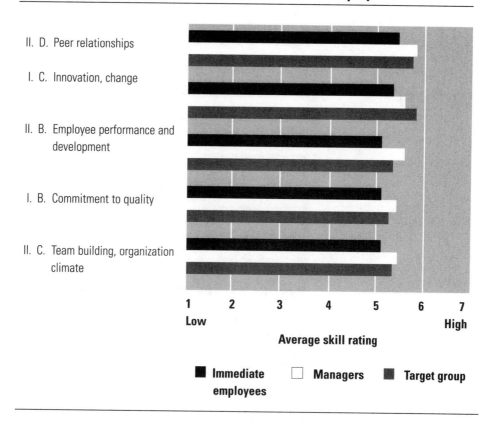

- Weight the skill gap by the importance rating to obtain the level of need. A skill gap with a high rating on importance will show a higher level of need than that same skill gap with a low rating on importance.
- Transform the level of need to a probability or percentile. Thus, the level of need appears on a scale from 0 to 100, with 0 meaning no need and 100 meaning highest possible need.

These results are presented in Figure 3.

Results

Interpreting needs assessment results is not always a precise science. A general rule of thumb is to concentrate on competency areas that score a level of need of 70 or above. These competencies are recommended as areas of immediate priority for training. In addition, within competency areas, items that show a level of need of 70 or

Figure 2. Mean ratings of the importance of skills, by target group members, their managers, and their immediate employees.

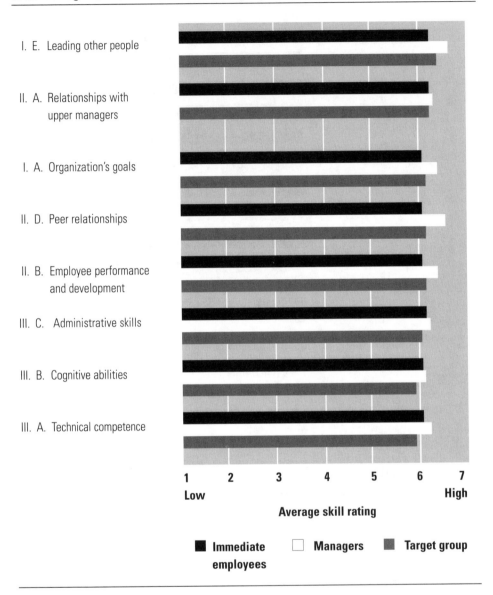

above are recommended as areas for further development. The rationale for setting training priorities, of course, is that training budgets are usually limited and the most urgent training needs should be addressed first.

Figure 2 (continued). Mean ratings of the importance of skills, by target group members, their managers, and their immediate employees.

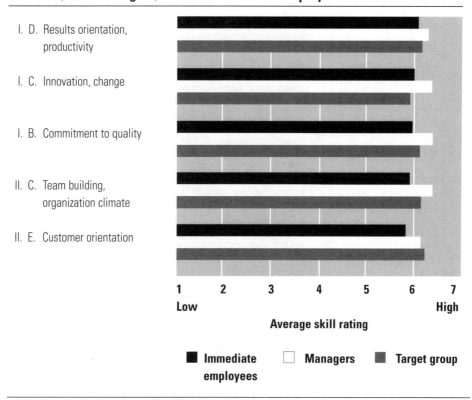

Selected results for AER are presented in Table 1. The needs assessment indicated that the highest level of need for training as reported by target managers, their managers, and their immediate employees was in the area of commitment to quality. Managers and employees of the people in the target group also indicated a high level of need for skills related to team building and organizational climate. In addition, the people in the target group and their immediate employees saw a high level of need in the competency area of employee performance and development. Managers of the individuals in the target group perceived a high level of need in the area of innovation and change.

In general, the needs assessment results revealed that the three rating groups saw fairly similar types of training priorities for the target group of managers. That is, all three groups gave relatively high level-of-need ratings to commitment to quality, employee performance

Figure 3. Level-of-need scores based on ratings of target group members, their managers, and their immediate employees.

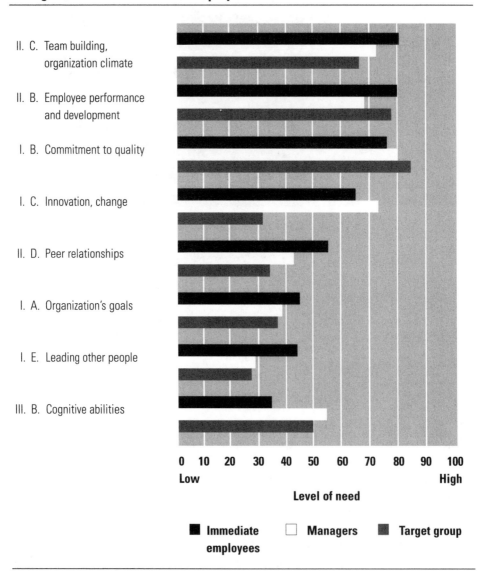

and development, and team building and organization climate. The discrepancies in the ratings between managers and immediate employees of the target managers are probably due to the different types of behaviors that the two groups experience in their interactions with the target group. For example, of all the rating groups, immediate employ-

Figure 3 (continued). Level-of-need scores based on ratings of target group members, their managers, and their immediate employees.

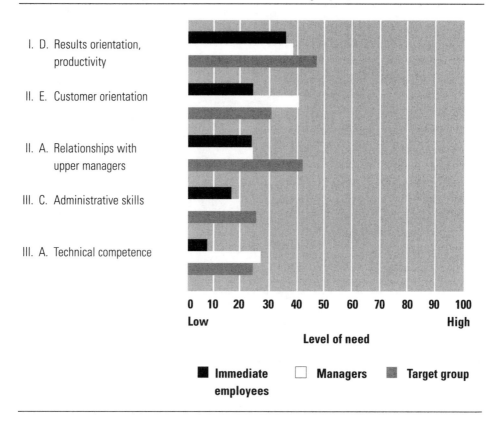

I. D. Results orientation, productivity

II. E. Customer orientation

II. A. Relationships with upper managers

III. C. Administrative skills

III. A. Technical competence

0 10 20 30 40 50 60 70 80 90 100
Low   High

Level of need

■ Immediate employees   □ Managers   ▨ Target group

ees gave the highest ratings to employee performance and development. It is most likely that they have the best perspective on this competency, because it relates to themselves as a group.

Intervention Description

Based on the results of the needs assessment, AER implemented a human resource development (HRD) intervention phased in over several years. This intervention consisted of extensive training in quality, interpersonal skills, and leadership. Although the needs assessment concentrated on determining needs of managers, all levels of the organization participated in the training.

The rationale for providing training throughout the organization was top management's conviction that a substantial commitment to training had to be made at all levels for the quality initiative to be

Table 1. Mean ratings for competency areas.

Competency area	Target group	Managers	Immediate employees
IB. Commitment to quality	85.392	80.098	76.462
IIB. Employee performance and development	78.373	69.097	80.138
IIC. Team building, organization climate	67.720	71.386	80.548
IIIB. Cognitive abilities	49.920	55.577	35.587
ID. Results orientation, productivity	46.841	39.389	35.399
IIA. Relationships with upper managers	42.782	24.656	23.961
IA. Organization's goals	37.949	38.786	43.636
IID. Peer relationships	34.483	42.968	56.526
IIE. Customer or client orientation	30.792	40.086	24.320
IC. Innovation, change	30.449	73.788	65.816
IE. Leading other people	26.746	29.450	43.043
IIIC. Administrative skills	25.656	19.696	16.409
IIIA. Technical competence	24.495	25.867	7.981

successful. The needs assessment was restricted to the managers, however, because the president of the organization felt that, as the drivers of the quality effort, these managers had the greatest need for focused and timely training. These managers participated in the training first so that they could model as well as support the subsequent training to be received by the rest of the organization.

The training occurred in two phases for both managers and other employees in the organization. Table 2 lists the specific training modules that were provided.

The training program's content was geared toward providing managers and employees with core courses and competencies related to working in cross-functional teams. Many of the skills related to teamwork, communication, leading and participating in meetings, and giving and receiving feedback.

Each unit of training represented two to three hours of training; units could stand alone or be combined with other training activities. The training used behavior modeling. The instructors attended a four-day certification seminar that covered facilitation skills, the behavior modeling process, basic program content, and implementation strategies. The training occurred at the organization's locations, and the frequency of training sessions depended on the organization, but ranged

Table 2. Training modules for managers and employees.

Phase 1	
Managers	**Employees**
The Management Support Role and Quality: The Leadership Role	Building Individual Commitment to Quality
Focusing Your Team on Quality	You Make a Difference
Facilitating Successful Meetings	Quality: The Individual's Role
Sustaining Momentum for Continuous Quality Improvement	Sustaining Momentum for Continuous Quality Improvement
Getting Good Information From Others	Giving Feedback To Help Others
Giving Constructive Feedback	Being a Team Player
Managing Change	Listening to Understand Clearly
Analyzing Work Processes	Analyzing Work Processes
Solving Quality Problems	Solving Quality Problems
Tools and Techniques for Solving Quality Problems	Tools and Techniques for Solving Quality Problems
Clarifying Customer Expectations	Clarifying Customer Expectations

from once a week to once a month.

The training involved presentations by an instructor-facilitator and skills practice. Each training session started with feedback and reinforcement of a previous session, an introduction, and an explanation of the rationale behind each key action, followed by brief behavioral cues on video. Participants learned to identify when to use the key actions in different situations and began to formulate action plans for both practice assignments and future on-the-job behavior. Skills practice offered participants different perspectives on how to use the key actions in work situations. They received feedback on their use of the key actions in the practice situations, and they were able to observe how others

Table 2 (continued). Training modules for managers and employees.

Phase 2	
Managers	**Employees**
Building a Collaborative Relationship With Your Peers	Positive Responses to Negative Situations
Confronting Issues With Your Manager and Peers	Resolving Issues With Others
Winning Support From Others	Keeping Your Boss Informed
Establishing Performance Expectations	Taking on a New Assignment
Resolving Team Conflicts	Working Smarter
Fostering Improvements Through Innovation	
The Challenge of Team Leadership	
Building a Foundation of Trust	
Launching and Refueling Your Team: Tools and Techniques	
Expanding Your Team's Capabilities	
Helping Your Team Reach Consensus	
Making the Most of Team Differences	
Forward Thinking	

used the key actions in turn.

The expected result of the HRD intervention was that the training would effect cultural change within the organization. AER had previously been managed in a dictatorial, almost militaristic manner and was inwardly focused. Top management felt that this work style was clearly incompatible with a quality and customer-focused organization. The training provided the tools for people at all levels of the organization to change their ways of thinking and behaving. Other goals of the training implementation were to increase teamwork and communication within and between the various organizational levels, increase employee involvement, become more outwardly focused, and foster a more participative management style to ensure that all the other goals were met. Finally, as a result of the culture change and the quality and customer focus, the ultimate expected outcome of the HRD intervention was improved earnings, reliability, and safety.

Conclusions

This needs assessment led to positive outcomes. Although the decision to train all levels of the organization to facilitate quality implementation had already been made prior to the needs assessment, the assessment did provide the following benefits:

- It demonstrated top management's commitment to the training at the outset.
- It helped managers buy into the training, for both themselves and their subordinates.
- It helped target critical skill gaps for managers, the key change agents for this quality effort.
- It helped send the message to middle managers that changes in attitudes and behaviors begin at the top and that their support would affect the success or failure of the organizational change.
- It allowed managers to see where they needed improvement from the point of view of their subordinates.
- It demonstrated true commitment to greater employee involvement in the organization, because employees' opinions were elicited.

Follow-up within the organization after training implementation indicated that the training had been successful as well. The organization experienced improvements in safety, reliability, and revenue.

Lessons Learned

Although the needs assessment at AER Inc. led to success, some recommendations for future assessments should be considered:

- Assess more than just the managerial group to obtain the buy-in of other groups in the organization as well. Such a process would also help to target training to immediate needs.
- Involve the external customer in the needs assessment. Particularly in the case of a quality initiative, it is important to model and reinforce the importance of the customer.

Questions for Discussion

1. What are your reactions to the approach used to identify the job competencies of managers and nonmanagerial personnel?

2. What was the value of having three rating groups assess the training needs of the target group?

3. What is your assessment of the training program that was implemented based on the results of the needs assessment?

4. What were the benefits to AER Inc. of conducting a training needs assessment prior to implementing any training programs?

The Authors

Lilanthi P. Ravishankar is market research manager at Zenger-Miller, an international supplier of training programs and services, headquartered in California. She is primarily responsible for the management of various research projects and data analysis and reporting. Prior to joining Zenger-Miller, she attended the master's program in sociology and demography at the University of Texas at Austin. Ravishankar can be contacted at the following address: Zenger-Miller, 1735 Technology Drive, San Jose, CA 95110-1313.

Darlene F. Russ-Eft is division director, research services, at Zenger-Miller. She is responsible for overall management of the research function at Zenger-Miller, which includes services in research and evaluation and needs assessment. Russ-Eft also serves on the adjunct faculty at the University of Santa Clara, University of California at Berkeley, and University of California at Santa Cruz. She holds Ph.D. and M.A. degrees from the Department of Psychology at the University of Michigan, and a B.A. from the Department of Psychology at the College of Wooster. An active member of numerous professional organizations, she is the author or coauthor of many research articles in major trade journals. She is currently chair of the Research Advisory Committee of the American Society for Training and Development.

References

Flanagan, J.F. (1954). The critical incident technique. *Psychological Bulletin, 51,* 327-358.

Flanagan, J.F. (1974). *Measuring human performance.* Palo Alto, CA: American Institutes for Research.

Assessing the Training Needs of Supervisors-Turned-Team-Leaders

Americana Insurance Company

William J. Rothwell

This case focuses on an assessment method called DACUM, which is an acronym for Developing a Curriculum. *The needs assessment involved the training needs of supervisors who were moving to a new role as team leaders.*

Background

Our division has piloted a team, and we have already made a nominal transition to teams because we have hung the label "teams" on our work groups. Now we need to turn the label into a reality. We feel that changing supervisory behavior is the key to that. Our reasoning is simple: Supervisors model behavior and set an example for hourly employees. Hence, for the team installation to be successful, supervisors must be trained to assume a new role as facilitative coaches and to model the behavior that will lead to cohesive, productive teams. But how can our supervisors be trained to become facilitative when they have long functioned directively, and when our corporate culture rewards controlling-oriented, top-down decision making?

This statement by Vice-President Thomasina King of the Americana Insurance Company underscores the challenge of making a transition from a functional to a team-based organization. It also dramatizes the vital role played by supervisors in this process. In this case, training needs assessment was only part of a larger performance improvement strategy intended to redesign supervisory jobs. Training needs assess-

This case was prepared to serve as a basis for discussion rather than to illustrate either effective or ineffective administrative and management practices. All names, dates, places, and organizations have been disguised at the request of the organization involved or the case author.

ment was focused on turning an ephemeral vision of the future into a concrete reality.

The Setting

The Americana Insurance Company remains financially stable and nationally competitive to this day. The firm sells insurance products in all 50 states through a national network of 2,500 independent agents. It also sells its products in Canada, in U.S. territories and protectorates, and in Europe to members of the U.S. Armed Services.

The company is organized into 13 divisions. Only four are considered "line" (or operating) divisions: Sales and Marketing, Information Processing, Service Before and During the Sale, and Service After the Sale. Other divisions are "staff" (or advisory) divisions, such as Human Resources, Accounting, and Law.

King is the vice-president of the Service Before and During the Sale Division. Her division consists of three departments: Underwriting, Service During the Sale, and Maintenance. The Maintenance Department maintains company office supplies, stores and retrieves millions of hard-copy insurance records, and oversees the physical maintenance of the corporate headquarters. It has a staff of 25. The Service During the Sale Department is the largest and is staffed by 200 of the division's 300 home office associates. The Underwriting Department is staffed by 75 underwriters and support staff.

A manager is charged with the responsibility for each department. The department manager of Underwriting is Philomena Steely; the department manager of Service During the Sale is Thomas Iron; and the department manager of Maintenance is Marjorie Smithson. All three department managers possess college degrees and were promoted from within the company.

The Problem

In 1991 Americana was facing stiff competition that resulted from a narrowing of profit margins on insurance products. Company leaders felt that to remain competitive, it was imperative to improve the quality of service to field associates (the term used in this company for its insurance agents) and policy owners (the term used in this company for customers and clients) and to empower home office associates (the term used in this company for employees). These goals were stated explicitly in the company's strategic business plan.

King believed that her operating division could best contribute to achieving these ambitious company goals by restructuring into teams.

She was convinced that the division's structure and the traditional work process hindered cycle time. (In this setting, cycle time refers to the time lag between collecting information from a prospective policy owner and issuing the policy.) Slow cycle time has grave implications throughout the industry; insurance policies not issued quickly are less likely to be accepted by prospective policy owners. As a result, the sale is never closed.

For years the company had issued policies in the following manner:

- *Step 1.* A field associate would make a sales call on a prospective policy owner. If the prospective policy owner was willing to take out an insurance policy, the field associate would take down important medical information about the client on a policy application.
- *Step 2.* The field associate would mail the policy application to the home office—the insurance company's headquarters—and await completion of the underwriting and policy issue process.
- *Step 3.* Upon arrival at the home office, the policy application would be routed directly to Underwriting. Underwriters would assess the risk to the company of issuing a policy to the prospective policy owner. If the risk was not acceptable, a rejection letter would be sent to the client. If more information was needed, an underwriter would ask the field associate who submitted the application to obtain that information. If the policy application was complete and the insurance risk was acceptable, the underwriter would forward the policy application for processing to the Service During the Sale Department.
- *Step 4.* Once the policy application arrived in the Service During the Sale Department, home office associates would create a policy owner file, establish financial accounts for record keeping, and issue a hardcopy insurance policy (a legal contract).
- *Step 5.* Once the policy was issued, it would be returned to the field associate who submitted the policy application. He or she would make a return visit to the new policy owner to deliver the policy. If the policy owner refused to accept delivery and did not sign the contract, the policy was canceled after a legally required grace period.

Portrayed in this outline format, the process appears to be simple enough. However, a dizzying array of additional steps could occur. The result was that an otherwise simple process could be transformed into one of immense complexity.

The process was prone to numerous delays that stemmed from many causes. For instance, policy applications could be misplaced in transit from one desk to another or from one department to another.

Home office associates handled enormous mounds of paperwork, which complicated processing. Another cause for delay was that field associates would forget to answer questions on policy applications, which would add time-consuming steps to processing. Yet another cause for delay stemmed from difficulties in confirming the medical status of prospective policy owners with notoriously difficult-to-reach physicians. Finally, extra steps could be added to processing policy applications when prospective policy owners customized the product to meet their individual needs. For instance, adding one rider to an insurance contract could mean lengthy delays in processing time, and many such riders were possible.

King was convinced that teams could slash processing time. She hoped that, if each team handled all steps in the process, policy applications would be subject to less delay and less opportunity to be misplaced while moving from one desk or department to another. Additionally, if home office associates did not specialize, but became generalists knowledgeable about all the steps, quality of service to policy owners and field associates would improve and the workers would be empowered.

Issues

Making a transition from a functional to a team-based structure poses a daunting challenge to any organization for several reasons. First, the organization's leaders may become so enthusiastic about teams that they forget to make a persuasive case for the change. Leaders should emphasize the business needs underlying the change. If they fail to do that, skeptical employees will wonder if "going to teams" is a legitimate effort—or amounts only to the pursuit of the latest management fad. (This reaction is especially likely when the leaders have been guilty of chasing fads before.)

Second, company leaders may fail to resolve differing opinions about teams among themselves. As a result, employees will receive mixed messages and be unsure what the leaders mean when they talk about teams. And if leaders lack consensus among themselves about the goals they seek, achieving these goals is nearly impossible.

Third, leaders may have trouble clarifying precisely how employees' daily work activities should change as the organization shifts from a functional to a team-based structure. Although they may be able to speak persuasively about the value of teams, can they model the desired behavior, set the proper example, and explain specifically what employees should do and how they should behave in teams? If not, employees will be bewildered. A transition to teams requires a clear vision, precise descriptions of desired behavior, and effective communication skills.

Fourth, leaders may entertain unrealistic expectations about how quickly a team-based structure can be installed. They may also lack reference points about where and how to begin the process. Such a large-scale change effort defies quick fixes.

Fifth, making a transition to teams calls for a culture change. It demands far more than individually oriented change strategies, such as training. Indeed, every part of the human resource subsystem—including selection, promotion, appraisal, and compensation policies and practices—must be reviewed and reengineered to support the change effort as well as any training designed to facilitate it.

Sixth, installing teams calls for intensive involvement by the people expected to change. Installation should not be handled dogmatically; rather, the process should match desired outcomes. If employees are to be empowered through the installation of teams, then the change process should also be empowering.

Finally, installing teams requires facilitators to think in future-oriented ways. They must avoid the temptation to reflect on past or present problems and must focus instead on desired future states that may have no historical counterparts. That can be difficult to do—and is clearly at odds with approaches to training needs assessment that adopt a "fix-it" mentality. Unlike some forms of traditional needs assessment that rely on comparisons between what has been happening in the past and what should be happening now, a future-oriented approach compares what should be happening in an uncertain future with what is happening now (Rothwell, 1984; Rothwell and Kazanas, 1994).

Target Population

The targeted population of this needs assessment consisted of the supervisors in the Service Before and During the Sale Division. Supervisors report directly to department managers. Maintenance has three supervisors, Service During the Sale has 10, and Underwriting has one supervisor to oversee support staff and five project chiefs overseeing underwriters. In this company, supervisors are promoted from within, do not possess college degrees, and remain in their jobs for lengthy periods. The median tenure of a supervisor in King's division is 15 years.

King focused her attention on the project chiefs and the supervisors in the Service During the Sale Department because they were directly involved in issuing insurance products in a way that was not true of the supervisors in the Maintenance Department. Project chiefs, although they did not possess supervisory job titles, functioned as supervisors over professional underwriters.

Action Items

This training needs assessment comprised the four action steps described in this section.

Step One: Framing the Change Effort

The goal of the first step was to build awareness among management about the possible definitions of teams and team leadership. No effort was made to translate these concepts into terms specific to Americana's culture or to discuss their implications for Americana's supervisors; rather, the aim was simply to frame the change effort by providing participants with background information.

To this end, Americana's training director, George Williams, searched for books, articles, and videotapes about teams and team leadership (e.g., Fisher, 1993). He then circulated the literature to King and to her department managers and supervisors. He also organized several briefing sessions to show and discuss videotapes on teams and team leadership issues to the same group.

Step Two: Planning To Build a Team Leadership Model

The focus of Step Two was planning for a retreat to build a team leadership model. The retreat would translate the general background information about teams and team leadership into terms unique to Americana's corporate culture and to the supervisors' roles in the division. The retreat would be the venue for the training needs assessment.

To that end, Williams drafted an agenda for a two-day retreat for King and all department managers and supervisors in her division (see Table 1). He then circulated it to them for review and comment. They checked their individual schedules and company work cycles and chose a date when the retreat could be held with minimal disruptions.

Before the retreat, Williams shared the agenda at a regular monthly staff meeting of supervisors in the Service Before and During the Sale Division. He fielded questions about the retreat and emphasized how important it would be in clarifying the team leader's role. (One supervisor remarked that it was "about time we defined the role, since we have already been functioning in teams for some time—and the teams aren't successful because supervisors and employees just continue to do what they have always done.") Williams chose to base his approach loosely on the so-called DACUM method (Norton, 1985).

Table 1. Agenda for the model-building meeting.

I. Introduction
   A. Objectives for the meeting
   B. Importance of the meeting
      1. Why the meeting is necessary
      2. Making the business case for a move to teams
      3. The importance of the team leader's role
   C. Organization of the meeting

II. Defining the team leader's role
   A. Listing activities
   B. Categorizing activities
   C. Verifying categories and activities
   D. Sequencing categories and activities
   E. Rating the importance of activities in the model
   F. Assessing individual strengths and weaknesses against the model

III. Implementing the team leader's role
   A. Identifying barriers to successful implementation
   B. Clarifying strategies to overcome the barriers
   C. Establishing action plans
      1. Assessing needs for new job descriptions
      2. Assessing selection criteria for team leaders
      3. Assessing training needs for team leaders
      4. Assessing performance appraisal criteria for team leaders
      5. Assessing rewards and incentives for team leaders

IV. Conclusion

Step Three: Building the Team Leadership Model

Williams functioned as group facilitator for the retreat, with assistance from two corporate trainers. As the agenda called for, he began by listing the retreat's objectives, explaining why it was important, and describing desired outcomes. King spoke a few introductory words of her own, stressing the importance of clarifying the supervisor's role in teams. She explained why the retreat would focus on the roles of supervisors and project chiefs.

Following the introduction, the model-building process began. Williams introduced Part II of the meeting in this way:

Williams: For some time I've been sending you books and articles about teams and team leadership. I've shown videotapes on the same subjects. We have taken field trips to local businesses in our industry to see how they are applying the team concept, and we've even had visitors from organizations in other industries visit us to brief us on their approaches to teams and team leadership.

Throughout that process, I was not interested in clarifying how we could apply these views—and, as we know, they were not consistent—to our corporate culture or to your jobs. But that will be the aim of today's session.

In this part of the meeting I would like you to brainstorm on the daily work activities of team leaders. I encourage you not to be critical. Save that for later.

For now, I'm going to go around the large table we have—there are 23 people in attendance here today—and ask each of you to list one activity that you believe should characterize the daily work of a future team leader. We'll keep going around the table, and each of you will list one activity as long as you are able to do so.

These activities can include what you are already doing as supervisors—if those activities are, you feel, what team leaders should do. The activities may also include utterly new ones, based on what you (as an individual) believe that team leaders should be doing.

As we progress around the table, my associates will help us. Corporate Trainer Joan Betters will write each activity you list on an 8.5-by-11-inch sheet of paper. Corporate Trainer Marty Larson will tape each paper on the wall in front of us so that you can keep track of what has been listed.

If you are unable to think of an activity, then just say, "Pass." This process should take about two hours. We'll take a break upon completion. If you need an individual break before that, feel free to leave—but please return soon!

Any questions?

King: Should my department managers and I also participate?

Williams: Absolutely. This process is meant to be highly empowering. You are all invited to participate. We are building a model of what team leaders should be doing in the future, not what supervisors are presently doing.

Steely: How will this help us?

Williams: The model we build collectively will become a specific vision of the future. It will become the basis for selecting, training, appraising, and compensating team leaders.

Iron: That sounds pretty ambitious for a single meeting.

Williams: It is. So respond carefully. However, you will have ample opportunity to refine this model in the future. It will not be cast in concrete; rather, it will be flexible, organic, and dynamic. But it will be more specific than any job description you have ever seen. And the process of establishing it will be highly participative, providing a chance for all the people affected by the new model to have a say in building it.

That opening set the tone for the session. After the session, Williams called a lengthy break. Participants were encouraged to leave the room to refresh themselves. Meanwhile, Williams worked with his associates—and with King and her managers—to establish mutually exclusive categories in which to collapse all the activities that were listed. The activities on the wall were then rearranged to fit into those categories.

Williams asked the participants to reconvene and explained to them what they would do next.

> We have collapsed all the activities on the wall into mutually exclusive categories. I will now ask you to examine each category carefully and determine whether it should be retained as it is, deleted entirely, combined with another category, or otherwise modified.
>
> After we have verified the categories, we'll turn to verifying the activities. We'll handle activities exactly as we previously handled categories, reviewing them one by one.
>
> When we finish, we'll take a break. Then we shall turn to sequencing categories and activities. I'll ask you to determine how the categories and activities should be arranged from easiest to most difficult for a novice to learn. At that point we'll adjourn for the day.

The events unfolded exactly as Williams described. By the end of the day, the participants had constructed a detailed wall chart of work activities that became the model of team leader activities (see Table 2 for a very abbreviated version of the model).

Between the first and second day, Williams and his trainers numbered each activity on the wall chart so that the chart could be reconstructed by a typist. They also used the activities on the chart as a basis for preparing a written questionnaire that listed all the team leaders' activities from the chart. At the opening of the second day of the retreat, Williams asked each participant to complete the questionnaire by rating both the relative perceived importance of each activity

Table 2. Abbreviated model of the team leader's role in Americana Insurance Company.

Category	Activities			
Leadership duties	Interview (involve team in what is needed and who is to be selected for vacant positions)	Conduct employee performance appraisals, guiding team members in providing information about the performance of their co-workers	Enforce the rules and help team members ensure compliance with rules among their co-workers	Carry out the disciplinary policy of the company, collecting input from team members about problem behaviors of their co-workers and documenting individuals whose performance is not adequate
Administrative records	Process payroll, making sure that adequate records are kept so that employees are paid on time	Keep attendance sheets	Prepare the budget for the team in compliance with company policy	Prepare and see to filling supply requisitions
Communications	Answer team questions or facilitate team investigations to answer questions	Handle phone calls	Communicate with team members, managers, and others in the company	Listen to team members, managers, and others in the company

to success in the team leader role, and how well he or she could conduct the activity at that time.

After completing the questionnaires, the participants were divided into small groups of three or four. They were asked to list the perceived barriers to successful implementation of the new role and to clarify strategies for overcoming the barriers. Each small group appointed one spokesperson, who accepted responsibility for summarizing group

Table 2 (continued). Abbreviated model of the team leader's role in Americana Insurance Company.

Category	Activities			
Coaching and motivating team members	Coach and motivate team members to preserve and enhance team and individual performance	Keep morale high	Demonstrate effective coaching behaviors in a way consistent with company training	Encourage team members to work together and to resolve conflicts constructively and creatively
On-the-job training	Oversee on-the-job training to ensure that team members receive appropriate training to do their jobs	Review errors and performance problems of the team	Make sure that team members are crosstrained so that each member is capable of performing all tasks of the team	Monitor team work flow and tell team members about work flow problems so that they can investigate and resolve those problems
Continuing education	Educate team members on new work procedures	Learn about company work flow and help team members learn about it	Identify changes in jobs or tasks and point them out, as necessary, to team members	Facilitate team interaction, helping team members work together effectively and cohesively

response   fi
participa

The
individua
to one in
ideas. It
addressin

Parti
them wer   barriers to successful installation. Among
them wer   time to make the change while getting the work out
successfully, lack of money to fund training, lack of company-specific

[handwritten margin notes:]
- Briefly describe core   10 min
- what drove needs assessment
- what went right/wrong
- what would you do differently

training on team leadership as described by the model, and lack of incentives to encourage the change.

During the afternoon of the meeting's second day, the participants were divided into five committees. Each committee was given the responsibility to establish an action plan consistent with the new team leader model for accomplishing all of the following:

- revise supervisory job descriptions
- establish a training plan and set training priorities for team leaders
- establish new performance appraisal criteria for team leaders
- establish rewards and incentives for team leaders
- establish new promotional criteria for team leaders.

King and her department managers preselected committee members to ensure that each committee would be staffed by a cross section of representatives from the division. A department manager was named ex officio member of each committee and served as an advisor, not a leader.

Williams explained to participants that they should not try to complete their committee assignments while at the retreat, but simply begin their deliberations. By the end of the retreat, however, each committee was encouraged to elect a leader, list probable work tasks, and establish timelines for reporting results. King informed the managers, supervisors, and project chiefs that the first report from each committee would be due at the next staff meeting in two weeks. A task force was then appointed to merge the five action plans into a single plan.

At the end of the session, Williams reviewed the retreat's objectives, highlighted what had been accomplished, and pointed the way toward future action. He emphasized that the model the participants had developed was not finished; rather, it represented a starting point for defining the team leader's role clearly.

Step Four: Installing the Model

The model of the team leader's role became a vehicle for making the change to teams in the division. Initially the focus was on clarifying the team leader's role. Committee efforts resulted in job descriptions for team leaders, a comprehensive training plan based on perceived group and individual needs, new performance appraisal criteria (and forms) for team leaders, appropriate rewards and incentives for team leaders, and new promotional criteria for team leaders. Subsequent efforts focused on redesigning the jobs of department managers, the division vice-president, and hourly employees so they would be consistent with a team orientation.

Conclusion

This assessment process was very successful. It provided an important starting point for launching the implementation of teams in the Service Before and During the Sale Division at Americana Insurance Company. The needs assessment was unique in that it was

- future oriented, geared to describing a job that did not yet exist in the organization
- involvement oriented, designed to encourage the people targeted for training and change to play an active role in defining their job responsibilities and assessing their own training needs relative to those responsibilities
- holistic, transcending a simplistic focus on training as a stand-alone performance improvement strategy.

Questions for Discussion

1. What were the relative advantages and disadvantages of focusing on supervisors (team leaders) instead of other job categories in this case study? What might be the relative advantages and disadvantages of focusing on hourly employees? department managers? the vice-president?

2. Why is it important to make the business case for any change effort?

3. How do an organization's strategic goals relate to making the business case?

4. How much do you agree that for change to be successful, the process of making the change must match the desired outcomes? Explain how that concept applies to this case study.

5. In the process described in this case study, the facilitator built a wall chart of future work activities with participants. What are the advantages and disadvantages of this approach?

6. As described in this case, participants were asked to use a questionnaire to rate the relative perceived importance of activities and their individual abilities to perform those activities. What are the strengths and weaknesses of using what amounts to a self-report as a basis for training needs assessment? How might that approach be improved?

7. How could activities become the basis for training? Explain the steps that would be necessary to construct instructional objectives based on the wall chart.

8. What knowledge, skills, and abilities would be required for a facilitator to carry out a needs assessment like the one described in this case?

9. How could the approach described in this case be used to identify job competencies, if competencies are understood to mean personal characteristics underlying successful performance? (For more information about competencies, see Dubois, 1993, and Spencer and Spencer, 1993.)

10. How might the approach described in this case be modified for assessing the future job requirements of executives? hourly employees? salespersons? technical workers? professional employees?

The Author

William J. Rothwell is associate professor of human resource development at the Pennsylvania State University, University Park campus. He earned a Ph.D. in education with a specialty in human resource development from the University of Illinois, an M.B.A. from Sangamon State University, an M.A. (and all courses required for a second doctorate) in English from the University of Illinois, Urbana, and a B.A. from Illinois State University. He has authored or coauthored more than 70 articles, 13 books, and five published training packages. Before entering academe, he served as a training director in both a public-sector agency and a private-sector corporation from 1979 to 1993. At present he consults with numerous organizations on training needs assessment, managerial competency assessment, succession planning, and large-scale change efforts. Rothwell can be contacted at the following address: Human Resource Development, Department of Adult Education, Instructional Systems and Vocational-Industrial Education, College of Education, The Pennsylvania State University, University Park, PA 16802-3202.

References

Dubois, D. (1993). *Competency-based performance improvement: A strategy for organizational change.* Amherst, MA: Human Resource Development Press.

Fisher, K. (1993). *Leading self-directed work teams: A guide to developing new team leadership skills.* New York: McGraw-Hill.

Norton, R. (1985). *DACUM handbook.* Columbus, OH: National Center for Research in Vocational Education.

Rothwell, W. (1984). Strategic needs assessment. *Performance and Instruction, 23*(5), 19-20.

Rothwell, W., and Kazanas, H. (1994). *Human resource development: A strategic approach.* Amherst, MA: Human Resource Development Press.

Spencer, L., and Spencer, S. (1993). *Competence at work: Models for superior performance.* New York: Wiley.

Using Performance Analysis To Assess Future Technical Training Needs

Specialty Chemical Unit

Catherine M. Sleezer

This case describes use of performance analysis for training (PAT)—a comprehensive needs assessment process—to determine training needs for technical employees. The model has three integrated components: a conceptual framework of the elements that affect decisions about training needs, a list of the phases and steps involved in determining training needs, and worksheets to guide the analysis.

Background

Most manufacturing firms are betting that the ability to implement new technology quickly will be vital to their success in the competitive marketplace of the future. This bet increases the importance of having highly trained technical workers. Business strategies for improving performance, such as implementing efficient tools, clever advertising, best management practices, and self-directed work teams, will be effective only if technical workers also have the knowledge and skills to adapt efficiently to future product, company, and industry changes.

This case describes a performance-analysis-for-training project that focused on the future training needs of technical workers in a strategic business unit of a service and manufacturing conglomerate. The business unit's decision makers recognized the critical nature of their challenge to train technical workers to meet future needs. They also recognized the key role of human resource development (HRD) in

This case was prepared to serve as a basis for discussion rather than to illustrate either effective or ineffective administrative and management practices. All names, dates, places, and organizations have been disguised at the request of the organization involved or the case author.

overcoming this challenge. The decision makers used this project to scope out the situation, build consensus among key players, and formulate specific training and nontraining changes for the future.

Organization Profile

The service and manufacturing conglomerate in this study provides products in areas such as chemicals, cellular mobile telephone services, computer-based services, and voice and data services. The conglomerate was facing a competitive business environment and, consequently, required the maximum contribution from each strategic business unit.

The strategic business unit described in this case produced chemical products and is referred to as the Specialty Chemical Unit (SCU). The SCU had few current performance problems to be corrected with training. However, the SCU's decision makers predicted that this situation would soon change. Several new manufacturing processes were in the planning or initial implementation stages. Further, the SCU's decision makers recognized that technological innovations could change their industry quickly in unpredictable ways. To support these new processes and to be proactive in adapting to future changes, the SCU's decision makers had made a commitment to provide each employee with 70 hours of training annually.

Industry Profile

The chemical industry was changing. The forces for change included increased offshore competition, new government regulations, and customers' requirements that SCU products and processes meet Baldrige Award or ISO 9000 guidelines. Leaders within the industry had informally discussed strategies for adapting to these forces. One such strategy was chemical operation certification. Industry leaders viewed certification as a competitive strategy: Their products would be made by certified operators. They also knew that government policymakers were considering chemical operation certification as a way to address worker safety and hazardous materials issues. Industry leaders agreed that industry-initiated certification was preferable to a government-mandated program.

Key Players

The key decision maker for this performance analysis was the SCU's manager of human resources. He was a recognized "fast-tracker" from corporate headquarters who was on short-term assignment to the SCU.

His focus was on learning about the SCU and determining how the SCU could make a stronger contribution to the conglomerate. Another person with a major decision-making role in the project was the plant manager. He was planning to retire in the next year and did not want too much change. Other people who helped plan the performance analysis included the human resource planning group, the manager of total quality, and SCU subject experts in chemical manufacturing.

The analyst role was filled by an external consulting team that consisted of a project director, a project manager, and two project assistants. The team's disadvantage of being external and not knowing the firm was balanced by the advantage of being able to perceive cultural issues that people within the firm might not see. The project director's biases included a belief that HRD could improve organization and individual performance. She was experienced in analyzing performance needs and in planning and implementing training and development efforts. The project manager also had a bias for using HRD to improve performance. He had worked on several needs assessment projects and was working on his doctorate in training and development. The project assistants had little practical experience in HRD but were graduate students in a training and development program.

The target population for this performance analysis project was the SCU's 106 technical workers.

Models and Techniques

The model used to guide this project was the performance analysis for training (PAT) model (Sleezer, 1990, 1993b). The model has three integrated components: a conceptual framework of the elements that affect decisions about training needs, a list of the phases and steps involved in determining training needs, and worksheets to guide the analysis.

The PAT model's conceptual framework includes three elements that affect decisions about training needs: the characteristics of the organization, of the decision makers, and of the analyst (see Figure 1). Relevant organization characteristics include its culture, politics, systems, and rhetoric. Decision maker characteristics that influence a performance analysis include expectations about training and support for it. And analyst characteristics that influence a performance analysis include the analyst's abilities and biases (Sleezer, 1993a). The premise of the PAT model is that it is through the interaction of these three elements that performance opportunities or needs are perceived, negotiated, and prioritized.

Figure 1. Elements that affect decisions about training needs.

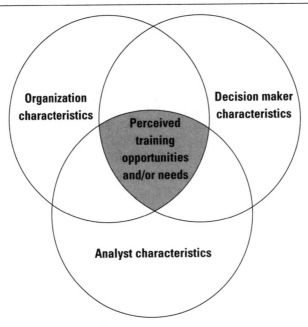

The PAT model's list of phases and steps in the process of analyzing performance needs is shown in Figure 2. The first phase, organizational analysis, focuses on determining where the training emphasis should be placed. Critically investigating the organization's performance needs, the causes of performance, and how performance needs should be addressed provides the basis for determining where training can be used as an effective strategy for improving performance. The second phase, work behavior analysis, focuses on identifying and documenting the specific behaviors needed to accomplish the work. The third phase, analysis of individual capabilities, focuses on determining which employees need training and the kind of training they need. Each phase of the process involves negotiation and discussion between the analyst and the decision makers. Thus, the process and output of each phase are influenced by the characteristics of the three elements in the conceptual framework: the organization, the decision makers, and the analyst.

The PAT model's worksheets detail specific activities to be completed during each phase and step of performance analysis for training. (See Figure 3 for an example of the worksheets.) Besides guiding the

Figure 2. Phases and steps of the performance-analysis-for-training (PAT) model.

Phase 1. Organizational analysis

Determine where in the organization or work group the training emphasis should be placed. The steps in this phase are as follows:

1. Identify perceived opportunities.
2. Determine the purpose and the parameters of the analysis.
3. Gather information about potential training opportunities and needs.
4. Gather anecdotal information.
5. Analyze information.
6. Report the findings to decision makers.
7. Decision makers acknowledge, prioritize, and determine the training opportunities and needs.

Phase 2. Work behavior analysis

Identify and document the specific behaviors needed to accomplish the work. The steps in this phase are as follows:

1. Identify the work to be analyzed.
2. Construct a work behavior analysis plan.
3. Conduct the work behavior analysis.
4. Gather anecdotal information.

Phase 3. Analysis of individual capabilities

Determine which employees need training and the kind of training they need. The steps in this phase are as follows:

1. Identify characteristics and capabilities of the group trainees.
2. Gather anecdotal information.
3. Gather information about nontraining causes of performance.
4. Synthesize and analyze information.
5. Report the findings to decision makers.
6. Communicate the findings and anecdotes to the people who will design the training.

---

needs assessment process, the worksheets serve to organize the information that is gathered throughout and to highlight key information. Together, the PAT model's three components provide an integrated, organized description of performance analysis for training.

Issues and Events

The decision makers and the consulting team agreed to work together to assess the SCU's future performance needs for technical workers. They also agreed to use the PAT model in accomplishing this task and to

Figure 3. PAT worksheet for Phase 1, Step 1.

Phase 1. Organizational analysis

Determine where in the organization or work group the training emphasis should be placed.

Step 1. Identify perceived opportunities.

This step occurs during the initial interviews between the analyst and the client. It is part of the discovery or sales process between the analyst and the client. Note that the information gathered in this step can be misleading because people at different places in the organization can have different perceptions of the opportunities and needs.

● Identify the perceived opportunities and the individuals who view them as important.

Perceived opportunities	Perceived by
_____	_____
_____	_____
_____	_____
_____	_____

● What is the product of the organization or work group? _____
_____

● Who is the client? _____
_____

● Analyze the information that has been gathered up to this point. _____

● Which of the perceived opportunities are related to the organization's bottom line? _____
_____

● Analyze the information that has been gathered up to this point. _____

● How are the perceived opportunities related to the bottom line? _____
_____

● Do the perceived opportunities seem to have a knowledge, skill, or attitude component that can be addressed with training? ☐ yes ☐ no

use the PAT worksheets to guide the implementation process. The following sections provide an overview of each phase in the assessment.

Phase 1: Organizational Analysis

The steps in this phase include identifying perceived opportunities, determining the purpose and parameters of the analysis, gathering information about potential training opportunities and needs, gathering anecdotal information, analyzing information, and reporting the findings to the decision makers. The final step is for the decision makers to acknowledge, prioritize, and determine the training opportunities and needs.

PROCESS. To begin this phase, the project director met with the manager of human resources and the plant manager. The project director presented an overview of the phases and steps of the PAT process (Figure 2) and of the worksheets for Phase 1. She also identified four possible methods for gathering the information that was needed to complete the worksheets: interview, observation, questionnaire, and review of written documents. The decision makers and the project director jointly decided to use observation, interview, and review of written documents. The SCU decision makers identified specific sources of information that they thought would be especially helpful to the consulting team and arranged to use plant publications and memos to inform SCU employees about the project.

Based on the decisions made during the planning meeting, members of the consulting team reviewed the following documents:
- publicly available information on the organization
- annual report
- job descriptions
- organization chart
- customer audits
- industry reports.

They also toured the facility, observed group meetings, and interviewed SCU employees, including 15 chemical operators, three group leaders, one supervisor, one clerk, two technicians, and eight engineers. The tour and the interviews provided background information about the organization and the people who worked there. This information included perceptions about the organization's systems, culture, politics, and rhetoric and information about the decision makers.

The consulting team used the PAT worksheets for documenting, synthesizing, and accessing the information systematically. These worksheets guided the team members as they analyzed problems and opportunities within the specific performance context. Team members individually filled in the worksheets for Phase 1 and then met to compare notes. This comparison produced many insights, as team members shared new information, revealed tacit assumptions, and clarified perceptions. The comparisons also revealed information that was missing and additional information that needed to be gathered to clear up inconsistencies.

The consulting team gathered additional information as needed to complete the worksheets, synthesized the information, and reported the results to SCU decision makers. The report identified the SCU's goals; knowledge, skills, and attitudes needed to achieve the goals; non-training issues that would affect the success of training; and potential future actions. The goals focused on the SCU's competitive position. The specific technical training needs that were identified included

- practical computer knowledge and skills
- knowledge and skills related to specific processes used in the SCU
- communication and teamwork.

The report described the following nontraining issues that could affect the technical training effort:

- Decision making, accountability for results, and rewards for performance were growing concerns.
- Operators did not always work as part of the team.
- Some manuals were not easy to read, and some work specifications were not current.
- Some employees expressed concern about how training would be implemented.

The report also identified potential future actions. One such action was to analyze which jobs and processes were expected to change significantly and to identify which changes represented the greatest risk to the SCU's future. Another potential future action was to consider how implementing chemical operation certification in the future would affect needs for technical knowledge, skills, and attitudes.

RESULTS. The decision makers approved the report. They also agreed on the performance opportunities and needs for which training resources should be allocated. Specifically, they decided that the next phase of the performance analysis for training would identify and document the knowledge, skills, and attitudes needed for chemical operation certification. This decision was based on the decision makers' perceptions that chemical operation certification was probably at hand and would have a significant impact on the SCU.

Phase 2: Work Behavior Analysis

The steps in this phase include identifying the work to be analyzed, constructing a plan for the work behavior analysis, conducting the analysis, and gathering anecdotal information.

PROCESS. In this case, the decision makers had already identified the work to be analyzed: the specific behaviors expected for chemical operation certification and the knowledge, skills, and attitudes needed to accomplish these behaviors. Therefore, the next step in this phase was to construct a plan for the work behavior analysis.

The work behavior analysis plan identifies the method (or methods) that will be used for analyzing the work. Because this project focused on chemical operation certification (which consists of complex, non-observable work behavior), the analyst chose subject matter analysis—as described by Swanson and Gradous (Swanson, 1994; Swanson and Gradous, 1986)—to document the specific work behaviors. Using this method involved gathering information on the topic of chemical operation certification from the literature and from experts. The reviewed literature consisted of articles, books, SCU publications, government documents, and association reports. Interviews were conducted with customers, government policymakers, leaders of the chemical manufacturers association, and individuals knowledgeable on this topic within the SCU and other chemical organizations. During the interviews, both factual and anecdotal information was gathered.

The subject matter analysis resulted in an organized report that included a table of current job responsibilities for specific SCU job titles and a table that showed the knowledge, skills, and attitudes that specific authors and industry sources predicted would be required for chemical operation certification. The information that had been gathered and organized was reported to the SCU decision makers.

RESULTS. After reviewing the tables and the report for Phase 2, the SCU decision makers had new insights about chemical operation certification and about how specific SCU jobs and job responsibilities would be affected by the certification. After asking questions of clarification and discussing implications for the SCU, they agreed that the information gathered during the first two phases of the project would provide the basis for implementing the PAT model's next phase.

Phase 3: Analysis of Individual Capabilities

The steps in this phase were identifying characteristics and capabilities of the trainees, gathering anecdotal information, gathering information about nontraining causes of performance, synthesizing and analyzing the information gathered, reporting the findings to the decision makers, and communicating the findings to the designers of the training.

PROCESS. There are several ways of identifying individual capabilities. The SCU decision makers and the consultant team chose to survey employees because each employee is a good source of information about the knowledge and skills that he or she needs. Furthermore, answering survey items can help employees realize that their jobs may change in the future and that each employee has some responsibility to prepare for the changes.

The consulting team developed the Technical Training Needs Assessment Survey. This survey incorporated information gathered during the first two phases of the project. The two-page survey included forced-choice items related to the employee's job and work shift, expected job changes, and the specific knowledge and skills needed in the future to perform the work. The survey also contained items on preferences for training delivery. The survey directions stated that information on individual surveys would be confidential and that only grouped data would be reported.

While pilot-testing the instrument, members of the consulting team interviewed employees to gather anecdotes, examples of positive and negative experiences, and information about the nontraining causes of performance. The team revised the survey instrument to include suggested changes. They also compared the information gathered in this phase with information that had been gathered during the first and second phases of the project.

The consultant team administered the survey over a two-day period to all 106 SCU technical workers. The completed surveys were analyzed using a computerized statistical package. Points were assigned to each descriptor: strongly disagree = 1, disagree = 2, agree = 3, and strongly agree = 4. Analysis of the survey data was limited to grouped data.

One survey finding was that employees expected changes to occur in their jobs over the next five years. Further, the findings showed a relationship between perceived future job changes and perceived training needs. Another finding was that employees with different job titles identified different knowledge and skills as having the highest priority. The top priorities for specific groups of employees were as follows:

- operators: key information into the computer
- group leaders: interpret computer data
- engineers: understand Material Requirement Planning (MRP) II
- technicians: know Occupational Safety and Health Act requirements
- clerks: use the computer and MRP II
- supervisors: record data, interpret statistical process control, and use statistical techniques
- managers: understand MRP II and interpret MRP II information.

The analysis of survey data also revealed knowledge and skill needs common to multiple job titles. The training needs common to more than three job titles included learning

- how to key information into the computer
- how to interpret computer data
- what the emergency chemical-handling procedures are
- what MRP II includes and how to input information into it
- how to interpret information from MRP II.

PAT worksheets for Phase 3 guided the analysis, and team members reviewed their filled-in worksheets when writing the report for this phase.

RESULTS. SCU decision makers expressed surprise about employees' perceptions of future job changes and their needs for new knowledge and skills. The decision makers were surprised to note the different learning needs within and across job titles.

They decided that providing the training as identified in the survey results would address future performance problems. They also noted that the PAT survey suggested to employees that job duties would be changing in the future. The decision makers discussed the importance of accurately communicating their specific perceptions about future job changes to employees and decided to work with the chemical operators in implementing the training.

Conclusions

Each phase in the PAT model provided specific information useful in making training decisions. Phase 1 provided information that could be used to verify the organization's strategic goals, to identify training and nontraining performance needs, and to identify potential solutions.

Phase 2 provided information useful in making decisions about implementing chemical operation certification. It also provided information about the specific work that chemical operators would do in the future and the specific knowledge, skills, and attitudes that would be needed.

Phase 3 provided information useful for targeting training to employees within specific job titles and for targeting training to meet knowledge and skill needs that were common across job titles. Phase 3 also provided the employees who completed the survey with information about future job changes.

Each component of the PAT model proved useful. The conceptual framework provided the consulting team with a perception of performance analysis as a process of negotiating and prioritizing needs, rather than as a process of looking for the "right" answer. The PAT model's phases and steps outlined a systematic process for analyzing performance needs. The PAT worksheets served as a tool for guiding the efforts of team members, organizing the information that was gathered, and comparing perceptions of team members.

Successfully implementing the PAT model required partnership between the decision makers and the consulting team. The process provided decision makers with an opportunity to scope out a future challenge, to build consensus among themselves, and to plan specific training and nontraining changes. Further, it provided a foundation for making decisions about technical training and the specific knowledge, skills, and attitudes that technical workers needed to meet the company's future performance goals.

A key outcome of the project was that the decision makers and technical workers had new, shared insights about how they could be stronger links in the SCU's performance chain.

An unexpected project outcome was that the project director was approached six months later by a conglomerate decision maker who had heard about the project. He wanted to know if she would consider implementing similar projects simultaneously in 50 plants located throughout the world.

Questions for Discussion

1. How did characteristics of the organization, decision makers, and analyst interact to influence the assessment process and product?

2. What would be the challenges in implementing performance-analysis-for-training projects simultaneously in 50 plants located throughout the world?

The Author

Catherine M. Sleezer is an assistant professor at Oklahoma State University. Sleezer's research and consulting interests include needs assessment, employee training, organization development, and economic evaluation of investments in human resource development. Sleezer has authored and coauthored articles on various topics in the field, including performance analysis for training, and evaluating and managing human resource programs. She is the editor of the theory-to-practice monograph titled *Improving Human Resource Development Through Measurement* (American Society for Training and Development, 1989). Sleezer can be contacted at the following address: Oklahoma State University, 413 Classroom Building, Stillwater, OK 74076.

References

Sleezer, C.M. (1990). *The development and validation of a performance analysis for training model* (Project No. 39). St. Paul: University of Minnesota, Training and Development Research Center.

Sleezer, C.M. (1993a). Training needs assessment at work: A dynamic process. *Human Resource Development Quarterly, 4,* 247-264.

Sleezer, C.M. (1993b). Tried and true performance analysis. *Training and Development, 47*(11), 52-54.

Swanson, R.A. (1994). *Analysis for improving performance: Tools for diagnosing organizations and documenting workplace expertise.* San Francisco: Berrett-Koehler.

Swanson, R.A., and Gradous, D. (1986). *Performance at work: A systematic program for analyzing work behavior.* New York: Wiley.

Assessing the Need for an Electronic Performance Support System

Kraft General Foods

Michael Venn, Barry Raybould, and Nicholas Bridges

This case is unique in that it describes a needs assessment for an electronic performance support system. In addition to the common assessment methods of steering committee, observation, and focus groups, this process included developing a conceptual demonstration of the technology to communicate the recommended intervention to decision makers.

Overview

This case describes a needs assessment for an electronic performance support system (EPSS) to support both the customer service function of Kraft General Foods (KGF) and the use of KGF information systems by customer service coordinators (CSCs). An EPSS is a computer-based tool designed to help people perform their jobs better. It is expected to improve human performance by providing the performer with integrated on-line information, advice, and learning experiences at the moment of need.

The needs assessment for the EPSS described in this case differs from traditional needs assessments in two important ways. Part of the purpose of a needs assessment is to communicate a proposed intervention in sufficient detail to help the decision makers in an organization determine if the intervention should be implemented. Because of the newness of EPSSs, most people do not understand the concept of an EPSS well enough to make a decision to build an EPSS based on a written description. Therefore, some type of interactive electronic

This case was prepared to serve as a basis for discussion rather than to illustrate either effective or ineffective administrative and management practices.

representation of the EPSS must be designed and developed as part of the needs assessment to communicate the recommended intervention to decision makers. This interactive electronic representation of a high-level EPSS design is referred to as a conceptual demonstration.

A second difference from traditional needs assessment involves selecting the sample size to be studied for the assessment. To determine what needs the EPSS should meet, one studies the errors commonly made when using the information system. The EPSS is then designed to support the system user in avoiding these performance errors. Far fewer subjects are needed to determine the usability weaknesses of an information system than to determine performance difficulties using traditional assessment techniques.

Background

Not only is the customer service function critical to the success of KGF, but it is a complicated job involving interaction with many internal and external personnel and customers. On a daily basis, CSCs use as many as seven different information systems. Additionally, the customer service function plays a key role in KGF's ability to respond swiftly to a rapidly changing business environment.

At the start of the needs assessment, there were plans for the computer systems used by the CSCs to be changing continuously over the next several years. Already, 600 pages of documentation on the systems existed, and this number was increasing monthly as new features were added to the systems.

The nature of the customer service function was also undergoing tremendous change. The role of the CSC had just been redefined in an attempt to standardize a new way of providing superior customer service. At the beginning of this assessment, training for the new CSC duties had already begun. Training took a total of 24 hours, although an increase to 28 hours had been recommended. The cost to train a single CSC was more than $5,300. The training covered roughly one-third of the tasks performed in this role. KGF management estimated that it took approximately six months for a CSC to become 80 percent competent.

Eventually, there were to be approximately 275 CSCs located in five regional customer service centers in the United States. Because the training effort had only begun, and the role of the CSC was still evolving, there were not many CSCs who had the content expertise to advise us on the CSC's role and needs. For the purpose of this assessment, we relied on the content expertise of three CSCs, a fourth CSC who had training responsibilities, and a CSC supervisor. KGF management felt these content experts would be able to adequately describe the new standardized CSC function and the needs of CSCs.

Purpose

KGF management was interested in pursuing an electronic way to maintain the documentation on how to use the computer systems, to distribute the most current documentation efficiently, and to support the performance of experienced CSCs through expert advice on how to do their jobs and through training in changes to their jobs. Management was advised by the training manager that an EPSS held much potential to accomplish these stated goals. They agreed to undertake a needs assessment for an EPSS to support the customer service function of KGF and the use of KGF information systems by CSCs.

Methodology

The method used to determine if a need for an EPSS existed was to identify and validate CSC and business goals and needs. Once a need was established, it was necessary to develop a conceptual demonstration to communicate the proposed intervention to KGF management.

Needs Assessment Team

A core needs assessment team consisted of an expert in the field of EPSSs, a training expert familiar with KGF, and two CSCs. A steering committee was formed to keep the needs assessment team apprised of the most current KGF business goals. The steering committee consisted of the vice-president in charge of the customer service function, the vice-president in charge of information systems development, a regional manager of the customer service function, the training manager for the customer service function, a member of the training staff who had extensive experience training customer service personnel, and a training manager expert in the field of measurement and evaluation.

Identifying and Validating Goals and Needs

To begin the needs assessment, the core needs assessment team and the KGF training manager participated in two days of meetings and observations. One and one-half days were spent in informal discussions and presentations with the steering committee, representatives from KGF's information systems department, members of the training staff, and CSCs.

The time spent with the steering committee was used to identify the business goals of KGF and the committee's perception of the kinds of problems the needs assessment was intended to solve. The members of the training staff described the nature of the current training and documentation, their insights into the need for a less traditional training and documentation intervention, their perceptions of the effectiveness of current training and documentation, their impressions of the performance difficulties that prevented CSCs from becoming proficient in less than six months, and their hopes for what an EPSS could accomplish.

The information systems representatives described the current information systems environment and the future direction of KGF information systems, along with requirements they had for any EPSS to be integrated with their information systems. The CSCs described the major tasks they performed, with whom they typically had contact, the main frustrations of their jobs, tasks that were error prone, and what their goals for an EPSS were.

To further define the needs of the CSCs and which tasks were error prone, the final half day was spent observing three working CSCs, and interviewing one CSC with training responsibilities and one CSC supervisor. Thus, including the two CSCs on the core needs assessment team, a total of seven CSCs were either interviewed or observed. Traditional needs assessment models would require a survey of a large, statistically significant sample of the population of 275 CSCs to determine the difficulty, frequency, and importance of individual tasks in the information system. Much smaller numbers are needed to study the usability of the information system, however. Nielsen and Molich (1990) indicated that almost half of all major usability problems can be detected with three participants. Virzi (1992) stated that 80 percent of usability problems can be detected with four to five participants, and all of the problems common to most users can be detected with 10 participants. Given that few of the CSCs trained to date had been on the job long enough to be considered experienced, and our sample included a trainer of CSCs and a CSC supervisor, both of whom had insights into the errors of other CSCs, our sample of seven CSCs was deemed adequate to determine CSCs' needs.

One result of identifying these needs was a listing of the most error-prone tasks for CSCs. The EPSS would be designed to support the CSCs in accomplishing these tasks accurately. The core needs assessment team broke down each error-prone task according to the root problem and the problems caused by the root problem. To tie the CSCs' needs to the business goals, these errors were mapped back to business goals that were negatively affected by the poor performance. The

Figure 1. Mapping an error-prone task to business goals.

Root problem: Customer service coordinator doesn't know how to make an adjustment.

CSC: ☑ Proficient ☑ Entry level

Problem		Goal
Customer doesn't get correct amount of product	▶	Provide superior customer service
⬆		
Warehouse has inaccurate inventory	▶	Maintain or increase profitability Provide efficient consumer response
⬆		
Credit department fixes adjustment, at a cost of $50	▶	Provide superior customer service Maintain or increase profitability
⬆		
CSC makes wrong adjustment	▶	Provide superior customer service
⬆		
CSC doesn't know how to make an adjustment		

mapping also indicated if an error was common among proficient CSCs, or entry-level, or both. (The desire was to address the needs of proficient CSCs.) Figure 1 shows an example of one of these mappings.

A focus group was held with two CSCs, a CSC supervisor, and a CSC with training responsibilities to validate this list of tasks and ensure that poor performance of the tasks would have a significant effect on the daily work of CSCs. Members of the steering committee were interviewed to validate that the problems were mapped to the business goals correctly and that poor performance of the tasks would have a significant negative impact on one or more business goals. The mappings were revised based on the comments received.

It was not necessary to validate the goals of the training department, as these goals were the views of the training manager, who was on the steering committee and therefore already involved in the process. It was not necessary to validate the future direction of KGF information systems, as this was a vision held commonly by the steering committee.

Developing the Conceptual Demonstration

With the goals and needs identified, it was necessary to develop a conceptual demonstration to communicate the results of the assessment to KGF management. This was done by gathering content, designing the EPSS and concurrently selecting software development tools that could support the design, and then evaluating the design for adherence to the identified goals and needs.

GATHERING CONTENT. Content was gathered by interviewing four subject matter experts who had expertise in the new standardized way of performing the customer service function. This group of subject matter experts included three experienced CSCs and a trainer of the CSCs. At this point, it was not essential to gather detailed content. However, content had to be defined well enough to determine how to design the EPSS to present the content appropriately.

DESIGNING THE EPSS CONCEPTUAL DEMONSTRATION. The conceptual demonstration is a nonworking representation of the EPSS screens and screen flows that show how the EPSS will eventually work. This demonstration presents the design of an EPSS in a tangible format to allow people to evaluate the design.

The conceptual demonstration was developed in ToolBook, a software program that allows one to create graphical screens and link them to other screens easily. This program made it possible to create the appearance of a working EPSS with minimal effort.

Designing the EPSS conceptual demonstration and selecting appropriate software that would be used ultimately to develop the EPSS was an iterative process. A high-level design of the EPSS was created based on the appropriate content and the current and future information systems environments. Software development tools that could support the initial design were investigated. A more detailed design of the EPSS was then created in a paper-based format. Again, software development tools that could support the design were investigated. CSC representatives were involved in design discussions and decisions throughout this process. Once the design was fairly stable, development of the conceptual demonstration in ToolBook was begun.

EVALUATING THE EPSS DESIGN. The conceptual demonstration was shown to two CSC representatives to determine if the EPSS met the needs of the new standardized CSC function. The conceptual demonstration was modified based on the CSCs' comments and then shown to the training manager to determine if the EPSS met the goals of the training department. No changes were made as a result of meeting with the training manager. An additional meeting allowed the steering committee to decide if the EPSS met business goals and needs. Finally, a meeting was held with representatives of the KGF information systems department to determine if the design of the EPSS could be implemented in the current information systems environment and be easily adapted to any future information systems environment.

Results

GOALS AND NEEDS. The business goals were identified as providing superior customer service, responding to consumers efficiently, producing error-free invoices, shipping orders complete and on time, and maintaining or increasing profitability. The meetings held with the CSCs and CSC supervisor identified that the key CSC needs for the EPSS were that it have a fast response time and be usable without interrupting the task in progress. The important goals of the training department were the abilities to update the training and documentation materials more efficiently, enable the CSCs to access information more quickly, and reduce the amount of paper documentation. Additionally, the initial meetings identified nine major error-prone tasks, each broken down into its root problem and the problems caused by the root problem, and then mapped back to the business goals. During the validation process, one of these tasks was eliminated because of insignificant negative impact on the business goals.

EPSS Conceptual Demonstration Development

EPSS CONTENT. As content was gathered, the team kept track of the recommended content of each EPSS module, how and when that content would need to change, and how each EPSS component would affect business. This content is not described here because it was specific to how KGF does business.

When the EPSS was designed, some content was excluded because it would have been impossible to support in the current KGF information systems environment. Other content was excluded from the EPSS for the following reasons:

- The content did not support a significant activity or problem.
- An EPSS was not an appropriate solution. (For instance, it is better to rewrite confusing system error messages than to create a help screen to explain them.)
- The content to support the problem was currently readily available.

INFORMATION SYSTEMS TRANSITION. Information systems for the customer service function at the time of this assessment ran on mainframe and AS/400 computers with a text-based user interface. The focus for the future was to move to a client/server environment in which information would be integrated and accessed by users through a graphical user interface (GUI). Therefore, an EPSS had to work in the current text-based environment, but be usable when KGF information systems moved to a graphical-based, client/server environment. It was important that the EPSS would not have to be redesigned or redeveloped once the transition occurred.

The future information systems strategy involved a transition from text-only screens linked to separate software applications, to a GUI in a client/server environment that would integrate data from multiple data bases into a single application. Therefore, the structure of the EPSS would have to change over time from linked modules to a performance support interface. In the linked-module approach, the EPSS is a series of modules that are linked to the software application. Each module may vary in size from a single help screen to an on-line manual or to a complete computer-based training lesson. Modules are accessed from a small program that is kept by the CSC as an open application. This program, called a launchpad, contains sufficient help to guide the CSC to the most appropriate EPSS module.

In a performance support interface, EPSS elements are incorporated into the design of the application software interface or consist of modules that are accessed directly from the software application. Links from the software application to appropriate EPSS modules are context sensitive.

EPSS MODULES. This section discusses the recommended EPSS modules. Technology requirements are identified for each type of module, as follows:

- *How Do I* provides step-by-step instructions on how to complete all the tasks in the application. These procedures are cross-referenced, using hypertext, to related procedures. The suggested technology was a hypertext engine.
- *Where Is* is an advisor that gives step-by-step advice on how to find information in the various computer systems used by the CSC. The advisor may refer to a knowledge base to provide this advice. The recommended technology was a hypertext engine or decision-tree-based expert system shell.
- *Who Do I Call* provides information on whom to call for a specific situation or responsibility. It is a data-retrieval module that finds information from a structured data base. A flat file structure may be adequate for the contact information, or a relational data base may be needed.

- *What Is* provides descriptive information on terms CSCs may encounter on the job or key concepts they must understand to perform the job. These terms are connected to a consistent web of related terms and definitions. The recommended technology was a hypertext engine.
- *Overview* consists of descriptions of key concepts and processes. A conceptual presentation provides a definition of a concept and a series of examples that illustrate items that fall either within or outside the definition of the concept. A process presentation describes a series of events that occur over time, and consists of a series of procedures performed by different people. Computer-based-training authoring software capable of displaying text, graphics, animation, video, and sound was the recommended technology.
- *Notepad* lets the CSC provide feedback to the EPSS data base administrator. This feature is critical to the design of the EPSS because of the constant evolution of the information systems the EPSS is designed to support. The job performer can ask questions not answered by the EPSS, report problems with the system performance, or report errors and inconsistencies in the content of the EPSS. If appropriate, changes are made to this knowledge base and distributed to all job performers. The suggested technology was electronic mail or more sophisticated groupware software.
- *News* lets the systems development group or the EPSS maintenance group communicate information to the EPSS users. For example, it provides information on what is new in the system, what is about to change, and how the change will affect the user. Electronic mail or more sophisticated groupware software was the suggested technology.

Figure 2 shows an example of how the computer screen would look with an application and the *How Do I* EPSS running concurrently. The application screen is on the left, the EPSS window on the right, and the EPSS launchpad below. This design allows users to view EPSS procedures and information while using the application, letting them work without interrupting the task at hand. When it is not necessary to view the application and EPSS at the same time, the application or the EPSS can be run full screen.

Conclusions

The EPSS conceptual demonstration was presented to the training manager, the steering committee, and the KGF information systems department for evaluation. All three meetings were successful, and it was decided to proceed with the development and implementation of the EPSS as presented.

Figure 2. Example of electronic performance support system and application running concurrently.

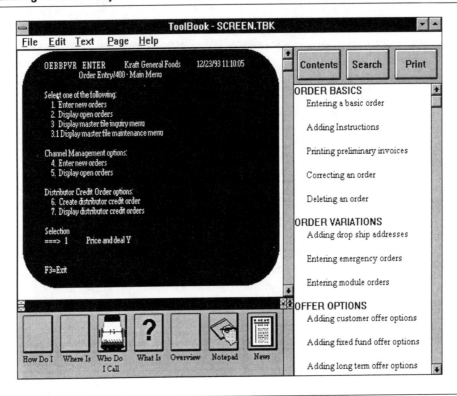

Through the implementation of an EPSS, the following benefits were anticipated: on-demand training and performance support, low-cost delivery of information, immediate access to current information, consistent structure of information, decrease in CSC errors, increase in CSC productivity, time savings resulting from getting answers from the EPSS rather than having to go to a colleague or supervisor, and reduction in formal and informal training.

Questions for Discussion

1. When developing ideas for the EPSS, how did the analysts ensure that the potential components met real business needs?

2. How was the project team set up to ensure that the real needs of the CSCs were addressed?

3. What are the differences in methodology between assessing the need for an EPSS and assessing the need for more traditional interventions?

4. What is an appropriate sample size for gathering information on the usability of an information system?

5. At what point of the assessment were technology issues addressed? Why?

The Authors

Michael Venn has spent 14 years teaching, designing instruction, and consulting in the training and education field. He has developed interfaces for information systems and on-line reference systems for several Fortune 500 companies. He has presented workshops, written articles, and developed courses on interface design, including the design of interfaces for computer-based training and on-line reference systems. Venn is an education manager with Arthur Andersen & Co, SC, and can be contacted at the following address: 1405 N. 5th Avenue, St. Charles, IL 60174.

Barry Raybould is the president of Ariel PSS Corporation of Mountain View, California, and has worked with many Fortune 500 corporations to help them develop their EPSS strategies. Raybould has written many articles on EPSSs in industry and professional journals, and is a frequent presenter at national conferences on EPSSs and technology-based training. He has designed and developed several award-winning performance support systems and is the editor of the annual *International Directory of Performance Support Authoring Systems* (Ariel PSS Corporation). He is author of a series of special reports on performance support system technologies and creator of the PSE (performance support engineering) methodology.

Nicholas Bridges is a training manager for Kraft General Foods, Northfield, Illinois.

References

Nielsen, J., and Molich, R. (1990). Heuristic evaluation of user interfaces. In *Empowering people: Proceedings of the ACM CHI'90* (pp. 249-256). New York: ACM Press.

Virzi, R. (1992). Refining the test phase of usability evaluation: How many subjects is enough? *Human Factors, 34,* 457-468.

A Quality Systems Needs Assessment

Formations in Metal Inc.

Russ Westcott

This case involved walk-through and one-on-one interviews to determine needs for a quality management system. Questions derived from both the ISO 9000 Series Standards and the Malcolm Baldrige National Quality Award literature were used in the assessment.

Background

This case discusses the examination of an organization's quality management system that used both the ISO 9000 Series Standards and the Malcolm Baldrige National Quality Award criteria. (The ISO 9000 Series includes the ISO 9001 standards that FIMI set as its goal.) The assessment results have formed the basis for continuous improvement. The initial assessment of an organization's system usually uncovers needs to improve leadership, the management of process quality, human resource development and management, strategic quality planning, information and analysis, customer focus and satisfaction, and quality and operational results. Such an assessment also compares what management says the organization does with what is actually done, as well as analyzing the extent to which the organization's mission, vision, values, and goals have been deployed throughout the organization.

At Formations in Metal Inc. (FIMI), a family-owned and -operated company, management was increasingly aware of significant changes occurring in their industry. As a job shop operation fabricating metal

This case was prepared to serve as a basis for discussion rather than to illustrate either effective or ineffective administrative and management practices. All names, dates, places, and organizations have been disguised at the request of the organization involved or the case author.

products in relatively small lots to customers' specifications, FIMI was accustomed to chaotic schedules, customer-demanded changes, a highly competitive marketplace, and a shortage of trained help. FIMI not only survived the Northeast's severe recession, but thrived. Rightfully, management concluded that they must be doing many things right.

Attention to customers' requirements had always been a mainstay of FIMI, and a primary reason for their success despite the overall business downturn. Finished products were of high quality. FIMI's management system had been effective, mostly because of the hands-on attention of the owners.

FIMI's management and workforce were maturing. More and more customers had indicated that future business would depend on assuring them that FIMI had a registered quality system in place (as defined by the ISO 9000 standards). Initially, FIMI management saw this development as a new threat to the company's growth and prosperity.

Organizational Profile

Since 1959, FIMI had built a reputation as a high-quality provider of fabricated metal products and established itself as the job shop of choice, with an increasing number of customers in the Northeast. With 65 employees running two shifts, and with managers wearing several hats, FIMI performed a daily act of juggling scheduling and production of hundreds of orders for a myriad of different-sized parts, made from dozens of different types of metal, finished in a variety of paints and textures. The "top-priority" label was prevalent throughout the plant.

The FIMI organizational structure was simple. The father divided his time among serving as president, selling to selected customers, and shepherding critical projects through the plant. The mother served as the financial and public relations officer. The daughter rotated through managing the various departments, learning the intricacies of each in preparation for ultimately taking over the company. The son-in-law, FIMI's former plant manager, now served as an outside salesperson. Other management and nonproduction personnel included a purchasing agent, inside salespeople (who provided price and delivery quotations and entered orders), an engineering and production planning group, a general manager of the plant, department supervisors, and a quality assurance specialist (for inspection and tool calibration). The production functions were cutting sheet metal, drilling and forming parts, assembling components, painting and finishing, and shipping and delivery. The roles and responsibilities appeared blurred to an outsider because all managers and many other employees assumed multiple roles.

Output measurements included number of orders received, number of products made and shipped, and profits. Financial results were not published.

Recent innovations had included the following:

- The networked computer system that built the customer data base now generated the paperwork that guided FIMI's multitude of jobs from quotations to customers through order entry, design, production routing, and finally shipping and delivery.
- A new laser sheet-metal cutting machine had greatly improved accuracy and quality and reduced waste.
- The new painting and finishing technology that was being tested would, when adopted, reduce the floor space needed for painting by more than 50 percent, and allow for much needed expansion of other functions.

Character Profiles

Ronald Caldwell, 63, was chief executive officer and president. He and his wife built the company from their garage. Since moving to its present location, a small town in rural New England, FIMI had expanded its building three times, and more space was needed.

Ron understood his business processes and capabilities completely; he knew his customers needed fast delivery of a staggering variety of small orders for a variety of different products. He had shaped FIMI to be highly responsive to the volatile marketplace. Ron spent at least one day each week on the plant floor following critical jobs and checking everything. He cherished FIMI's well-deserved reputation.

Like most business owners, Ron could clearly comprehend the return on investment for a new piece of processing equipment, but he was much more cautious about investments in the softer side of the business. For example, he was less certain about the wisdom of buying the new computer system than about buying the considerably more expensive laser cutting equipment. Despite a traumatic conversion to the computer system, however, he was glad he had agreed to modernize. Ron admitted to not knowing much about how the new system worked, leaving that up to his daughter.

It took a year and much persuasion from his daughter and wife before Ron agreed to take the journey toward the most comprehensive ISO standard, ISO 9001. However, he acknowledged that customers were beginning to talk about future business depending on whether or not suppliers, such as FIMI, were ISO 9000 registered. The problem was not that Ron was against improving quality. He already ran a high-quality operation. But FIMI depended on relationships and individuals' skills and memory, whereas ISO 9001 requires documented systems and documented management reviews, internal audits, and a corrective action system. Reluctantly, Ron agreed to proceed.

Elaine Caldwell, 62, partner in life and in the business, served as FIMI's financial officer, office manager, and public relations person. It was Elaine who met with the Chamber of Commerce. Her picture was more likely than Ron's to appear in news articles about FIMI. Elaine provided the steady hand and mind that helped the business stay on course. Recently, when Ron became ill temporarily, Elaine and her daughter ran the operation for two months without a problem. When the quality initiative was first proposed a year ago, Elaine voted to move ahead. Now, with an even sharper focus on ISO 9000, Elaine was 100 percent in agreement to begin.

Lydia Treadwell, 36, university-educated daughter of Elaine and Ron, had been at FIMI full time for less than two years. She was on rotation, spending several months in each department of the business. Lydia was the resident guru for the new computer system and the management representative for the quality initiative. During Ron's illness, it was Lydia who moved the ISO 9000 planning forward so that only Ron's "OK" was required when he returned to work.

Issues and Events

Running a job shop business is not easy. Each day can reveal a potential disaster resulting from poor estimating, customer changes, fragile customer loyalty, equipment or people problems, or scheduling glitches. The job shop manufacturing business is not for the faint of heart.

Companies, like FIMI, that had not focused on military or space customers had not generally been required to meet military specifications. But FIMI's customers were getting registered to the ISO 9000 standards, and these customers were stating that future business might depend on FIMI's quality system also being registered.

With no business coming from overseas, FIMI had not been concerned with ISO 9000 and had totally ignored the Malcolm Baldrige National Quality Award criteria. Ron felt that pursuing either the ISO or the Baldrige criteria amounted to needlessly spending money that could go for expansion.

Then, almost overnight it seemed, there was a groundswell of companies rushing to bring their systems into compliance and seeking registration to one of three ISO 9000 standards. At the same time, the state in which FIMI is located initiated its version of the Baldrige award.

Clearly, to remain competitive, FIMI had to explore these options. Believing they already had in place a quality management system producing high-quality products, FIMI agreed that it was logical to assess the present system against the ISO 9000 standards and the Baldrige criteria.

Target Population for the Assessment

Sixteen top management, supervisory, and administrative personnel—25 percent of all employees—were interviewed in depth. Various other members of the workforce were asked brief questions about their work. Every aspect of the business except financial results was assessed. All management personnel, except the quality assurance person, had two or more years of experience with the company, and a few had been with FIMI since 1959.

Action Items

Three sales visits were needed to clarify FIMI's needs and to satisfy the owners that conducting an assessment would be cost-effective, that hiring an outside consulting firm was most appropriate and the consultant's proposal addressed the company's needs, and that the proposing consultant had the necessary experience and solid references. Concurrence of the three family owners was achieved a year from initial contact.

Planning and Scheduling

Using a custom-designed assessment instrument (structured interview questions), two consultants spent three days each with FIMI personnel gathering data. Two of the three days were spent assessing the company against the ISO 9001 standards. The final day focused on collecting additional data related only to the Baldrige criteria. After analyzing the data and preparing the formal report, the consultants met with management for two hours to present the assessment feedback, conclusions, and recommendations for action.

Conducting the Assessment

Auditing for compliance with an ISO 9000 standard means reviewing the quality system documentation for compliance with the chosen standard (usually done off site) and reviewing the actual quality processes being performed to see if they conform to the documentation. Virtually no documentation of the quality system existed at FIMI, so an audit could not be performed. Only an assessment of how the quality processes compared directly against the ISO standard made sense.

The assessment included the following steps:

- *Step 1.* Sixteen people, including the owners, other management, and staff, met for a two-hour awareness session covering an introduction to ISO 9000 and the Malcolm Baldrige National Quality Award. The consultants emphasized what meeting the ISO 9001 standard would mean to FIMI and its employees (i.e., business survival), briefly outlined the process they planned to take, and noted that the assessment was to uncover those areas that needed to be addressed in order for FIMI to comply with the standards and was not a performance review of the employees.

- *Step 2.* Escorted by Lydia, the consultants conducted a two-day, structured walk-through of the plant's processes, starting with a customer's first contact for a quotation and proceeding through order entry, purchase of materials, engineering, production scheduling, production, and shipping. Supervisors and workers at each step were interviewed briefly, using prepared questions derived from the ISO 9001 standard (see Table 1 for sample questions). Because of the standard's emphasis on measurement, the plant manager and quality assurance person were interviewed in depth.

  Also during these two days, the consultants
  — traced actual orders through the system
  — reviewed records and recordkeeping
  — reviewed document files and controls thereof
  — examined traceability (i.e., the ability to trace back from detection of a defect through all the previous steps and processes to the lot of raw material from which the part was ultimately formed so that one can identify other parts that may have originated from the same processes or the same material and segregate these parts for further inspection or recall them for rework or replacement)
  — observed purchasing practices, especially how vendors were selected
  — examined training practices and records
  — requested evidence of management reviews, internal audits, corrective action practices, document control, training procedures, and other management responsibilities required by the standard, and noted what was missing.

- *Step 3.* On the third day, the consultants met individually with each member of management for nearly an hour each. These structured interviews focused on collecting additional data for assessing FIMI against the Baldrige criteria (see Table 2 for sample questions).

Table 1. Sample questions used to assess compliance to the ISO 9001 standard.

- Is there a clearly defined, documented, and deployed quality policy?
- Are there documented procedures and records for periodic management review of the suitability and effectiveness of the quality system?
- Is there a quality manual defining responsibilities, authority, and accountability of functions and personnel affecting quality?
- How does the contract review system ensure that inconsistencies between customers' requirements and organizational capabilities are detected and resolved?
- Are there procedures established and maintained to control and verify the design of the product to ensure that customers' requirements are met?
- How do document controls ensure that obsolete documents are identified and removed from work areas?
- Is there a documented system for selecting suppliers that ensures that authorized suppliers can meet specified requirements?
- Are there procedures for product identification and traceability that ensure control of the identity of the product and its components during all phases of the process?
- Do the procedures provide in-process controls to ensure
  - verification of goods by inspection, test, or other method, in accordance with the quality plan or documented procedures?
  - product conformance through use of process monitoring and process controls?
  - product, or components thereof, pending verification, are subject to controlled urgent usage?
  - identification and segregation of nonconforming product at various vital in-process stages?
- Do calibration procedures ensure that the inspection, measuring, and test equipment is capable of the accuracy and precision necessary?
- Do records demonstrate effective operation of the quality system, including achievement of required quality levels?
- Are there procedures to establish, plan, schedule, initiate, conduct, and report results of internal quality audits?
- How does training cover requirements for requalification or recertification?
- Are there clearly defined procedures for the establishment and use of statistical process control techniques?

- *Step 4.* Toward the end of the third day, the consultants drafted their overall observations and presented an oral summary of their findings to the management group. Presentation of the formal assessment report was scheduled for two weeks later.
- *Step 5.* Off site, the consultants analyzed and categorized the data collected and summarized their observations, findings, and conclusions relative to each of the major elements of the ISO 9001

Table 2. Sample questions used to assess FIMI against the Baldrige Award criteria.

- How do senior executives demonstrate leadership, personal involvement, and visibility in goal setting, planning, reviewing quality performance, communicating with employees, and recognizing employee contributions?
- How does the organization evaluate and improve the scope and quality of its data, and how does it shorten the cycle from data gathering to access?
- How does the organization evaluate and improve the scope, sources, and use of benchmark and comparative data?
- How are strategic plans and goals implemented, evaluated, reviewed, and improved?
- How are key quality goals and improvement methods for human resource management practices identified?
- What practices and specific mechanisms, such as teams or suggestion systems, does the organization use to promote employee contributions to quality objectives?
- How does the organization assess needs for the types and amounts of quality education and training received by all categories of employees?
- How are designs of products, services, processes, and administrative procedures developed so that customers' requirements are translated into design requirements?
- How are overall product and service performance data analyzed, root causes determined, and results translated into process improvements?
- What approaches are used to define and communicate the organization's quality requirements to suppliers?
- How are quality assessment findings used to improve products or services, systems, processes, practices, and supplier requirements?
- How does the organization determine the most important factors and requirements in maintaining and building relationships with customers, and develop strategies and plans to address them?
- How are standards that define reliability, responsiveness, and effectiveness of employees' interactions with customers determined?
- How does the organization use comparisons of trends in customer satisfaction and in market share of customers to improve its customer service and satisfaction practices?

standard and the Baldrige criteria. A formal report was prepared. Excerpts are in Table 3.

- *Step 6.* The consultants conducted a two-hour feedback session with FIMI management to present the results and facilitate initial planning for ISO 9001 implementation. Subsequently, FIMI engaged the consultants to guide FIMI on the journey to ISO 9001 registration.

Table 3. Excerpts from the assessment report.

- Overall, the systems in place are effective in that the processes generally produce products that meet customers' requirements—except for timeliness of delivery. The major deficiency is a lack of quality system documentation.
- There was no evidence of formal management review or follow-up of quality results and trends.
- People seemed aware of their own and others' responsibilities. However, except for the production Traveler Sheet, no other procedural documentation exists.
- Estimating, order entry, and verification procedures appeared to be reasonably planned and understood by the people involved. However, procedures need to be documented. Also, in one observed order, the customer requirement (release quantity) was missed. The responsible people guessed that this may have been a change order not processed or that a confirming order was different from a verbal order. No formal procedure existed for documenting and following through the correction and future prevention of such an error.
- No evidence was found that quality considerations figured in the selection of acceptable vendors, nor are records kept to show why vendors remain acceptable.
- Traceability is difficult to maintain under present practices, especially if lots are divided when parts are sent for special services or when partial shipments are made.
- No evidence was presented that internal quality audits are done.
- A training plan is under development for key processes; however, it does not include adequate provision for requalification or records.

Models and Techniques

Instruments

Although the structured interview questions were prepared specifically for FIMI, the literature is replete with checklists and sample questions. The consultants used the prepared questions in walk-through and one-on-one interviews.

Respondents were not asked to fill out questionnaires. The questions served as a checklist to ensure that the consultants covered all the necessary elements and criteria. The questions were not always asked exactly as printed, nor in the sequence printed, and were frequently supplemented by follow-up questions to probe or clarify a respondent's reply.

Protocol

The consultants followed basic auditing protocol to the extent possible, but the interviews were less formal and followed a discussion format more than is typical in a traditional audit. In the interviews, the consultants refrained from providing suggestions for improvement or critiquing the processes employed. The objective of walking through a typical order-processing cycle was to observe the process in use, record data, and not be judgmental. The overall objective of the assessment was to pinpoint the areas in which FIMI did not meet, or did not adequately meet, the ISO 9001 standard and the Baldrige criteria.

Data Collection

Both consultants took notes during the walk-through and the individual interviews with management. Responses were collected for each of the questions on the checklists. Interviewees' additional comments were noted as they occurred in the discussions. Toward the end of the third day, the consultants quickly reviewed their observations, extracted the key findings, and reported these orally to management. Off site, the consultants later rewrote, combined, and compressed all observations and notes, recording them against the appropriate questions, and prepared the formal report of findings and conclusions. Finally, the consultants returned to FIMI to present the report to management and solicit feedback.

Although some assessments and audits employ a rating scale, this approach was deemed inappropriate for FIMI. FIMI either did or did not comply with the standard.

Method of Delivery

The road map in Figure 1 shows the principal steps needed for FIMI to achieve registration to ISO 9001. The plan recognized four key factors, which could also apply to other small companies:

- No company time was available for extensive formal classroom training.
- No knowledge or time was available to struggle through the initial documentation of the quality system.
- No person could be allocated exclusively to the implementation process.
- Funding of the implementation would have to be spread over 20 months.

Accordingly, the consultants were retained for three consultant-days per month to facilitate steering committee meetings, prepare the initial drafts of documentation, and provide guidance in following the steps toward registration. Monthly billing spread the financial burden. Management and workers received just-in-time, on-the-job training from the consultants as the documentation progressed. The consultants assisted in selecting a registrar, developing FIMI's internal auditors, and

Figure 1. Road map for the ISO 9001 trip (estimated time of arrival: 20 months from now).

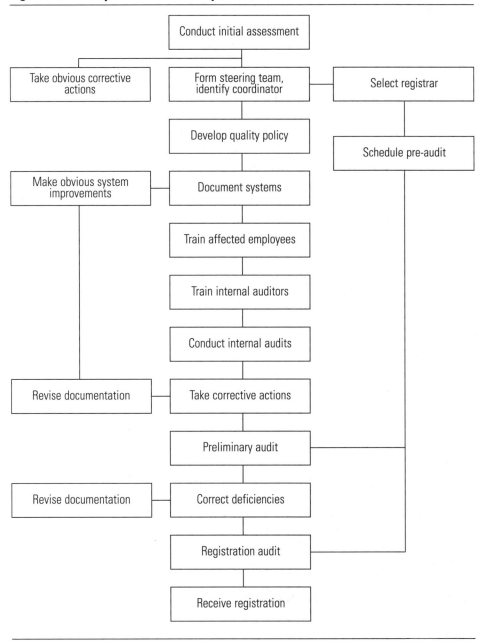

prepping FIMI for the registrar's pre-audit and final audit. Over time, FIMI personnel gradually absorbed complete responsibility for revising, printing, and controlling the official FIMI Quality Manual and Quality Procedures, as well as for training operators in accordance with the documented procedures.

Costs and Benefits of the Initial Assessment

The immediate benefit of choosing qualified consultants to conduct an assessment rather than choosing an ISO registrar's team to conduct an audit was that FIMI saved at least $5,000. Moreover, because FIMI did not have a documented system, a full audit would have been a waste. Finally, FIMI needed to know quickly about any deficiencies and the estimated cost to comply, and the consultants were available sooner than a registrar would have been.

After assessment, FIMI estimated the costs as:

Assessment	$ 3,500 (paid)
Consultants' guidance over 20 months	36,000
Registrar's pre-audit and final audit	16,000
	$55,500

FIMI estimated that they could reasonably expect to recover all their costs through process improvements within a year from registration, approximately 32 months from starting the assessment.

Had FIMI chosen not to proceed through to registration, the needs assessment alone would have been well worth the cost. It pointed to more than 25 areas needing improvement in a system the owners had considered to be of high quality. Lydia observed that the introduction of documented procedures alone would greatly facilitate crosstraining of personnel, which is critical in a small job shop operation. Elaine noted that poorly identified and controlled documents, and the resultant errors in the shop, would be eliminated through proper document control procedures, and the prevention of just one such error would easily absorb the cost of the assessment.

Procedures for Analyzing the Data

Although the data collected for this type of assessment can be voluminous, the analysis process involved no mysterious or esoteric techniques. Analysis was simplified because of the extensive description of the requirements (the ISO 9000 standards and the Baldrige criteria) and the prepared checklists based on those requirements. Essentially, data collection involved ascertaining whether the area being observed met or did not meet the requirements. The analysis was less a matter of ascribing meaning to the data than a matter of categorizing and compressing the data to a "yes" or "no" for each requirement, with examples to back up the conclusions. Statistically, it did not matter whether there was one instance of observed noncompliance or 14. One was significant. The structure of the standards provided the structure of the report.

Conclusions and Recommendations

The no-frills approach that was employed enabled FIMI to implement a fully compliant quality system in time for final audit. Registration was achieved in the first pass—a very cost-effective outcome. FIMI is now entirely consultant-independent and has a fully functional system of continuous improvement, corrective actions, controls, internal audits, and management reviews. Ron, Elaine, and Lydia are pleased with the outcomes.

By combining the Baldrige criteria with the ISO 9001 assessment, FIMI owners have identified a long-range vision of where they want to take the company and how they will manage the transformation effectively. Unlike companies that choose to meet only ISO 9000 requirements, FIMI has expanded its horizons by using the Baldrige criteria as a model of how to operate a successful enterprise. FIMI now has its eye on the state's quality award as a next goal.

Integrating training with the gradual implementation of the required quality systems precluded a need for costly formal training programs and eliminated the "fade-out" problem (i.e., the gap between instruction and application). Learning by doing, with guidance and coaching from the experienced consultants, enabled FIMI to assimilate the process with minimum pain and cost. Employees did not have to be pulled off their jobs for extended time periods to accomplish the objective. Straightforward assessment processes (structured interview questions and ABWALL—Assessment By Walking Around Looking and Listening) were appropriate for the size of the business and the sophistication level of FIMI's processes. Virtually everyone in the company was involved and fully informed every step of the journey.

Consultant's Reflections

FIMI's objective was to make a "go" or "no go" decision as to whether to seek ISO 9001 registration. Because of the foreseeable competitive pressures, they were predisposed to select "go." However, even though the decision implied survival, understanding the investment in time and dollars was crucial. Without the assessment, no reasonably accurate estimate was possible.

Communication of the results was easy in FIMI's open environment and cooperative culture. Virtually everyone was involved in the assessment process and aware of the outcome. Cooperation of all personnel was outstanding. They disclosed and discussed everything freely with the consultants. There was no evidence they felt anxious about the assessment process or the questions asked, and apparently they did not feel that they were personally under scrutiny.

Questions for Discussion

1. How would you categorize the data gathered at FIMI? Were they quantitative or qualitative? Were they objective or subjective?

2. Were the steps taken at FIMI different from training needs analysis? How so? To what extent do you think the data collected might aid a training person at FIMI in structuring a training program?

3. If you were the owner of FIMI, what might you have done differently, and why?

4. How would you describe management support of the assessment? How important was communication of the assessment process throughout FIMI?

5. Do you have any suggestions for improving the process described?

6. To assess a company substantially larger than FIMI, how would you change the process described, and why?

7. If you agree that it is so, why do you think that relatively few internal human resource development people are currently involved in assessing and implementing quality initiatives, such as ISO 9000 registration, the Malcolm Baldrige National Quality Award, total quality management, and continuous quality improvement?

8. What knowledge, skills, and experience from human resource development and training are applicable to assisting in a quality initiative?

9. If you wanted to expand your horizons, what steps could you take to involve yourself in the quality arena?

The Author

Russ Westcott, president of R.T. Westcott & Associates in Old Saybrook, Connecticut, has more than 30 years' business management experience with aerospace companies, financial services, information services, manufacturers, retail stores, government, and utilities. Since 1979, his firm has provided quality and performance improvement consulting services to small businesses. Westcott is active with the American

Society for Quality Control, the Quality Consortium, and the National Society for Performance and Instruction. Westcott's articles on quality topics have appeared in *QNET, ASQC Quality Management Forum, BusinessHartford, BusinessWest, Quality Edge, Middlesex County Business Review,* and the *Business Times.* He can be contacted at the following address: R.T. Westcott & Associates, 263 Main Street, Suite 308, Old Saybrook, CT 06475.

Developing Managers in the Former Soviet Union

Izhorsky Zavod

Donna L. Wiley

Management development has been a critical need in the former Soviet Union since perestroika. This unique case describes a needs assessment of Russian managers that uses interviews to conduct an organization analysis, a strategic job analysis, and a person analysis.

Background

Since the late 1980s, dramatic changes have occurred in the republics of the former Soviet Union and the countries of Eastern Europe. Because of the fall of communism and the breakdown of the command economy, enterprises in this region are facing unprecedented challenges during the transition to a market economy. The challenges these enterprises are facing include privatizing, eliminating vertically integrated monopolies, removing the vestiges of central planning, deregulating prices, introducing currency convertibility, and establishing a financial infrastructure (Ivancevich, DeFrank, and Gregory, 1991).

Perestroika dramatically changed the position of managers in Eastern Europe. They are now expected to compete in a market-oriented environment. They must comprehend the complex social, political, legal, and economic dimensions of the market economy. To do so, they must develop expertise in such market-based fields as strategic planning, marketing, accounting, and finance, as well as radically alter their values and practices concerning the management of human

This case was prepared to serve as a basis for discussion rather than to illustrate either effective or ineffective administrative and management practices.

resources. They are expected to play a variety of new roles—efficient manager, entrepreneur, forecaster, negotiator, external monitor, and motivator. In addition, globalization has made the Eastern European economy more interdependent with the rest of the world's economies, so that managers must now be able to develop and implement global strategies for dealing with a diverse set of global partners. All of these changes are occurring in the midst of chaos in the Eastern European monetary, supply, and distribution systems (Ivancevich et al., 1991; Prokopenko, 1992).

Need for Management Development

Recent circumstances have created a tremendous need for management development. The lack of critical management skills is a serious impediment to the implementation of a full market economy. Firms cannot produce the quantity or quality of products needed to compete successfully in the world market because of their managers' lack of general business-practice skills. Thus, management development has been called the most urgent priority for human resource management efforts (Bailey, Shenkar, and Bangert, 1992; Ivancevich et al., 1991; Prokopenko, 1992).

Such efforts are hampered by the lack of existing management education and training systems, including the lack of professional trainers, modern training facilities and equipment, and management training literature and materials. Eastern European managers have not had the opportunity to study Western markets, laws, and business practices. Although simple replication of Western systems is not the solution, it is believed that some Western management models, tools, and techniques can be applied in specific situations (Ivancevich et al., 1991).

Western Assistance in Eastern European Management Development

Given this tremendous need for management development and the lack of internal resources to fulfill this need, several Western initiatives have been created to assist in the training and development of managers in Eastern Europe. These include programs developed by American and European academic institutions either to assist in setting up educational programs in Eastern Europe or to bring Eastern European managers to training programs at Western institutions of higher education.

Although there appears to be consensus about the need for management development, there is disagreement about how it should be conducted. Several criticisms have been leveled against these Western initiatives. Many programs have been criticized for offering ready-made packages that were developed without the involvement of local Eastern

European participants (Elenurm, 1992). Many of the Western program designers have lacked the information needed to design a training program specifically tailored to the needs of Eastern European managers because they have not had the opportunity to conduct a thorough needs assessment. In contrast, this case describes an opportunity to conduct a systematic needs assessment. This assessment was used to design and implement a management development program for a group of managers from a large, state-owned steel production facility in St. Petersburg, Russia. In the spring of 1991, the Institute of Research and Business Development at California State University, Hayward (CSUH), was asked to design a management development program for Izhorsky Zavod (IZ). The following sections outline the major steps of the needs assessment process and describe the training program that was implemented based on the results of the needs assessment.

Organizational Profile

IZ is a very large, state-owned, vertically integrated steel production facility, founded in 1722 by Peter the Great to build the Russian navy. Employment in 1991 exceeded 26,000 people. The plant produces steel and alloy products as diverse as table silverware, heavy excavation equipment, and nuclear reactor pressure vessels. Because of safety and environmental concerns about nuclear power plants following the Chernobyl disaster, orders for these vessels have fallen dramatically. In addition, low-cost raw materials from the Ukraine are no longer guaranteed. Distribution systems are unreliable, and problems are caused by the nonconvertibility of the ruble.

Needs Assessment Process

In July 1991, four CSUH business professors were invited by IZ's top management to visit their facility in order to design a management development program to fit the enterprise's unique training needs. A planning meeting was held before the group traveled to St. Petersburg. The group decided to focus their analysis on Goldstein's (1986) three levels: organization analysis, job analysis, and person analysis.

Organization Analysis

The organization analysis centered on four issues: the specific goals of the organization, the training climate, the relevant external system factors, and resources available for training. Interviews were conducted with top executives of IZ to collect information about the organization. These interviews were conducted by holding several meetings of the management team and the CSUH team. The meetings were fairly unstructured and highly interactive, with all members participating in both asking and answering questions. Although at least one of the Russian managers spoke fluent English, and one of the American professors (a Russian émigré) spoke Russian, a translator was used to ensure mutual understanding. The interviews were taped for later review. During the time the CSUH team spent in St. Petersburg, there were also several opportunities for informal interaction with IZ top management. The trust and respect that developed from these informal interactions were invaluable in creating a climate of openness during the more formal discussions.

The top executives were asked to describe their organization's current situation and their short- and long-term goals for the organization. Goals included privatizing, gaining access to financial resources and raw materials, creating joint ventures, and converting to more consumer-oriented products. Another key goal was decentralization. Because of the increasing threat that IZ's most talented managers would leave the organization and look for opportunities to start their own businesses, top management's long-range goal was to spin off large divisions into relatively autonomous profit centers, giving each division's manager more control over his own business. In top management's own words, the company was striving to operate on three basic principles: "to produce the best quality product; to take professional responsibility for our work; and to take the initiative as professionals and create change."

The organization's training climate was determined by reviewing the history of and past commitment to training at IZ, by visiting the training facilities, and by assessing the commitment of resources to the current training proposal. This analysis revealed tremendous support for training and for organizational change.

In 1980, a new general director, Vladimir Vasilyev, was appointed at IZ. Like the enterprise directors in the study by Ivancevich et al. (1991), he has played a key role in his firm's economic progress. However, unlike most Russian enterprise directors, he is relatively well read in Western literature and is not averse to taking risks. In 1985, before glasnost and perestroika, he recognized the need for creating new ways of doing business. He created a new center for management education (one of the first in Russia). Recently, the company has instituted computer training, with a classroom equipped with IBM-compatible computers and Hewlett-Packard printers.

Management development programs are conducted at IZ's company retreat on the Gulf of Finland. Although training is well supported and accepted throughout the organization, there is a lack of access to knowledge about Western management practices, which motivated this particular training request. General Director Vasilyev made it clear that he was willing to commit whatever resources were necessary to make this management development program successful.

The relevant external factors affecting this enterprise were obvious. According to Goldstein (1986), instructional design is affected by legal, political, social, and economic factors. In Russia during the summer of 1991, all of these factors were in chaos. In 1988, IZ had essentially declared itself independent from the Ministry of Steel Industries. Although top management had been seeking to implement the principles of a market economy ever since, the lack of legislation and infrastructure had made this virtually impossible. Management was proceeding to act based on the assumption that such an economy would someday exist.

Job Analysis

In a typical training needs assessment, the job analysis specifies the tasks to be performed and the knowledge, skills, and abilities (KSAs) required for performing a job as it currently exists. This description is then used as a basis for the instructional objectives. This type of job analysis was not possible in this case because the job (i.e., manager in a market-based economy) did not currently exist. Therefore, a more appropriate form of job analysis was used—strategic job analysis, which is the specification of the tasks to be performed and the KSAs required for effective performance of a job as it is predicted to exist in the future (Schneider and Konz, 1989).

The first step in strategic job analysis is to gather information about the kinds of issues in the job, the company, and the larger environment that may affect the job in the future. This information was gathered during the interviews conducted with top management (discussed in the preceding section), as well as in interviews conducted with the potential trainees (discussed in the next section). Clearly, the major issues facing both the organization and the job of manager were related to making the transition from a command economy to a market economy. Both groups were asked how this transition would affect IZ. Indeed, almost every facet of the organization would change. No longer would goals be dictated by the central plan. The organization would now be responsible for deciding what products to make, where and how to locate raw materials, and who its customers would be. The huge monolithic organizational structure would have to be completely redesigned.

The second step in strategic job analysis is to revise the current tasks and KSAs in light of expected future changes. Both top executives and the group of managers who would be attending the training program were asked how the role of manager at IZ would change as a result of the Soviet Union's transition to a market economy and the resulting changes at IZ. Because of the organization's goal of decentralization, the jobs of these managers would change dramatically. They would ultimately be responsible for directing their divisions as relatively autonomous profit centers. Both groups were also asked to identify the specific knowledge and skills that they felt managers would need to function successfully in the new environment and that they hoped to develop as a result of this training. Knowledge of strategic planning, marketing, financial management, and the privatization process was viewed as essential. Knowledge and skills involved in new product development and innovation would be required to fulfill the goal of conversion to consumer products. Effective use of human resources was also identified by top management as a key issue for the future, so knowledge and skills in new techniques of managing people were also identified as key KSAs.

Because these managers had never operated in a market environment, their perspective on precisely what their jobs would be and what skills would be needed was somewhat limited. Therefore, the KSA analysis was supplemented by researching the academic and business literature on the changing role of managers in Eastern Europe. In addition, the CSUH faculty had already conducted two executive training programs for Soviet managers and had gained considerable insight into the challenges facing these managers. This insight was valuable input for the needs assessment and program design processes for the IZ program. The validity of this analysis is substantiated by Prokopenko's (1992) report identifying the most immediate and extensive training needs of Eastern European managers. His list, which follows, parallels almost perfectly the KSAs identified in the current analysis:

- general management (in market conditions)
- strategic management (planning, portfolio analysis, and feasibility studies)
- industrial restructuring (downsizing, privatization, business valuation, and small-enterprise development)
- marketing and sales management (pricing, advertising, distribution, and international markets)
- financial management (sources of funds, equity, capital markets, and cash flows)

- accounting and auditing
- organization development and change management
- problem analysis and decision making
- innovation, technology transfer, and product design management
- human resource management and motivation
- information technology (management information systems and computerization)
- environmental management
- productivity, value-added concepts, profits, and quality management
- negotiating skills
- business law.

IZ's top managers expressed their view that training in human resource management and motivation was extremely important, as they believed motivating their employees in this new market-oriented direction was key to their future success.

Person Analysis

Person analysis determines whether individual employees need training and exactly what training is required. The first step in this process for the IZ program was the selection of training participants. The selection was made by IZ top management. According to Deputy Director Leonid Karlyukov, the key selection criteria were creativity and flexibility. The group of 16 managers chosen included department chiefs of metallurgy, machine shops, maintenance, economics, foreign trade, and computers. They were quite young, considering their high-level positions, with ages ranging from 28 to 50.

During the visit to IZ, interviews were conducted with the participants, both individually and as a group. As with the top executives, there was ample opportunity for informal interaction with several members of this group. This interaction was critical in establishing trust and rapport. For the majority of this group, this was their first encounter with Americans, and they were nervous initially. At least one manager recounted an example of being sanctioned in earlier times for interacting with foreigners, so these interactions required a completely new mind-set for these men.

The managers were asked about their backgrounds, such as their education, functional expertise, and managerial experience, as well as current challenges they were facing on their jobs. They were also asked about their attitude toward the changes that were taking place in the organization and the potential opportunity to study Western business practices in the United States. Other goals of the interviews were to assess their English proficiency and their preexisting knowledge and skill levels. All of the prospective trainees were well educated, with many holding advanced degrees, primarily in engineering fields. Although they were quite young, they had risen to significant levels of responsibility and authority within the organization, some managing entire divisions consisting of several thousand employees. Based on their level of education and job responsibilities, it was clear that this was an extremely intelligent, fast-learning group. It was also clear that the IZ managers were highly motivated. They viewed the changes taking place in the Soviet Union (the Soviet Union dissolved during the program) as having potentially very positive professional and personal consequences. They perceived that learning about Western business practices would place them at a great advantage, both in their own company and in the labor market in general. One manager noted, "This program is important not only for my own survival, but for the survival of my children."

Most of the managers, however, had very little exposure to Western business practices. English proficiency was another main consideration. One of top management's secondary goals for the program was that the trainees should become proficient in English. Top management had been adamant that the classes be conducted in English and planned for the participants to study English intensively before the beginning of the program. From the meetings held with the prospective trainees, it became obvious that the majority would not be able to comprehend lectures conducted solely in English. The resolution of this problem is discussed in the section on program design.

A final assessment technique was the administration of Acumen (Acumen International, 1990), a self-report diagnostic tool that measures several dimensions relating to managerial style. Acumen measures style with the following scales: humanistic-helpful, affiliation, approval, conventional, dependence, apprehension, oppositional, power, competition, perfectionism, achievement, and self-actualization. Studies have demonstrated that effective managers—as measured by variables such as peer evaluations, number of promotions, and salary increases—display a different profile on the Acumen than ineffective managers. Specifically, effective managers consistently score high on the achievement, self-actualization, humanistic-helpful, and affiliation scales (Cooke and Rousseau, 1983; Gratzinger, Warren, and Cooke, 1987).

This instrument was translated into Russian and administered to the prospective trainees via personal computers at IZ's computer laboratory. The results, given in Table 1, showed that these managers scored extremely high in the power and competition dimensions, but scored low in all of the dimensions related to effective management among Western managers. These scores were confirmed in class discussions held during the training. In general, the managers viewed their employees as lazy and untrustworthy—attitudes not consistent with the organization's strategic human resource management goals. Therefore, the role of the manager and motivational and leadership techniques were heavily emphasized in the program content.

Table 1. Acumen results for the 16 participants.

Dimension	Mean percentiles
Power: tendency to be authoritarian and controlling	81.22
Perfectionism: need to seek perfection	80.00
Competition: need to be seen as the best and to maintain a self-centered attitude	76.33
Apprehension: tendency to experience anxiety	55.00
Approval: need to seek others' approval and support	52.00
Self-actualization: level of self-esteem, interest in self-development	50.22
Oppositional: tendency to take a critical, questioning attitude	47.88
Achievement: need to achieve and have an impact	46.12
Dependence: tendency to be compliant, passive, and dependent on others	41.77
Humanistic-helpful: inclination to see the best in others, to encourage their growth and development, and to be supportive	38.22
Conventional: need to conform, follow the rules, and meet the expectations of those in authority	36.33
Affiliation: degree of friendliness, sociability, and outgoing tendencies	31.06

Cost of the Needs Assessment

The Institute of Research and Business Development paid the cost of airfare for the four faculty involved in the needs assessment process. IZ paid the in-country costs for the visit. The only additional costs for the needs assessment team were opportunity costs for the two weeks they were in Russia. Time was also spent planning the needs assessment visit and analyzing the results after the trip was completed. This time was not billed to the client, as it would be in a typical management development project. However, IZ did pay in hard currency for the entire training program that resulted from this assessment.

Training Program Design

Based on the needs assessment results, the following goals were developed for the participants in the management development program designed for IZ:

- to acquire knowledge and skills in the essential aspects of a market-economy business system
- to acquire strategic management and marketing skills required to operate autonomous divisions
- to acquire skills in innovation and new product development
- to understand the basic aspects of a joint venture and to make business contacts that might lead to the formation of joint ventures
- to improve English proficiency
- to learn new human resource management skills.

A subsidiary goal of the program was to provide the Russian managers with some understanding of U.S. culture and to provide an opportunity for the U.S. faculty to learn something about Russian management practices, culture, and way of life.

One of the first design decisions was program length. There was unanimous agreement that a program of short duration (two to four weeks) would provide only a superficial look at U.S. business practices and would not achieve the company's objectives. Based on the training staff's experience with an earlier program, it was decided that three months was too long for trainees to be away from their families. Therefore, after calculating the minimum number of hours needed to cover the proposed topics and to provide an opportunity for visiting U.S. companies, the team designed a nine-week program, consisting of approximately 230 hours of classroom instruction. The curriculum was divided into eight general categories: overview of U.S. business, economics, finance, accounting, management, marketing, human resource management, and quantitative business methods, with additional sessions on innovation, privatization, and joint ventures.

Lecture was the primary training method used, because of the tremendous number of concepts and ideas to be conveyed. However, faculty were encouraged to play the role of facilitator rather than instructor, using activities and group discussions requiring application and input from the Russian trainees. The focus of the discussions was how Western ideas could be adapted to their organizational and environmental context. Based on the needs assessment results, it was determined that most participants were not proficient enough in English to comprehend lectures conducted in English. However, two of the 16 group members were highly proficient and had translating experience. They alternated as translators for the classroom portion of the training program, translating the instructors' information to the rest of the class and the class's comments back to the instructor. Several other members of the group were proficient enough to comprehend much of the class material and to respond in class. Although this was a slow process, it worked quite well with a group this size. It was still possible to hold quite lively, participative discussions.

The second training method was the playing of a business game. BRANDMAPS (Chapman, 1991), a sophisticated, competitive, computer-simulated marketing strategy game, was used to integrate the various topic areas and their application. This game allowed the trainees to practice many of the market-economy concepts they were learning in the classroom. The trainees were divided into competing teams in order to view the operations of a company in a competitive environment. They were able to witness the effects of their own strategic decisions as well as the effects of external factors. Woodall (1992) has criticized such experiential activities because they are based on Western organizations and cultural perspectives. However, the objectives of this particular program were to gain knowledge and skills in the workings of a market economy. In addition, IZ was already involved in joint ventures with Western countries and anticipated more in the near future. Thus, it was felt that this type of game would help achieve the objectives of this program.

A third major component of the program was visiting U.S. businesses. Sixteen days of the program were spent on company tours, which provided opportunities for the trainees to see the concepts that they were learning in class in actual practice. The group visited a variety of companies in manufacturing, high-technology, and financial industries, including Hewlett-Packard, Raychem, NUMMI, Posco Steel, Bechtel, Pacific Bell, and the Pacific Stock Exchange. Participants had the opportunity to speak to people at all levels, from top executives down to line managers and employees. Although the participants were very impressed by the manufacturing facilities and technologies they observed, their questions most frequently pertained to human resource management issues. Invariably, they asked how the companies motivate and compensate their employees. At NUMMI, the General Motors-Toyota joint venture, they were able to see firsthand the concepts of autonomous work teams and employee involvement put into practice, and were able to observe the outstanding results NUMMI attributes to its employees' commitment and participation.

Conclusions and Recommendations

The main conclusion to be drawn from this case study is that it is possible to apply state-of-the-art management development practices in programs for Russian managers. The key to the success of this particular program was the opportunity to conduct a relatively thorough needs assessment, which allowed the program to be tailored as closely as possible to the needs of the organization. The opportunity to actually see the work site, hold direct discussions with top management, and meet the potential participants provided valuable information that would have been impossible to obtain otherwise. However, the opportunity to obtain such information is becoming increasingly difficult. This particular assessment occurred just prior to the breakup of the Soviet Union. Since the breakup, such enterprises rarely have had access to hard currency to fund these programs. Western economic aid programs, such as those of the U.S. Agency for International Development, are available, but tend to target areas outside the major urban centers.

Even with a thorough needs assessment, there continue to be obstacles that training programs for Russian managers must face. First, language is a barrier to the effectiveness of any program. The optimal solution is to have participants who are fluent in English. If this is not feasible, another solution is to translate as much of the class material as possible—particularly overhead transparencies, lecture outlines, and handout materials. If a translator must be used, this person should be familiar with business terminology.

Second, group composition is another key consideration. This program demonstrated the advantages of involving managers from a single company only, so they had common interests and concerns and common frames of business reference. In previous programs mixing managers from different companies, it was very difficult to meet the participants' very diverse training needs. However, even with a group of participants from the same company, individual needs varied according to their functional responsibilities. A recommendation for future programs is to make group composition as homogeneous as possible (e.g., similar job experience or similar company backgrounds).

Third, although the plant visits were very successful, they provided only a superficial look. The participants suggested (and other programs have included) adding internships in which participants spend a short, intensive period in one company. This would allow a more in-depth, realistic view of Western business practices in operation. Even though such internships would involve logistical difficulties, they should be considered.

Finally, it should be emphasized that the learning that occurs in these programs is bidirectional. The faculty involved in this program learned a great deal about both Soviet business operations and Soviet culture. As Ivancevich et al. (1991) and other authors have emphasized, Western academic and business partners must understand their Eastern European counterparts before management development efforts can be maximally beneficial.

Questions for Discussion

1. What additional needs assessment methods would have been useful in this assessment process? what additional information?

2. Could an adequate needs assessment be conducted if analysts were unable to visit the organization? What methods would you recommend?

3. Given the needs assessment results obtained in this case, what other human resource development interventions would you recommend to this enterprise? What other training delivery methods would you recommend for use in this training program?

The Author

Donna L. Wiley is a professor in the Department of Management and Finance at California State University, Hayward. She teaches in the areas of human resource management and human resource development. She has taught in three management development programs for managers from the former Soviet Union. She participated in a conference held for Russian women in business at Russian State University for the Humanities and taught a course on theories of management at the Academy of National Economy in Moscow. She has presented several papers and written articles and book chapters on her experiences. She is also the director of graduate programs for the School of Business at California State University, Hayward, which is currently preparing to open the first Western-accredited M.B.A. program in Moscow. Wiley can be contacted at the following address: Department of Management and Finance, 25800 Carlos Bee Boulevard, California State University-Hayward, Hayward, CA 94542.

References

Acumen International. (1990). *Acumen.* San Rafael, CA: Author.

Bailey, E.K., Shenkar, O., and Bangert, D. (1992). Human resource practices in a transitional economy. In *Proceedings of the Third Conference on International Personnel and Human Resources Management* (Vol. 2), unpublished manuscript.

Chapman, R.G. (1991). *BRANDMAPS.* Englewood Cliffs, NJ: Prentice-Hall.

Cooke, R.A., and Rousseau, D.M. (1983). The factor structure of Level I: Life Styles Inventory. *Educational and Psychological Measurement, 43,* 449-458.

Elenurm, T. (1992). Innovative learning: A way to train managers for the market economy. In *Proceedings of the Third Conference on International Personnel and Human Resources Management* (Vol. 2), unpublished manuscript.

Goldstein, I.L. (1986). *Training in organizations: Needs assessment, development, and evaluation* (2d ed.). Monterey, CA: Brooks/Cole.

Gratzinger, P.D., Warren, R.A., and Cooke, R.A. (1987). *The optimal and ineffective manager: Satisfaction orientation traits are important predictors of leaders' effectiveness.* San Rafael, CA: Human Factors ATG.

Ivancevich, J.M., DeFrank, R.S., and Gregory, P.R. (1991). The Soviet enterprise director: An important resource before and after the coup. *Academy of Management Executive, 6*(2), 42-55.

Prokopenko, J. (1992). Transition to a market economy and its implications for human resources management in Eastern Europe. In *Proceedings of the Third Conference on International Personnel and Human Resources Management* (Vol. 2), unpublished manuscript.

Schneider, B., and Konz, A.M. (1989). Strategic job analysis. *Human Resource Management, 28*(1), 51-63.

Woodall, J. (1992). Models and methods of management development in Poland and Hungary. In *Proceedings of the Third Conference on International Personnel and Human Resources Management* (Vol. 2), unpublished manuscript.

The Dark Side of Organizations

Promo Inc.

John A. Zuber and Richard A. Swanson

In the previous cases, the needs assessment resulted in a specific initiative or program to improve the organization. This case is unique in that, although the process and methodology appear to have been proper, there were no programs or changes implemented as a result of the needs assessment. This unhappy ending occurred because of management's failure to support the process properly and the reaction to the negative results of the process. These are important issues that must be addressed in any needs assessment undertaking.

Overview

Surveys of organizational culture and climate have become an important diagnostic tool in helping business managers identify problems and guide organization development interventions (Burke, 1982; Sleezer and Swanson, 1992). Although interviewing is the most popular technique for acquiring information to guide change strategies, the other common diagnostic tool is the paper-and-pencil employee survey (Burke, 1982). This case presents the rationale for using employee surveys in the diagnostic phase of improving organizations and then illustrates how the "dark side" of an organization can affect the organization development process. Finally, recommendations to assist practitioners in managing the dark side effectively are presented.

Assumptions Underlying Organization Development

In the new-world economy, corporate America is scrambling to meet the unrelenting demand for ever-increasing productivity, quality,

This case was prepared to serve as a basis for discussion rather than to illustrate either effective or ineffective administrative and management practices. All names, dates, places, and organizations have been disguised at the request of the organization involved or the case author.

and innovation. Competition and instant marketplace shifts are the most significant drivers of these trends, although the high costs of waste, rework, and unmet customer expectations are also important factors (McLagan, 1991). As U.S. corporations strive to improve their productivity, quality, and innovative capability, they are recognizing that knowledge has a critical role in this process.

Contemporary organization development theorists are in harmony with this goal. They see their contribution as "a systemwide application of behavioral science knowledge to the planned development and reinforcement of organizational strategies, structure, and processes for improving an organization's effectiveness" (Cummings and Worley, 1993, p. 2).

The general change model of organization development has four phases: entering and contracting, diagnosing, planning and implementing, and evaluating and institutionalizing (Cummings and Worley, 1993, p. 60). The four phases are not generally emphasized equally. For example, Cummings and Worley (1993) devoted a single chapter each to Phases 1 and 4 in their book, while devoting three chapters to the diagnosing phase and 10 chapters to the planning and implementing phase.

Changes involving teamwork, sharing information, or values opposed to the culture of the dominant group often require that companies make fundamental changes in their values, beliefs, and organizational practices. These latter changes, in turn, often require fundamental paradigm shifts in the way employees think, not only about their work, but also about themselves and their organizational relationships.

Many factors limit the success that organizations have in implementing strategies aimed at changing employees' values, beliefs, and practices. It is useful to place these factors into two broad categories: limited organizational resources and cultural attributes of the organization (Senge, 1990).

Strategies to minimize resistance produced by an organization's climate and culture should begin with an organization diagnosis. This will help determine those current values, assumptions, and beliefs that are discordant with the new ways of working and valuing that are advocated by management. The required diagnostic information can be gathered through interviews, employee surveys, observations, and examination of existing documentation (Swanson, 1994). Although each of these methods has its strengths and weaknesses, and although together they provide an important mosaic made up of overlapping and validating data, employee surveys are uniquely suited to this task because respondents are less likely to distort perceptions when answering questions anonymously, large numbers of employees can be given the opportunity to participate and provide feedback, and information generated by climate surveys can be interpreted and summarized through statistical procedures, which tend to be given credibility in business environments.

Once these limiting values, beliefs, and practices have been identified, managers and practitioners are in a position to use this information to develop strategies for producing real and fundamental change. Schein (1985) has developed an approach to thinking about culture that is very useful in helping organizations adapt. He defines organizational culture as the learned behavior of a stable group of people as they cope with their external environmental and internal problems. He views culture as existing at three levels. The first level includes artifacts or the organization's daily practices, activities, and rituals. The second level includes the organization's values or conscious explanations about what is happening at the artifact level. The third level is the employees' basic assumptions, which are commonly held worldviews that exist at the unconscious level. Schein postulates that these worldviews drive the organizational practices that we see.

This model provides the practitioner with a systematic approach for understanding and modifying an organization's culture to support new approaches and innovations. The underlying theory is that to manage resistance to change effectively, it is critical first to identify and change the underlying assumptions that are driving the values, beliefs, and practices hostile to the change effort. Changing basic assumptions is a difficult and lengthy process but is required for true and lasting change (Heilpern and Nadler, 1990).

For example, managers who believe the organization's overriding purpose is to make near-term shareholder return will generally assume that there is a cost associated with increasing the quality of products or services. Management may not trust employees to make important decisions regarding the work they do, and thus may have a difficult time implementing a quality program focused on process improvement.

Consequently, for many organizations, survival depends on knowing not only what new technologies and programs to employ, but also what new values, beliefs, and practices will be needed to support these innovations. Employee surveys for determining organizational climate and culture help organizations take the first step in this process. However, although employee surveys have been known to go awry and do not always fulfill expectations, there is little documentation of these instances.

Background

This case is based on extensive observational and interview data related to an organization development effort in a private-sector organization. The focal point is the contribution of a relatively inexperienced external consultant who became part of an established companywide quality improvement team. The consultant, joining the effort at the second phase of the change process—diagnosis—had the important task of directing a companywide survey of all employees to assess the organizational climate. The purpose was to help the organization move on to Phase 3, planning and implementing.

Organizational Profile

Promo Inc. is a privately held, medium-sized organization of 1,100 employees. Located in the Midwest, the organization provides products and services in the direct-mail industry. Promo was founded in the late 1960s and is still headed by the founding chairman and chief executive officer. It is made up of three divisions, Mailing, Printing, and Envelope, which work together to provide its customers a "total package" of products and services, including envelope production, high-speed printing, data processing, and personalization of preprinted forms. Promo had revenues of more than $90 million in the last fiscal year.

The Mailing Division provides data processing, personalization of printed forms, and lettershop services. It is divided into traditional departments, including warehousing, accounting, account services, human resources, data processing, bindery, and lettershop. Typically, the division receives a mailing list from a customer such as a large credit card company and then downloads this information into a computer. The computer then drives high-speed printers, which personalize preprinted letters or forms with the names and addresses from the customer's list. The lettershop function involves inserting the letters or forms into envelopes, applying postage, and presorting the mail in accordance with postal regulations.

Apart from the company's primary facility is a satellite production operation. The company's greatest strength is being able to process large jobs in a short period of time. It also has a reputation for being able to do difficult jobs, such as inserting a pen into an envelope, which often requires modifying and reprogramming equipment.

These strengths have helped the organization build a customer base including large financial, credit card, and insurance companies. However, Promo is currently facing a threat common throughout the mail industry—its inability to maintain quality control in the face of customers' demands for increasingly complex jobs. This push is primarily due to technology becoming increasingly sophisticated in its ability to discriminate between different populations and target a potential customer's needs with more accuracy. For example, five years ago, a two-million-piece mailing might have had five "splits," or five different combinations of inserts targeted for different segments of a population. Today, that same mailing might have 100 splits. This increase in complexity has multiplied the probability of operators making mistakes by a factor of 20, and has severely taxed the Mailing Division's processes.

As a consequence of this increased complexity, Promo Inc. has not been able to maintain an acceptable standard of quality, and has lost many of its most valued customers. Mistakes also generate rework, which in the previous fiscal year involved postage, labor, and material costs of more than $300,000. These difficulties have resulted in layoffs and low morale as the company's health and future have come into question. To combat this threat, Promo's management team began a total quality management (TQM) program three years ago and has made improving quality an important goal.

An additional threat to the company is high turnover. The yearly turnover rate in the Mailing Division production areas has been over 90 percent. Turnover in administrative areas has been 20 percent and in the satellite production facility has been 60 percent. This turnover rate has been estimated to cost more than $600,000 per year in training and orientation costs, plus costs associated with mistakes that new employees typically make. Management also believes the high turnover rate contributes directly to Promo's inability to consistently provide a quality standard acceptable to its customers.

Industry Profile

Promo's culture is highly integrated, with few values, beliefs, and practices contrary to the dominant culture permitted. In general, the direct-mail industry has what might be characterized as a "sweatshop" orientation. The industry's practices and values are based on the assumption that workers are a commodity and can be purchased in whatever quantity desired for the market price. They are not valued as an investment. Employees are inadequately trained, paid minimum or close to minimum wage, forced to work 45- to 60-day stretches without a day off during busy periods, and laid off the moment production demands decrease. Other industries that have practices and policies similar to these include the agricultural and textile industries.

Using Deal and Kennedy's (1982) four dimensions to define a culture, Promo's culture would be characterized as valuing activity over results-oriented action, individualism over teamwork, decisions that minimize risk or maintain the status quo, and feedback that is based on compliance.

This culture served Promo Inc. well before the internal and external environments began to increase dramatically in complexity. When Mailing Division employees operated slow but reliable electromechanical inserters and printers, when jobs were not complex, and when customers' expectations were not so demanding, Promo functioned well and grew to become one of the top 100 privately owned companies in its state. However, many of Promo's past strengths have turned into weaknesses. With the introduction of high technology, frequent changes in postal regulations, and complex jobs, Promo's antiquated practices are increasingly causing employees to make mistakes, resulting in rework, poor quality, missed deadlines, and wasted materials.

The Employee Survey

In March, a survey was commissioned by Promo's TQM Steering Committee, whose membership included the director of human resources, the director of data processing, the director of production, the manager of management information systems, and the assistant director of finance and accounting. The committee's goal was to determine the causes of high turnover rates in the Mailing Division and to develop and implement strategies to solve the turnover problem.

The committee members began this project by identifying, through a cause-and-effect diagram, a number of probable reasons for the high employee turnover rate. They decided, however, that the best way to prioritize these causes and to discover other possible contributing factors was to develop a survey instrument that would systematically measure employees' perceptions regarding the general characteristics of the organization. At this time, the steering committee determined the survey could also provide benchmark information regarding Promo's TQM program, and could be re-administered later to assess progress. An outside consultant was given the task of designing and developing the survey instrument, administering it to employees, analyzing the data, and providing feedback sessions.

The steering committee chose an outside consultant because the organization did not employ anyone who was experienced and skilled in implementing culture surveys, and because there was a low level of trust between management and employees. Management and employees perceived external consultants to be more knowledgeable about the survey process, to have a lesser stake in the outcome, and to be more trustworthy. The steering committee and the external consultant worked together to determine the final design framework and survey items.

Design of the Employee Survey

The survey instrument was designed around 16 possible causes of turnover that the TQM Steering Committee had identified, along with additional organizational factors derived from approximately 20 individual interviews with employees. The result was a 102-item survey, made up of both forced-choice and open-ended items, which was organized into the following general categories: management leadership, supervisory effectiveness, interpersonal and departmental relationships, productivity and accountability, communications, employee career development, training and development, job satisfaction, working conditions, employee compensation, and employee turnover. The survey instrument included a page asking employees to provide information regarding their job in the organization, their department, their sex, their shift, and the length of time they had worked for the Mailing Division. To ensure anonymity for people who worked in small departments, and to avoid the problems associated with employees feeling they were excluded from the process, the steering committee decided to administer the survey to all 480 Mailing Division employees.

The survey instrument was pilot-tested with a small group of employees. The pilot test revealed that some items were not clear and needed to be revised. The pilot test also revealed that the survey took, on average, 20 minutes to complete.

Administering the Employee Survey

The director of human resources and the external consultant administered the survey to small groups of employees over two days in August. Great care was taken to assure employees that they were taking the survey anonymously and that the completed surveys would be processed by people outside the Mailing Division and Promo Inc. Employees were also informed of the purpose of the survey and the steering committee's decision that the results of the survey would be completely disclosed to all employees.

Survey Results and Analysis

The survey analysis was divided into three separate reports, each having a specific purpose. The Employee Survey Data document presented the results of the survey according to department, job, shift, and seniority variables. Being 500 pages in length, it contained by far the most information of the three reports. Its contents included the survey instrument as it was administered to employees, the 11 survey categories and their respective item numbers, and the outputs of five statistical programs written to process the data (i.e., means tables including standard deviations and number of responses given for each item). This document did not include anecdotal responses to open-ended items, assessments of the data, or recommendations. This report was the least user-friendly and was intended to be used as a data resource for future organization change strategies, TQM projects, and research.

The Employee Survey Report analyzed the data primarily by job classification. It was organized according to the 11 survey categories and presented a survey summary. Not every question or item was included in this analysis. Most items left out were omitted because they were similar to other items. The data in this report were represented by bar graphs and accompanied by relevant anecdotal statements made by employees. The 12 parts of this report also included sections analyzing problems to identify underlying causes. This report was developed to be easily understood by the general workforce and was designed to be used in the feedback sessions.

The Executive Summary was intended to give a quick overview of the survey results. Its contents, taken from the Employee Survey Report, further summarized the results of the 11 survey categories and specified general recommendations for developing a plan to reduce turnover and improve productivity.

Dissemination of Survey Results and Analysis

One week before disseminating the results and analysis of the survey, Promo fired the executive vice-president of the Mailing Division. The president stated the reasons were poor management and the poor performance of the division. The executive vice-president had been in the position for one year and was hired from outside the direct-mail industry. At this time, Promo fired an additional 12 Mailing Division employees, including managers, supervisors, and lead operators. This action was said to be a cost-saving measure critical to the division's survival. Records show that personnel "house cleaning" of this type occurs once or twice a year within Promo.

In the first week of October, five survey feedback sessions were held for management. The first feedback session, presented to the president, consisted of going through both the Executive Summary and the

Employee Survey Report. In general, the data were a fairly strong indictment against management. The problems employees identified and reported feeling most strongly about varied across departments and roles, but generally included wages, mandatory overtime, pressure to meet or exceed standards, and benefits. It was difficult to judge the president's reaction to the data, analysis, and preliminary recommendations. He asked a few questions about the data, but seemed more interested in discussing his undocumented and largely unknown vision for the organization, a vision unrelated to the problems the survey had identified. He also expended a great deal of energy justifying his decision to fire the executive vice-president.

The TQM Steering Committee was then given the results and analysis of the survey, and feedback sessions to Mailing Division managers followed. These sessions took approximately two hours apiece. Reactions to the data and analysis were mixed. It appeared as though everyone was caught off guard by the employees' anecdotal responses, which indicated that many employees were extremely angry with the policies and practices of Promo and the Mailing Division. The director of personnel and the director of data processing were the most willing to discuss the identified problems contributing to turnover, and were eager to begin developing strategies. Other managers responded less favorably. The production manager at one point stood up and stated, "It's only the opinions of employees, not necessarily fact." He later stormed out of the meeting stating that he did not want to listen to any more nonsense. The manager of management information systems and the assistant director of finance responded by bringing into question the validity of the study and the efficacy of employee surveys in identifying problems.

Despite the earlier decision to provide all employees with the results of the survey, and having already guaranteed employees that this would be done, the steering committee decided that production employees should be given only a sampling of the results. The committee members said that employees might not react positively or appropriately if provided access to the full Employee Survey Report. They decided instead to provide employees with an abbreviated verbal report from their managers. It took two months for these feedback sessions to take place, and the consultant was told not to attend any of the sessions.

Development of Action Plans

The steering committee met twice with the consultant to discuss developing priorities and strategies to reduce turnover. However, the agendas of these meetings were generally controlled by three committee members who continued to challenge the validity of using employee feedback as a basis for guiding change. As a result, very little effort was spent on prioritizing the identified issues and developing solutions. At the end of the second meeting, the director of human resources asked in frustration, "Are we really interested in doing anything about the turnover rate?" After a pause of several seconds, he said his remark was not meant to be rhetorical and conceded that the committee apparently was not serious about doing anything.

The steering committee never met again to discuss possible action plans for reducing turnover, nor were the survey data ever used to establish benchmarks for the organization's TQM effort. The employee survey, which had cost approximately $20,000 to develop, implement, and analyze, was shelved.

The Dark Side of Organizations

Change efforts in U.S. companies today are generally comprehensive, involve new practices that are not congruent with existing norms and values, have pervasive influence on the way people work, are difficult to explain, take years to implement, and have effects that are not easily separable from other influences in the environment (Walton, 1975). Consequently, one should not associate the success of employee surveys with the success of the strategies they help develop. The criterion used to determine the usefulness of an employee survey is solely whether it produced an action plan to address identified problems. This limited definition of success suggests that it would be useful to analyze why Promo's survey failed to produce an action plan. Several reasons inherent in Promo's culture and the survey process itself contributed to this failure. They include incapacity to act, need to minimize risk, hostility of leadership to change, and problems associated with negative findings.

Incapacity To Act

As stated earlier, one of the central characteristics of Promo's culture is its preference for activity over real action. The latter term refers to work designed to have some positive effects on the organization; the former refers to nondirectional activity, or giving the illusion of making contributions to the organization's goals. Factors that led to the development of Promo's incapacity to take action include a highly centralized power structure and the inability of managers to balance conflicting priorities because of unclear and uncommunicated organizational strategies (Shaw, 1990).

The external consultant had participated on five other projects aimed at identifying Promo's problems, developing solutions, and implementing actions. In every instance, these projects stalled after problems were identified or solutions were developed. In none of these projects were solutions actually implemented. Thus, he knew about Promo's incapacity to act but naively anticipated that a companywide survey would break the logjam of smaller interventions.

Need To Minimize Risk

Another characteristic of Promo's culture that significantly contributed to the survey's demise was the Mailing Division's preference for decisions that minimize risks. This risk-aversive behavior came from the perception that failure could result in severe consequences, including the loss of one's job. This perception was a result of executive management routinely firing and demoting managers without clearly stating reasons related to performance. Managers maintain low profiles to avoid the possibility of being the object of executive management's scrutiny, which they believe can have only negative outcomes.

This preference for low-risk activity made it difficult for the steering committee to act on the survey data because the data indicated that significant organizational changes and resources would have to be expended to reduce high turnover. The fact that these actions could pay handsome returns did not matter. Again, the consultant was rationally weighing the true odds of success rather than the severe organizational consequences to people associated with failure—even perceived failure.

Hostility of Leadership to Change

Corporations attempting to make organization-wide changes involving their cultural values and beliefs need champions to take high-visibility roles in these initiatives (Garcia, 1989). Firing the relatively new and well-liked executive vice-president was a significant event in the failure of the survey and the larger TQM initiative. He had come to Promo from a nonmanufacturing industry that carried a different set of values, beliefs, and assumptions. He wanted to improve the working conditions of employees and viewed them as an integral part of the corporation. His departure meant there was no longer anyone at the executive level who supported the findings of the survey, which indicated that turnover could be reduced by providing better benefits, pay, and working conditions. In addition, because he was not replaced, the steering committee did not have anyone within the Mailing Division to resolve the impasse they struggled with, nor anyone to hold them accountable for developing an action plan to reduce turnover.

The consultant did not fully discern the wide gap in commitment between the vice-president and the rest of top management until the vice-president was gone.

Problems Associated With Negative Findings

In writing about the problems inherent in social science research, Carter (1971) stated that survey data that do not agree with management's anticipated results can result in management deciding not to accept the findings. He listed five possible reasons clients may use to reject data generated by surveys: psychological characteristics of the clients, poor quality of the research, nonfeasibility of implementing the recommendations, past negative experiences with social science research, and inappropriateness of the data or researcher to generate policy recommendations. In Promo's case, the psychological characteristics of the client were critical.

The problems identified by the survey were not in themselves unexpected. What did catch management off guard was the intensity of feelings communicated through the survey, and the clear messages sent to management about what employees thought was wrong with the company. For example, an anecdotal remark from one employee was that "employees are treated as cattle, with no concern for their families or feelings. They are simply something to use to meet an end." Remarks such as these probably caused many of the managers to perceive that there would be a significant psychological cost to their self-concepts if the data were accepted. Maybe this is why they decided to take out most of the anecdotal remarks from the report before making it available to employees. This may also be the reason for the emotional response from the manager who referred to the responses as "only the opinions of employees, not necessarily fact."

The negative nature of the findings also would have made it very difficult for any of the managers or directors to approach the president for resources to support efforts guided by the data. They understood it would be very difficult for the president to accept findings that challenged his value system. Consequently, they perceived supporting the survey's findings as extremely hazardous.

The organization development consultant naively assumed that the negative information was good in the sense that it provided the route to a good outcome. He did not fully anticipate the immediate effect of the negative information.

The reasons for the employee survey's failure to produce action were rooted in both the characteristics of Promo's culture and the inherent difficulty of presenting negative findings to management.

Conclusions

As explained earlier, this case study focuses on the diagnosis phase of organization development. When this phase unravels, the issues point back to Phase 1, entering and contracting. Heilpern and Nadler (1990) suggest that the following five statements are the test for when an organization contemplating an intervention with values contrary to the dominant organizational culture should move beyond Phase 1:

- The current state is intolerable.
- Management is willing to make the investment over time.
- The organization is prepared to stick with the intervention permanently.
- The intervention is important to the success or survival of the business.
- Senior management understands that the intervention cannot be delegated to middle management.

According to these criteria, it is doubtful that a TQM initiative should have been started at Promo Inc. However, these five criteria would have provided a useful tool to begin discussing possible changes in Promo's culture, and would not have been as threatening a first step as the employee survey itself turned out to be. We recommend that the critical first phase be completed successfully before beginning any diagnosis or intervention that attempts to change the basic cultural attributes of an organization.

In addition, the consultant assigned the task of developing the employee survey should have discussed possible findings with the president (the person who actually controlled organizational resources) before beginning the study. Such a discussion would have provided an assessment of the president's willingness to support various organizational reactions and adaptations for each possible survey result. A determination could have been made a priori that the solutions for addressing some of the possible outcomes of the survey were not tolerable. The consultant and the president could then have made an informed decision regarding whether to proceed with the development and implementation of the survey.

Of course, the critical incident that precluded any chance of the employee survey being useful was the firing of the executive vice-president. The consultant was not privy to information that might have led him to anticipate this action and had assumed the executive vice-president would champion the effort to develop strategies in response to the survey data. The external consultant had assessed the vice-president's willingness to address problems in the Mailing Division and knew he wanted to improve the working conditions for employees. Consequently, the consultant did not attempt to balance the survey report in terms of positive and negative findings; in the absence of the executive vice-president's support and leadership, the report's overwhelmingly negative findings caused upper management to become defensive. This lack of balanced reporting was perhaps another mistake on the part of the consultant.

In conclusion, general recommendations to practitioners implementing employee surveys are as follows:

- Articulate the goal and hold on to it. A clearly stated organizational goal should direct the nature of a climate survey. Connections between the goal, the survey, the data reporting and dissemination, and the follow-up actions are critical.
- Establish ownership of the employee survey at high levels of the organization. Employee surveys generally address organization-wide problems and function as a preliminary information-gathering step in developing strategies to transform the underlying "deep structure" of organizations. Because there are very few shortcuts in developing, implementing, and managing these interventions responsibly, these efforts almost always require an investment of organizational resources over time and a commitment from the true gatekeepers of the organization's power and resources. It is critical to establish ownership and commitment at this level before beginning the project.
- Build contingency plans into the contract. It is important to discuss the climate survey's different possible outcomes and appropriate contingency plans so that the controllers of the organization's resources can make informed decisions regarding their degree of commitment to the project. It is important to document this level of commitment and write it into the consulting contract.
- Balance positive and negative findings. In order to minimize middle management's likely resistance to negative data, every effort should be made to balance the survey's findings in terms of strengths and weaknesses of the organization. Building this balance into the survey report decreases the probability that psychological defense mechanisms will prevent managers from examining the data objectively. This will lead to greater commitment and cooperation in developing and implementing the change strategies—and improve the probability of success.

Questions for Discussion

1. What were the critical incidents that contributed to the failure of this climate survey to produce an intervention?
2. What key questions should a practitioner ask before beginning a climate survey?
3. What could the practitioner in this case study have done differently to increase the probability of success?
4. What is the utilitarian value of climate surveys?

The Authors

John A. Zuber is a product development specialist with Personnel Decisions Inc. and a research associate with the University of Minnesota Human Resource Development Research Center. His expertise includes work and organization analysis, design and development of training systems, team building, coaching, management training, evaluation systems, and statistical process control. Zuber has recently developed a model for implementing new technology that the State of Minnesota is using to help organizations increase their productivity and competitive position in the global market. At the University of Minnesota, he teaches graduate-level courses in training in business and industry. Zuber holds bachelor's and master's degrees from the University of Minnesota and is presently pursuing a Ph.D. at the University of Minnesota in the field of human resource development. He can be contacted at the following address: 58 Malcolm Avenue, Minneapolis, MN 55414.

Richard A. Swanson is a professor with and director of the Human Resource Development Research Center at the University of Minnesota and senior partner of Swanson & Associates Inc. Swanson is an internationally recognized authority on organizational change, human resource development (HRD), the analysis and evaluation of work behavior, forecasting the financial benefits of HRD, and trainer training. He received his doctoral degree from the University of Illinois. During Swanson's 25 years of experience, he has performed consulting work for several of the largest corporations in the United States in the areas of strategic human resource planning, personnel training, organization development, and quality improvement.

Swanson has published more than 150 articles on HRD. He is coauthor of *Performance at Work: A Systematic Program for Analyzing Work Behavior* (Wiley, 1986), *Forecasting Financial Benefits of Human Resource Development* (Jossey-Bass, 1988), and *Performance Appraisal: Perspectives on a Quality Management Approach* (American Society for Training and

Development, 1990). He recently published *Analysis for Improving Performance: Tools for Diagnosing Organizations and Documenting Workplace Expertise* (Berrett-Koehler, 1994). He has served as editor of the *Journal of Industrial Teacher Education* and the *Performance and Instruction Journal,* and is the founding editor of the *Human Resource Development Quarterly.* In 1995 he assumed the presidency of the Academy of Human Resource Development. In 1993 Swanson received the American Society for Training and Development professor's network national award for his "Outstanding Contribution to the Academic Advancement of Human Resource Development."

References

Burke, W.W. (1982). *Organization development: Principles and practices.* Boston: Little, Brown, & Co.

Carter, R.K. (1971). Clients' resistance to negative findings and the latent conservative function of evaluation studies. *The American Sociologist, 6,* 118-124.

Cummings, T.G., and Worley, C.G. (1993). *Organization development and change* (5th ed.). St. Paul, MN: West.

Deal, T., and Kennedy, A. (1982). *Corporate cultures.* Reading, MA: Addison-Wesley.

Garcia, J.E. (1989). OD interventions that work. *Personnel Administrator, 34*(6), 90-94.

Heilpern, J., and Nadler, D.A. (1990). Implementing total quality management: A process of cultural change. In D.A. Nadler, M.S. Gerstein, and R.B. Shaw (Eds.) *Organizational architecture: Designs for changing organizations,* (pp. 137-154). San Francisco: Jossey-Bass.

McLagan, P. (1991). The dark side of quality. *Training, 28*(11), 31-33.

Schein, E.H. (1985), *Organizational culture and leadership: A dynamic view.* San Francisco: Jossey-Bass.

Senge, P.M. (1990). *The fifth discipline: The art and practice of the learning organization.* New York: Doubleday.

Shaw, R.B. (1990). The capacity to act. In D.A. Nadler, M.S. Gerstein, and R.B. Shaw (Eds.) *Organizational architecture: Designs for changing organizations,* (pp. 155-174). San Francisco: Jossey-Bass.

Sleezer, C.M., and Swanson, R.A. (1992). Culture surveys: A tool for improving organization performance. *Management Decision, 30*(2), 22-29.

Swanson, R.A. (1994). *Analysis for improving performance: Tools for diagnosing organizations and documenting workplace expertise.* San Francisco: Berrett-Koehler.

Walton, R.E. (1975). The diffusion of new work structures: Explaining why success didn't take. *Organization Dynamics, 3*(3), 2-22.